Into the
I
Of All

Into the
I
Of All

An Ultimate Yoga

Copyright 2011 by Muni Natarajan

All rights reserved. No part of this book may be reproduced in any form or by any means, electronic or mechanical, including photocopying, recording, or by any information storage and retrieval system, without permission in writing from the publisher.

First Edition
Printed in the United States of America

Interior design and illustration: Muni Natarajan

This book is dedicated to
Satguru Sivaya Subramuniyaswami,
who told me, "The only reason you
took birth on this earth was
to know your Self."

Acknowledgments

To Satguru Sivaya Subramuniya, the yoga master
who was my teacher. To all the nameless, good people who
influenced the content of this book. To Rozalina Brightly for her
hours of tedious proofreading. And to my wife and best friend,
Mary Beth, who asked me—before I started this project—
"Why don't you write down what you were
taught in the monastery?"

Table of contents

Introduction

Part One: The Basic

Step 1   **Bliss** • *The feeling of the one life force*
Step 2   **Enjoying** • *Savoring bliss*

Step 3   **Self** • *The "I" of all: our one essential identity*
Step 4   **Beholding** • *Sensing Self*

Step 5   **Being** • *The one life force at its blissful source*
Step 6   **Countering** • *Doing to be*

Step 7   **Love** • *A sense of oneness felt as bliss*
Step 8   **Blessing** • *Spreading bliss*

Step 9   **Balance** • *The stillness of equilibrium*
Step 10 **Centering** • *Becoming still*

Step 11 **Awareness** • *Consciousness individualized*
Step 12 **Flowing** • *Moving awareness at will*

Step 13 **Breath** • *Life of body, leader of mind*
Step 14 **Rhythmizing** • *Using rhythm to vitalize breath control*

Step 15 **Wisdom** • *Insight applied in the fulfillment of need*
Step 16 **Wait Watching** • *Catching distraction*

Step 17 **Needs** • *Useful aims of desire*
Step 18 **Needalizing** • *Identifying needs*

Step 19 **Experience** • *The means by which we know*
Step 20 **Facing** • *Confronting fear and desire*

Step 21 **Opposites** • *The parameters of thought*
Step 22 **Luminating** • *Leading thought with intuition*

Step 23 **Thought** • *The middleman in the pecking order of power*
Step 24 **Redoing Doubt** • *Moving from doubt to faith*

Step 25 **Intuition** • *The sage behind the scenes*
Step 26 **Inneracting** • *Personifying thought-forms*

Step 27 **Now** • *The only experience of time*
Step 28 **Spiraling** • *Focusing into* now *absorption*

Part Two: The Deep and Wide

Step 29 **God** • *An unfixed concept of a fixed reality*
Step 30 **Questioning** • *Opening the mind to change*

Step 31 **Soul** • *An unfixed concept of a changing entity*
Step 32 **Searching** • *Using the mind to learn*

Step 33 **Chakras** • *Seven centers of power*
Step 34 **Ascending** • *Moving awareness up*

Step 35 **Bodies** • *The five sheaths of the soul*
Step 36 **Internalizing** • *Moving awareness in*

Step 37 **Motive** • *A desire voiced as a reason for action*
Step 38 **Motivation Evaluation** • *Inviting forethought*

Step 39 **Yogas** • *Variations on a theme*
Step 40 **Innerrelating** • *Using yogas together*

Step 41 **Yoga** • *Yoking awareness back to source*
Step 42 **Tuning the body** • *Preparing for meditation*

Step 43 **Sat Guru** • *A spiritual teacher*
Step 44 **Appreciating** • *Taking the best and leaving the rest*

Step 45 **Virtue** • *Being good*
Step 46 **Gauging Good** • *Assessing a degree of virtue*

Step 47 **Three Realms** • *The physical, mental and spiritual*
Step 48 **Clarifying** • *Assessing a level of living*

Step 49 **Three States** • *The outer, inner and deeper within*
Step 50 **Planning** • *Using the mind to fulfill a need*

Part Three: The Relative

Step 51 **The Conscious State** • *The waking level of mind*
Step 52 **Observing** • *Watching the conscious mind*

Step 53 **The Subconscious State** • *The subliminal level of mind*
Step 54 **A Purification by Fire** • *Burning emotion away*

Step 55 **The Superconscious State** • *The mystical level of mind*
Step 56 **Innersearching** • *Exploring being*

Step 57 **Hidden Hybrids** • *Subconscious amalgams*
Step 58 **Seeing** • *Anatomizing memory hybrids*

Step 59 **Sleep** • *A release of waking consciousness*
Step 60 **Gloaming** • *Dwelling on the threshold of sleep*

Step 61 **Externalization** • *Absorption in outer life*
Step 62 **Defying Discontent** • *Intensifying inner life*

Step 63 **Internalization** • *Absorption in inner life*
Step 64 **Cooling** • *Withdrawing from hot and cold*

Step 65 **Vibration** • *The oscillation of consciousness*
Step 66 **Sensing** • *Reading vibration*

Step 67 **Nada** • *Sound: the first manifestation of life*
Step 68 **Eeeing** • *Listening to an inner sound*

Step 69 **Mantra Japa** • *The repetition of empowered sound*
Step 70 **Empowering** • *Doing mantra japa*

Step 71 **Affirmation** • *A repeated declaration of an aspiration*
Step 72 **Shaping Fate** • *Creating and performing an affirmation*

Step 73 **Determination** • *Will: a tool and a fuel*
Step 74 **Juxtaposing** • *Comparing willing and willful*

Step 75 **Sex** • *The great connector, baby maker*
Step 76 **Unrepressing** • *Eliminating buried confusion*

Step 77 **Concentration** • *Focusing*
Step 78 **Stepping In** • *Following a path to meditation*

Step 79 **Meditation** • *Intuiting*
Step 80 **Flowering** • *A meditation*

Step 81 **Samadhi** • *Awareness absorbed*
Step 82 **Being Aware** • *Holding awareness aware of itself*

Step 83 **The Yogas of Spine and Mind** • *Unnecessary pursuits*
Step 84 **Settling In to Learn** • *Leaning on the spine*

Step 85 **Powers** • *Liabilities going in, assets coming out*
Step 86 **Impersonalizing** • *Seeing the impersonal in the personal*

Step 87 **The Shining Ones** • *The higher beings of inner realms*
Step 88 **Praying** • *Conversing with the Shining Ones*

Step 89 **Worship** • *Surrendering in communion with God*
Step 90 **Worshipping** • *Giving up, going in*

Step 91 **Evil** • *An impermanent consequence of ignorance*
Step 92 **Coming to Terms** • *Accepting or rejecting indoctrination*

Step 93 **Sufferance** • *A catalyst for introspection*
Step 94 **A Water Purification** • *Washing emotion away*

Part Four: The Absolute

Step 95   **Evolution** • *A journey through time*
Step 96   **Goal Digging** • *Assessing the quality of current desires*

Step 97   **Involution** • *A non-journey in now-awareness*
Step 98   **Side Stepping** • *Accessing the in-tell of intelligence, now*

Step 99   **The I's** • *The many false identities of the one and only Self*
Step 100 **Deidentifying** • *Relinquishing false identities*

Step 101 **Transparency** • *The absence of personal presence*
Step 102 **Gracefulizing** • *Learning from the past for the future, now*

Step 103 **Simplicity** • *A condition of clarity*
Step 104 **Differentiating** • *Looking past life to death*

Step 105 **A Final Focus** • *The last use of thought*
Step 106 **Deepening** • *Seeking the source of being*

Step 107 **The End** • *The final yoking of yoga*
Step 108 **Pulsing** • *Following the upward surge of life force*

Afterwords
Glossary

The Goal of Yoga:
To realize life's fullest potential by merging with life's ultimate essence in the "I" of all.

Introduction

When I first heard about yoga, I was immediately fascinated. Nobody had to convince me it was a good thing. From the moment I caught even a glimpse of what it was all about, all I wanted to do was get started with a committed practice.

A friend of mine introduced me to a friend of his who had a sister with a telephone number of the only yoga instructor she knew of in the small town where I lived. Back then, in the mid-sixties, yoga was not yet a household word—even though it was gaining prominence more quickly than any of us realized at the time.

I got that number, called it and arranged to attend my first yoga class. Before I knew it, I was sitting in the tidy living room of a charming home, listening to a soft tamboura drone, adjusting to the scent of Indian incense, and trying to look comfortable hunching cross-legged on the floor next to four strangers that were not male, under forty or there for the first time like I was. Naturally, I was feeling more than a little self-conscious.

As our host and teacher entered the room, she took sympathetic note of my newbie presence and, with the grace of a bird in flight, glided over to perch by me before assuming her pillowed seat facing the class.

Emma was her sweet name. Emma was a slim and distinguished 45-to-50-years-of-age sort of lady with a soft voice and kind eyes. Looking at me as if I were her sixteen-year-old son who had just done something bad, she said that she was the one I had talked to on the phone, that she was really glad I had come, and that if, "during our time together," there was mention of menstrual cycles, pregnancy issues or hot flashes, not to worry, these matters shouldn't concern me. I said, "ok," and she got up to start the class.

After about three sentences of good-natured banter, Emma got right down to the business at hand. "There is no one system of yoga, as yoga is taught today," she said, "and no one fixed criterion by which the relative quality and authenticity of today's many yoga systems might be evaluated." At first, I just assumed this was the up-front disclaimer Emma thought she had to get said should any of us be unhappy with her class. Now, 45 years later, I know it was not a disclaimer at all. It *was* and *is* the truth.

I'll never forget Emma and that first yoga class. Together, they launched me into an odyssey I've not left for these last two thirds of my life—nor will I. This is so because I know the journey of yoga is well worth the trek, as I think you will see for yourself should you decide to travel it with me for the length of this book and beyond.

It's true there is no one system of yoga as yoga is taught today. It is also true there is no one criterion by which the relative quality and authenticity of today's many yoga systems might be evaluated. These conditions of vagueness exist because the goals and paths of the numerous yoga systems now in existence vary *so* much the only thing that could be said they all have in common is they all consist of physical *or* mental or physical *and* mental disciplines that originated in India.

Although it might seem logical to assume India should have produced at least *some* books thoroughly describing *some* of these systems of yoga, she has not done so (arguably) in a fashion that is completely understandable to the Westerner. This is primarily because—not being much of a proselytizer—she never really wanted to. Plus, she just tends to *do* what she *does* better than she explains it.

For thousands of years, the yoga teachers of India have followed an oral tradition of instruction, almost exclusively. Even today, many Indian yoga adepts insist the essence of their instruction cannot be conveyed in written word and the physical presence of a qualified teacher is always necessary for a student to learn correctly and completely.

Because too few qualified Indian yoga instructors have taught extensively in the West, and because the first literature written in English about India's yoga consisted primarily of translations composed by English speaking scholars who were either biased or insensitive, the past century has witnessed a largely unguided reformation of yoga in the West.

Today yoga is deeply immersed in this reformation, reconstructing itself *outside* India in much the same way it created itself *inside* India more than two thousand years ago—through each sincere aspirant's individual experimentation with disciplines designed to awaken intuitive wisdom from within a mystic core that is always and equally available to everyone, everywhere. In this process of experimental reconstruction, an edited version of an old yoga is being realized as a living phenomenon with an infinite potential for growth, but only in the lives of those who take it seriously enough to work with it in practice—practice being its most valid visa of entry, the true means by which its "end of ends" might be realized.

Although some traditionalists have asserted that some value has gone missing in this transformation of old to new, anyone who has practiced yoga with sincerity will readily agree that, although yoga's absolute truths have never changed and never will, the methods by which those truths are realized can and must change with changing times.

So it is that this book is not a codified presentation of an ancient tradition "set in stone," but is instead a collection of living and growing teachings presented as a journey of 108 steps. The substance of this journey comes from my own experimentation with yogic principles and practices conveyed to me by my teacher, Satguru Sivaya Subramuniyaswami, during the 37 years I lived and served in his monasteries.

The yoga my teacher taught was a comprehensive system drawing from an ancient wisdom and practice that was taught to him by his teacher who was taught the same thing by his teacher and so on back some 2,000 years or so, or so I was told.

This "one comprehensive system" included instruction from the traditions of *hatha, karma, japa, nada, bhakti* and *raja yoga*. Therefore, this book will include a dose of all these, but as they were taught to me—as interrelated components of a one way.

Yoga's highest goal should be *to realize life's fullest potential by merging with life's ultimate essence*. In India's tradition of tacit intimation, I'll say no more than this about that for now, so as to allow yoga to be for you what you make of it.

You do not have to agree with all that you read here. In fact, I encourage you not to. I encourage you, as my teacher encouraged me, to question everything put before you. Put it all to the test of your own experimentation so that in the end you will have a bundle of applied wisdom as useful to you as my bundle of applied wisdom—partially represented here in this book—has been to me.

Each of the 108 steps of this book's path is a chapter. These 108 chapters are sequential and grouped in twos. Each group of two consists of a "principle" chapter followed by a "practice" chapter. This structuring will allow you to learn of a principle in one chapter—then, in the next chapter, have an opportunity to generally or specifically apply that principle in practice. The titles of the "practice" chapters are *italicized* to further distinguish them from the "principle" chapters.

Each practice chapter will include instructions for journaling—writing by hand in a journal to be used only in conjunction with performing the exercises in this book. This journaling will provide a way for *you* to pull upon *you* to get from *you* far more than any book could ever give, though a good book can give a lot. This is to say: To make the most of the best of *you*, please do the journaling.

The "I" writing this book will be a "we" for the most part. I have chosen to write from this perspective because I have been taught and I firmly believe none of us ever acts alone. We all do what we do with the assistance of unseen helpers on "the other side."

Also, please understand that when "we" refer to "he" we also mean "she." Establishing this preliminary understanding of gender in a grammatical and syntactic reference should allow us to proceed along the path of this book with the established understanding we are always addressing and referring to both women and men equally.

So now that you are at least somewhat set to go, let us—you, me and our helpers in between—begin our mystical journey of 108 steps from we to one, into the "I" of all.

PART ONE
THE BASIC

1
Bliss
The feeling of the one life force

Who could ever question the innate sanctity of a child's bliss and the blessed effect that bliss has upon others? And who would not want to take that bliss and pass it on—just by reveling in it and letting that reveling spread of its own accord?

Once we perceive bliss as the feeling of the force of life, we can see it everywhere—where it is obvious and where it is not. It is obvious in love, but not in lust. It is obvious in peace, but not in war. It is obvious in selflessness, but not in selfishness. Yet still it's there, everywhere.

Clearly, pure bliss is apparent in the lives of small children who have not yet learned to abstain from an unrepentant and unpretentious enjoyment of their inherent joy. And clearly that bliss is obviously there in the upliftment those children spill over onto us as their bliss becomes our bliss by no intentional effort of theirs whatsoever.

Certainly, it is a turning-point day when we let it be okay to unabashedly seek our own bliss in the better of its many guises, but especially as itself, naked and pure—like a child would experience it. On that day, we learn to live without lack and give without loss by simply allowing ourselves an enjoyment of a bliss so abundant it overflows us onto others as blessings.

At first, we experience bliss in things we *do*.

Say, for instance, we are listening to some music we love on the radio. That listening is a *doing*. And it is a *doing* that we are inclined to keep on doing because we feel bliss while we are doing it. And while we are listening to that music we love, we say to ourselves, "Ahhh, this music is pure bliss."

Suddenly, someone comes along and changes the channel to a station playing music we hate. What happens to our bliss? Is it not gone along with our beloved music? Usually.

That's the tricky thing about feeling bliss through *doing*. Whatever is being done can appear to be the cause of the bliss felt during the *doing*. Once bliss is perceived in its pure and virgin state, however, it becomes apparent that *doing* could not possibly cause bliss, because bliss precedes *doing*. This is not immediately obvious, of course. But somewhere along the line, each of us discovers it is true: *Bliss stands alone without a cause.*

Experiencing this causeless bliss is easy. It requires only a perceptual adjustment. If we can acknowledge to ourselves that bliss *can* be experienced for no reason and we can allow ourselves to drop the very idea we have to *do* something to feel bliss, we'll find we've found bliss right then and there, without even looking for it.

Once we have identified bliss as a fundamental quality of life, we can more easily enjoy it as a backdrop to our *doing*. In this new enjoyment, we know that regardless of what happens in our *doing*, even if that *doing* should undo itself in disaster, the bliss behind it will remain intact and safe in *being*. As a result of this knowing, our life shifts gently as does our consciousness so that we are inclined to act appropriately and live gracefully—all through a *doing* anchored firmly in *being*.

2
Enjoying
Savoring bliss

In this practice, entitled "Enjoying," we will isolate and relish the bliss of *being*. In preparation for this enjoyment, we will perform an action called the *full wing flight*.

In addition to enhancing the lung's exchange of oxygen and carbon dioxide, which is the primary function of the body's respiratory system, this *full wing flight* helps to stop random thought, de-emphasize negative emotion and clear the way for an unobstructed perception of the feeling of *being*, which is the feeling of bliss.

The practice of the *full wing flight* shapes up around a well-known yogic breath control called the *complete breath*. This *complete breath* is performed by inhaling slowly and steadily through the nose, first filling the lower part of the lungs (expanding the abdomen slightly); then filling the middle part of the lungs (expanding the lower ribs, breastbone and chest slightly); and finally filling the highest portion of the lungs (expanding the upper chest and pulling the abdomen in slightly). The exhalation that follows is simply a reversal of the inhalation.

To accomplish the physical action that should occur in conjunction with the *complete breath* during the *full wing flight*, assume a standing position to lift your arms out and up, like a bird spreading its wings, so that each hand draws an invisible 180-degree arc from the bottom, where the arms hang limp, to the top, where the palms of the hands are pressed lightly together in prayer formation above the head.

This lifting of the arms gets coordinated with the *complete breath* in the following manner (see figure 1): As the arms are raised one third of the way up the 180-degree arc, the first phase of the *complete breath* is performed. As the arms are raised up the second third of the the arc, the second phase of the *complete breath* is performed. As the arms are raised up the last third of the arc, the final phase of the *complete breath* achieves a full inhalation. That full inhalation should then be held for a few seconds before an exhalation begins an exact reversal of the procedure just described.

Performing this breath control with the three-phase arm motion helps the unified fluidity of the exercise by giving it a dance feel. It also allows for more air to be drawn into the upper lungs during the third phase of the inhalation.

In the following practice of "Enjoying," you will also be assuming a posture called the "corpse pose" in English and *shavasana* in Sanskrit. When you are in this position (see figure 2) you are lying flat on your back with your arms relaxed to the sides of your body (palms facing up) and your feet set slightly apart.

Enjoying

• In the top right corner of the first page of your journal, write the date and time of this practice you are now beginning. In the top left corner, write "Three Enjoyable Events."

• Sitting in a casual and comfortable position, take a few moments to reflect upon the most recent events of your life. Go back no more than three days. Recall specific occasions that were ethereally enjoyable such

Figure 1: *The three-phase arm motion of "full wing flight"*

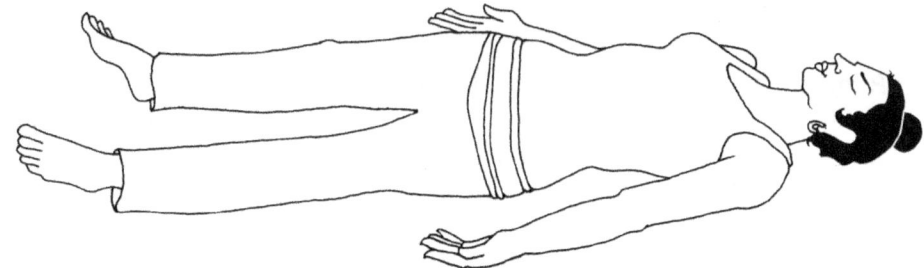

Figure 2: *The "corpse pose" known as* shavasana *in Sanskrit*

as when you watched a sunset, chilled out in a hot tub or relaxed in a hammock on a Sunday afternoon. Then describe these three events in your journal under your title: "Three Enjoyable Events."

Example: "It was about 6:45 in the evening on May 16, 2009. I had been driving on the interstate for at least three hours heading home from Lake Tahoe to San Francisco. With an hour of travel still ahead of me, I decided to take a break. Pulling off the road at the first 'rest stop' I could find, I got out of my car, walked a bit to stretch and sat down at a picnic table to watch the sun's last sinking out of twilight into night. As I gazed into the final dazzling brilliance of this evening phenomenon, I lost track of time. If sunsets lasted forever, I'd still be there. But they don't and I'm not. Soon enough, I was back on the road dealing with fast traffic and the like. It was dark. All I could think about was getting home."

• When you have finished your writing, stand up and practice the *full wing flight* three times—more if you like. Then lie down in *shavasana* for about ten minutes. (Careful! A soft surface might invite sleep.) Allow yourself to bask in bliss.

A note: The *full wing flight* is not the cause of the bliss you are feeling. That bliss was there first. The *full wing flight* simply relaxes and invigorates the physical body so the underlying and ever-present bliss of *being* can become more apparent.

• As you enjoy your *shavasana*, recall the three events you just recorded in your journal and reflect on each one separately. Once you have caught the enjoyment of each event, drop the event and hold the enjoyment. Be sure to do this with each event.

• Remaining in *shavasana*, strive to catch and hold the one feeling that was the same through each of your three experiences of enjoyment. That one common-denominator feeling is the bliss of *being*. Try to hold that bliss for at least five minutes without getting distracted.

• When you feel like it, sit up, open your journal and write the question: "What do I have to say to myself right now?" Leaving your journal open in your lap, close your eyes and mentally ask: "What do I have to say to myself right now?" As you hold yourself in the bliss of *being*, wait for mental impressions to arise. As they arise, open your eyes and record them in your journal. If nothing arises, write nothing.

We are not looking for ultimate wisdom here. All we are trying to do is catch a knack for being inwardly receptive to the intuition that is forever available to us in and through the bliss of *being*.

3
Self

The "I" of all: our one essential identity

Although an unexplainable truth can only be known through experience, the very existence of that truth and the possibility of its experience can suffer obscurity if it is not announced in concept first. Therefore, paradoxically, an unexplainable truth must sometimes be "announced" in explanation before it can be experienced.

Upon hearing the explanation of an unexplainable truth—even if that explanation is, "It's unexplainable!"—those who have not experienced that truth will have to accept that explanation in faith, reject it in doubt, or reform it into a question left open for an answer yet to come.

However it is received, that truth stands announced—in concept. If that announced concept is either accepted or contemplated, it beckons. If it is rejected, it awaits. Sooner or later, a beginning development of that concept into experience will mark the start of a mystical expedition into the unexplainable.

A concept can never be absolutely true. And that's all right because the value of a concept is not in its content but in its connection. A concept of a truth is connected to that truth by a thread of logic that will eventually work itself out to give itself up to an *experience* of that truth, which will be absolute. Take, for instance, the classic yoga teaching about "the Self." One conceptual announcement of that teaching might go something like this:

We all share a one life force that comes from a one life source, which is also our one identity that we'll call "Self" for now, though any name would do. This Self is beyond the grasp of consciousness, transcends time, form and space and defies description. Although it cannot be experienced because it precedes experience, it can be merged with from within being and acknowledged, after that merging, as Self Realized.

In this one relatively short paragraph, there is a lot of concept to accept, question or reject. Yet even if all of this concept is completely rejected, it does not go away. It takes its stand in memories we think we have forgotten but haven't. There, it awaits its opportunity to offer us a beckoning into the depths of yoga.

If we have worked out doubt enough to wholeheartedly accept that a given concept of Self offers at least an idea of a certain experiential possibility, and we can therefore allow ourselves to forthrightly seek Self based on a plan derived from this concept, even the heavy demands of everyday life cannot weigh us down into thinking Self Realization is too much to hope for, because we can now hope for anything. We can now hope for anything because we have replaced a dark doubt with a bright faith that makes any reasonable aim seem obtainable.

From a grounded faith in reasonable possibility, we can see clearly that inner and outer experiences do not have to contradict each other, but can actually share mutual support, as they most certainly do in the lives of mystics who are the way they are because their *outer* listens to their *inner* and their *inner* listens to their *outer* while they reside in *being* in between.

Whether or not we choose to accept the concept we will all

become mystics sooner or later, we must at least concede that, while we are not, things may not be as they seem.

Because physical life is by nature so overwhelmingly mesmerizing and all-consuming, most of us are easily drawn into what seems like a necessary identification with the body and its urgent needs. Our "I" seems to be the body. And our life seems to be only physical.

We think to ourselves: "If I can't eat, I'll die in a matter of weeks. If I can't drink, I'll die in a matter of days. If I can't breathe, I'll die in a matter of minutes." Physical survival becomes our paramount concern. We assume, if the body dies, we die.

"Such is not the case, of course," some of us might be taught to speculate. Certainly, when we hear, read or think we are more than a physical body, we might intuitively sense this to be true. But do we know this beyond the shadow of a doubt? Is that small spark of intuition enough to fortify us against a "gut fear" of physical death?

"I'm not afraid of dying," some of us might stoically assert. But aren't we? Is it not a fear of our own physical demise that lies at the root of most of what we do in physical life, including getting educated, finding a job, buying a house, caring for a family and saving for retirement? Would we not feel a primal fear of death if any of these "necessities of life" were threatened?

Something must happen within us to turn this earth-bound thinking and feeling around. Something must happen and something does happen. This is the promise the sages of old have boldly made—that every one of us will experience our way up and out of the identification with the physical body that stimulates a disproportionate fear of death.

For a few of us, this transcendence might get triggered through a revelatory event—such as a near-death experience or an otherworldly dream. An extraordinary incident like this can mold its changes within us abruptly. Suddenly we are filled and thrilled with a confident knowing that we are not the physical body, that we wear the physical body like a set of clothes and that we have worn many physical bodies through many lives.

More often, however, this transcendence surfaces gradually, smoothly and unobtrusively as a gentle shifting of focus. We simply find ourselves realizing our lives really aren't so burdened and our problems really aren't so many. In this realization we give ourselves permission to become intrigued with the possibility of enjoying an internalized life that is far more substantial and fulfilling then the externalized life we have been living. When we arrive at this threshold of a new life, however we get there, we are ripe for merging with the "I" of all.

Yet seeking something that cannot be experienced (because it precedes experience) can be intellectually frustrating. We are left to wonder just how to go about getting what we already have, or being what we already are. Even if we are told in no uncertain terms that dropping the urgency of searching is key and the most efficient thing we can *do* is *be*, we are not usually willing to trust such simplicity until we have exhausted all of our other options.

There are two common meditations prescribed by teachers to help us deflate our infatuation with "other options." One centers upon the question: "Who am I?" The other focuses on the statement: "I am." Both of these meditations short-circuit *doing* by focusing upon the "I" that does. In this flipping of awareness back upon itself we are encouraged to either be who we are ("I am.") or question who we are ("Who am I?"). Through both of these approaches we are drawn within to delve back into the energies that precede thought and action until we can delve no more.

4
Beholding
Sensing Self

In this practice, entitled "Beholding," we will endeavor to gain a sense of the one timeless, formless, spaceless Self that precedes the many roles we live in the play of life.

The sequence of exercises we will be performing in the preparation portion of this practice will include a breath control called the *cleansing breath*. To perform the *cleansing breath*, sit up straight, inhale deeply and hold your breath for about four seconds. Then, as you exhale slowly, force air vigorously through tightly pursed lips in a series of short exhalations separated by brief pauses until all the air in your lungs has been completely expelled. This comprises one "round" of the cleansing breath, which may be repeated.

Like the *complete breath* in *full wing flight*, this *cleansing breath* yields both physical and psychological benefits. Physically, it assists in a more complete elimination of toxin-laden carbon dioxide from the lungs. Psychologically, it affects an immediate cessation of thought and emotion as it invites—in its aftermath—a calm focus of awareness.

Beholding

• In the top right corner of the next available page in your journal, write the date and time of this practice you are now beginning. In the top left corner, write "Roles of my Life."

• Sitting comfortably with your journal in your lap, pen in hand, think of yourself as an actor and your life as a play. As you perceive yourself in this way, identify the various roles you have taken on in the performance of your life. As these roles occur to you, write them down in your journal under your title: "Roles of my Life."

At first, this list will accrue quickly since certain obvious roles—like brother, daughter, mother or husband—will be easily identifiable. As the list gets longer, however, your searching will have to become more introspective. Follow this searching all the way through to its natural conclusion—past your work roles of boss and bossed, paper pusher and problem solver; and your weekend roles of lawn mower, window washer and leak fixer—into your deeper more psychologically imposed roles like victim, hero, looser, warrior, coward and the like.

• When your list is as complete as you think you want to make it, perform the *full wing flight* three times, followed by three rounds of the *cleansing breath*. In the pleasant exposure to the bliss of *being* these practices reveal, lie back in *shavasana* (the "corpse pose").

Once you are settled, imagine yourself living without playing any of the roles you have listed. Ask yourself, "Who is the 'I' that's left when no roles are played?" And wait for an answer. After about ten minutes, replace that question with the statement, "I am," and allow your intuition to guide you into a sense of the essence of all.

- When you feel the time is right, sit up and open your journal. In the top left corner of the next page in that journal, write "Free Writing 1." Then close your eyes. Visualize a vacant space in front of your face. Allow that emptiness to be filled with whatever comes. As impressions arise, open your eyes and write those impressions down under "Free Writing 1." Even if what you perceive is visual imagery, try to describe that imagery in words.

5
Being
The one life force at its blissful source

To *be* in bliss for a short period of time, *unintentionally*, is not an experience that needs be accomplished. It accomplishes itself. To *be* in bliss for a longer period of time, *intentionally*, is an accomplishment that takes some *doing*.

When we are in a state of *being*, we are not *doing*. Nevertheless, to purposely sustain *being* for even five minutes requires dealing with an urge to physically, emotionally or mentally *do* something else instead. This urge to *do* arises because that primal energy of life we become in a blissful state of *being* is imbibed with an indissoluble compulsion to creatively manifest itself out into something tangible.

When this itchy urge to *do* sits face-to-face with our intentional attempts to *be*, we feel ourselves getting pulled out when we want to stay *in*, caught in a battle we can't seem to win between the *inner* of *being* and the *outer* of *doing*.

As we attempt to intentionally sustain *being*, this "urge to *do*" will surface in a number of ways. The body will fidget to fight an inclination to move. The imagination will spin out thoughts and images of all those unfulfilled desires it would like us to "do something" about. Memory will cough up a plethora of "unresolved issues" it has been storing away for us to settle some day. And all of this will arouse a whole array of emotions that will battle to steal our full attention. In this way, something seemingly simple—striving to intentionally sustain a state of *being*—becomes confusingly difficult, due to challenges posed by memories, thoughts, emotions and urges that pull us toward *doing*.

For this reason, much of our yoga practice, especially in the beginning, has to do with "fighting fire with fire," so to speak—using *doing* to cancel out *doing* until only *being* remains. "Fighting" in this context means *countering*—*countering* an outwardly directed *doing* with an inwardly directed *doing*. The "I am" and "Who am I?" meditations described in Chapter 3 are prime examples of this *countering*. The *doing* in these meditations is of the thinking sort. By thinking the "I am" thought or asking the "Who am I?" question, we are *countering* the urge to *do* another thought or question instead.

Through the consistent exercise of a yoga well anchored in *countering practices*, we develop *countering habits* that mature our *efforts to be* into an increasingly sustainable *state of being*. Living in *being* feeds life back to life, vitalizes physical, mental and emotional health, and permeates experience with bliss.

This is all great news, of course. Yet we feel compelled to clarify that, in a yogaless world, all would be just fine—though not quite as fine as it might be. This is to say that yoga is not a requirement of life but an enhancement of life that has its place toward the end of our infatuation with the manifestation of life. In this understanding we can see why and how yoga consists of sensible practices derived from natural processes.

We are benefiting from these natural processes all the time. Look at how we automatically de-stress distress by "zoning out"—as in pulling in a deep breath, letting out a long sigh and relaxing back into a trouble-free moment just before an episode of anger, frustration or anxiety pushes us into overload. This natural adjustment is the inspiration behind a number of powerful yoga practices designed to assist us in our withdrawal of awareness from thought or emotion into *being*.

All the yoga practices in this book have been devised (not by me, they are ancient) as extensions of natural processes (like gaining relief from "zoning out") that happen automatically and unintentionally and are governed by an innate intelligence that is preordained to assist us in maintaining physical health, mental sanity and spiritual consciousness.

6
Countering
Doing to be

In this practice, entitled "Countering," we will turn *doing* back upon itself toward *being*. In this effort, we will be performing the *trataka* gaze, the *sigh breath*, some *Aum chanting* and a *flower blessing*. While these four techniques are plenty effective when practiced separately, their integration yields an especially powerful means of *doing* to *be*.

Trataka is the practice of fixing the gaze of open eyes on a physical object. In a sophistication of this practice, the eyes are closed and the physical object previously gazed upon is visualized. In our use of *trataka* here, we will keep the eyes open. *Trataka* supports a focus of awareness with a focus of eyes.

The *sigh breath* is a simple and pleasurable breath control performed by inhaling a quick but deep in-breath through the nose and exhaling a long, leisurely sigh-of-relief out-breath through the mouth. The primary purpose of the *sigh breath* is to calm stress and release negative thought or emotion.

Aum chanting is one of yoga's most powerful *countering practices*. The mantra *Aum*—pronounced "aa" (as in law), "oo" (as in zoo), and "mm" (with mouth closed and teeth lightly touching)—is the first and most powerful of the *bija* mantras.

Bija mantras are single-syllable "seed sounds" of primal potency. These "seed sounds" can be used alone or they can be put together in different combinations to form longer mantras in the same way that letters get joined to form words, and words get joined to form sentences.

By itself, *Aum* is a mantra of transmutation. "Transmutation" here refers to the development of a lower energy up into a higher energy. During the chanting of *Aum*, this moving up of energy can be felt quite literally, since its first sound, "aa," vibrates within the chest; its second sound, "oo," vibrates in the throat; and its third sound, "mm," vibrates in the head.

The *flower blessing* is a *countering practice* specifically used to nullify negative emotions felt by one person toward another. In preparation for this practice, 108 flowers or flower petals must be gathered, and a simple altar must be prepared. At the center of this alter should be a picture of the "target" person—the person you have chosen to focus upon. If a picture of this person is not available, his or her name written on a piece of paper will do.

To perform the *flower blessing*, inhale deeply and hold your breath for a few seconds. Then, as you breathe out, audibly chant *Aum* in the manner described above. As soon as you feel the peace *Aum* reveals, place a flower or a petal in front of the picture (or piece of paper) at the center of your altar. Repeat this process until all of your flowers or petals have been used.

Now that we have described *trataka, sighing, Auming* and *blessing with flowers*, we'll use them to *counter*.

Countering

- Search your memory for a person who has stirred negative emotions within you. Then, prepare an altar for a flower blessing focused upon this person.

A note: Constructing an altar dedicated to a person that stirs your negative emotions will probably be the last thing you want to do. Consequently, performing this practice in any fashion—poorly or not—will be a significant achievement.

- In the top right corner of the next available page in your journal, write the date and time of this practice you are now beginning. In the top left corner of this page, write "My Benediction."

- Sit up straight and perform the *sigh breath* (as described at the beginning of this chapter) three times. Then take a moment to think about the person centered on your altar. Let any negative emotions stimulated by this deliberation rise up.

- As you are feeling these negative emotions, fix your *trataka* gaze on the picture (or piece of paper) at the center of your altar and perform the *flower blessing* with *Aum chanting* until all 108 flowers or petals have been placed on your altar. When you are done, perform the *sigh breath* at least three times.

- When you are ready, open your journal. Under your title, "My Benediction," record your reflections, having performed the countering exercise of *flower blessing* supported by *sigh breathing, trataka,* and *Aum chanting*. As you write, let your intuition surprise you with a knowing you didn't know you knew about yourself, the person you have just blessed and the primal life force that fuses the two of you together in oneness.

7
Love
A sense of oneness felt as bliss

Love is almost too general a term to be useful if it is not put into context. So let's do that. Let's put love in context.

In a physical context, love might look a lot like lust; in an emotional context, it could be conceived as a sharing of intimacy; in an intellectual context, it might be understood as a mutual fulfillment of practical needs. In a spiritual context, however—which would be the context of yoga—love could very well reveal itself as *an inability to draw lines of separation*. The *experience* of this latter more broad-based and unconditional love might be described as *the enjoyment of an inescapable sense of oneness felt as bliss*.

But this blissful enjoyment of oneness would not be of the up-and-down sort. Ups and downs—as in mood swings—are emotional. Although emotional "ups" are fun enough as they occur, they are never long lasting and are forever followed by "downs" that happen in compliance with an inner law that states, "That which goes up must come equally down before cycling back around to center."

Because yoga practices are always all about getting back to center one way or another, they tend to simplify our lives. Take, for instance, this bliss we have discussed so much thus far. The bliss of *being* and the bliss of a deep, broad and unconditional *love* are the same. Simple!

Once we have caught the idea that the bliss of *being* is not different from the bliss of a deep love, we know that when we are feeling one of these we are feeling the other, and that when we are feeling emotion (negative or positive) we are feeling neither.

The *countering* exercises of *Aum chanting* and *flower blessing*, described in Chapter 6, are good examples of practices designed to release us from an entanglement with the push-and-pull of negative and positive emotions so we can fall back into the one central bliss of *being* that is forever radiating a one unconditional love.

Getting stuck off center is all too easy. Staying stuck off center is even easier. Staying stuck off center is how egos get formed, for an ego is nothing but an off-center, false sense of self that forms itself when awareness stays away from home so long it forgets where home is.

The longer awareness stays stuck off center, the harder it is to get unstuck, for wherever it is, it builds from there its own version of *being* and its own version of love—counterfeit replicates of the originals to be sure—as it nurtures a desire to remain as it is and a fear of loosing what it has become. As grim as this scene might seem to be, it is a necessary prerequisite to an effective involvement with yoga or some such practice. Yoga is not the only way out of an ego, of course, but it *is* a way that is most effective.

Living life easily with a sense of centeredness is *yoga in action*. Such living springs forth spontaneously from a faith in *being*. Since a faith in *being* is inspired by the *being* experience and the *being* experience is inspired by a faith in *being,* which inspires more *being* experience, which inspires more faith, *yoga in action* is—as we can all discover for ourselves—a lifestyle that grows from within itself.

8
Blessing
Spreading bliss

In this practice, entitled "Blessing," we will discover how simply relaxing the body allows a release of thought and emotion that lets the bliss of *being* and love spontaneously flow out as blessings to all.

In the sequence of exercises that make up this practice, we will be performing a breath control called *ujjayi*. We will also be assuming a physical posture called the *jackknife* (also known as the "boat pose," or *navasana* in Sanskrit).

The *ujjayi* breath control is sometimes referred to as the "ocean breath" because its performance sounds like the sum-total monotone of a nearby sea or the quiet wind-tunnel roar of a conch shell's inner spiral. Many yoga teachers say *ujjayi* is "throat breathing" rather than "nose breathing." What they mean by this is that in *ujjayi* we focus upon slightly constricting the passage of air through the throat while we are breathing through the nose. This constriction of air produces *ujjayi's* distinctive wind sound as it softens and slows the breath to yield a curious effect of soothing and calming the nervous system, even though it increases oxygenation and builds internal body heat. *Ujjayi* is one of yoga's most popular breath controls and perfect for this practice of "Blessing." To catch the knack of performing *ujjayi*, hold a hand mirror up close to your face and fog it up with an out-breath through a mouth open wide. That action applied with the mouth closed during controlled inhaling and exhaling is *ujjayi*.

The *jackknife* requires the performance of both the *ujjayi* and the *cleansing* breath controls. In preparation for assuming the *jackknife*, sit on the ground with your legs together and extended forward. In this position, inhale deeply with *ujjayi*. As you begin to exhale, switch to the *cleansing breath* as you lean back to balance on your sitting bones while raising your extended legs as high as you can without rounding your back (see figure 3). To stabilize your balance in this position, straighten your arms forward and up until they are approximately parallel to the ground with the palms of your hands open and facing each other. When

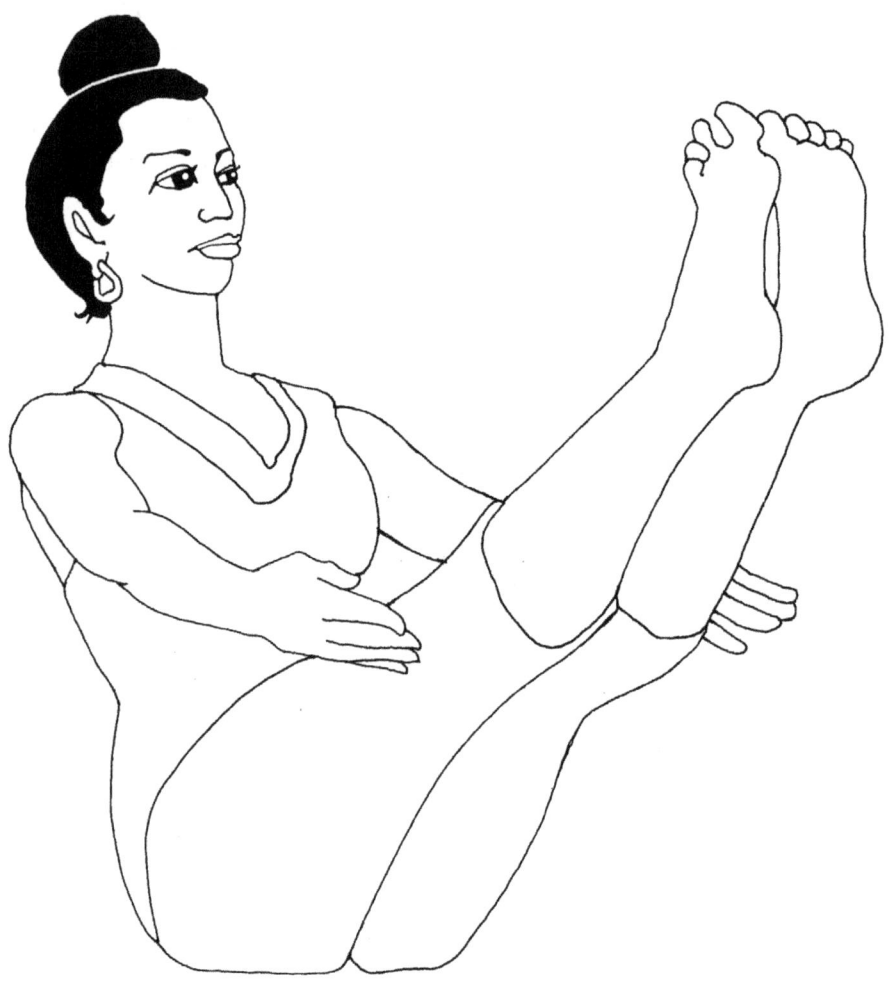

Figure 3: *The jackknife—also known as the "boat pose" or* navasana *in Sanskrit*

you have concluded your *cleansing breath* exhalation while holding this posture, lower your body into a reclining position of physical rest. This sequence constitutes one round of *jackknife*, which may be repeated.

Blessing

- In the top right corner of the next available page in your journal, write the date and time of this practice you are now beginning. In the top left corner of this page, write "A Blissful Blessing."

- Lie on your back with your arms to your sides. Raise both arms straight up to a 45-degree angle (without bending the elbows) and clinch your hands into fists. Then rotate your clinched fists at the wrists, five times clockwise and five times counterclockwise. When you are finished, lower your arms and raise your straightened legs up until your feet are about six inches off the ground. Then, as you did with your clinched fists, rotate your feet at the ankles, five times clockwise and five times counterclockwise. Following this, perform the *jackknife* five times.

- Remaining on your back in *shavasana*, perform *ujjayi*—slowly, deeply and luxuriously. During the exhalation of this soothing breath control, hold only the thought of *letting go* as you feel the release of physical tension, wherever in your physical body that tension might be. Do this for at least five full rounds of *ujjayi*. (One round of any breath control consists of one inhalation and one exhalation.)

- As you relax and enjoy the aftermath of these tension-releasing exercises, feel the bliss of *being* circulating through the nervous system of your entire physical body. After about five minutes, visualize this bliss flooding out through the skin of your body into the world. Try not to get consumed in a method of doing this. Just let it be done, knowing the *being* of you knows what to "do." Continue this practice of blessing for at least 15 minutes.

- When you are ready, sit up, open your journal and—under your title, "A Blissful Blessing"—record your reflections on sharing bliss.

9
Balance
The stillness of equilibrium

Yoga literally means "to bind back." This binding back or yoking of yoga is a withdrawal of *we* into *one* that occurs as *doing* merges back into *being* and *being* merges back into Self.

Before all this merging can occur, however, *being* and *doing* must come into balance. Once this balance has been established, there is a sense of centeredness.

When we are *not* experiencing centeredness, our awareness of *doing* overshadows our awareness of *being*. When we *are* experiencing centeredness, we are equally aware of *being* and *doing*. When we cultivate this centeredness as an intentional practice, *being* gradually overshadows *doing* because centeredness favors *being*.

Being overshadowing *doing* does not mean *doing* doesn't get done. It only means *doing* gets done effortlessly from within *being*, *as if nothing is happening*. Also, under the influence of *being*, *doing* occurs with maximum efficiency.

When our yogic *countering* practices have canceled out a sense of *doing* to the extent that at least a little bit of *being* can be felt all the time, that feeling of a "little bit of *being*" has a chance to grow until it *so* dominates *doing*, *doing* doesn't *seem* to exist at all. And all we are aware of is *being*, even while we are active.

There is a beautiful yogic *countering* practice called *centering* that goes after centeredness directly. In this practice, we discover that thought and emotion find equilibrium when the body becomes balanced, and that a calm and blissful sense of centeredness arises of its own accord when this three-point stabilization of body, mind and emotion gets sustained long enough to be consciously enjoyed.

In the next chapter, we will be providing a detailed description of this centering exercise. For now, just to get a sense of the benefit of a practice like this, try standing on one leg for about thirty seconds. Then try to stand on the other leg for the same amount of time.

Isn't it revealing how even a meager attempt to become physically balanced in an awkward position demands that breath be suspended, thought be stopped and emotion be quelled? Whether or not you can find equilibrium standing on one leg, just trying will yield a sense of what physical centeredness feels like, as well as a respect for the stilling effect a centering of the body can have on thought and emotion.

As we will discover again and again throughout this book, the physical realm provides our yoga practice with a variety of tangible hooks and handles for grabbing, holding and maneuvering our non-physical awareness.

10
Centering
Becoming still

In this practice, entitled "Centering," we will seek to find stillness in balance. In this easy effort we will be including the performance of two physical postures called *vrkshasana* and *sukhasana* in Sanskrit.

Since *vrksha* means "tree" and *asana* means "posture," *vrkshasana* is often referred to in English as, not surprisingly, the "tree posture." To assume *vrkshasana* (see figure 4) bend the right leg at the knee, place the right heel at the inside top of the left thigh and allow your right foot to rest on the inner left thigh, toes pointing downward. (If necessary, rest a hand on a nearby wall while moving into this position.) Then, as you balance on your left leg, join your hands in prayer position (palms together) at the level of your heart in front of your chest. After a comfortable period of time, move into the alternate version of this position to stand balanced on your right foot.

While you are achieving equilibrium in *vrkshasana*, you might find it helpful to focus your eyes upon one unmoving, physical object. As you become comfortable in *vrkshasana's* balance, your breath will *want* to pause. Let it, as you enjoy the poise of suspended stillness.

Also in this practice, we will be focusing upon developing a sitting posture for meditation. There are a variety of these seated positions. For now, we will be working with a physically undemanding one called

Figure 4:
Alternate versions of the "tree pose" known as vrkshasana *in Sanskrit*

sukhasana in Sanskrit. Although *sukhasana* literally means "joy pose," it is usually referred to in English as the "easy pose."

To assume *sukhasana* (see figure 5), sit in a simple cross-legged position with either leg folded over on top of the other. Resting your hands on your knees in any fashion that is comfortable for you, lift the crown of your head and feel your spine straighten as you visualize your body being pulled up from above, as if by a puppeteer's string. As you relax into this pose, rock back to front and side to side to locate your natural center of gravity. If you find it difficult to straighten your spine in this position, raise your seat up by slipping a pillow or a folded blanket under your sitting bones.

Figure 5: *The "easy pose" known as* sukhasana *in Sanskrit*

Centering

- In the top right corner of the next available page in your journal, write the date and time of this practice you are now beginning. In the top left corner of this page, write "Seeking Center."

- Perform *vrkshasana* (the "tree pose") until you have established a strong sense of physical balance. Be sure to assume both the left version of this posture (balancing on the left leg) and the right (balancing on the right leg). When you are finished, get up and walk around a bit. As you walk, try to maintain that balanced feeling you established in *vrkshasana*. This should be an easy and pleasant experience.

- After a few minutes of this balanced walking, sit down in *sukhasana*. In this seated posture for meditation, focus on establishing the same balance you achieved in *vrkshasana*. Feel how this balancing of the physical body brings calm to thought and emotion.

- Once you have become comfortable and balanced in *sukhasana*, perform several rounds of the *complete breath* (described on pages 4 and 5). Then relax in *ujjayi* as your breathing shallows toward suspension of its own accord.

A note: As this natural stilling of breath is cultivated, it will encourage a further calming and balancing of mind, body and emotion. When you sink and settle into the center of all this stilling, you will experience for yourself just how fluidly and easily the yoking of yoga can occur—especially as you discover how this yoking *wants* to happen and needs from you only your permission.

- After about 20 minutes or when you are ready, open your eyes and your journal and—under your title, "Seeking Center," record your reflections after having stood, walked and sat in balance. As you reflect, consider the efficacy of *centering* as a *countering* method of finding and holding *being*. How does its aftermath of feeling compare with what you experienced after letting go, chanting *Aum*, blessing with flowers, meditating "Who am I?" or "I am," and simply seeking bliss?

11
Awareness
Consciousness individualized

Awareness is an important quality of *being*, for it gives *being* its sense of identity and perception. The nature of this identity and perception is our true nature.

We say "true nature" because each of the many roles we play in life has a persona perceived as a nature. And each of these natures has a potential to mesmerize us into thinking that nature is our true nature, just as each role we play has a potential to mesmerize us into thinking that role is our true identity. Yoga breaks us loose from all of this mesmerizing to ground us in the one nature of our one true identity.

This "true identity" is both absolute and relative. As an absolute identity, it is Self. As a relative identity, it is *awareness*. *Awareness* is a functional extension of Self. Because *awareness* is a quality of *being*, its nature is the nature of *being*. Since the nature of any thing is comprised of that thing's qualities, the nature of *being* consists of *bliss, love, stillness, balance, peace, power, rapture, awareness* and more. All of this is provable through experience.

In concept, it has always been a basic tenet of yogic thought that *awareness* and *consciousness* are *not* the same thing. From this yogic perspective, *consciousness* is a basic property of life—wherever there is life there is *consciousness*. *Awareness*, on the other hand, is *conscious consciousness*, a specific chunk of that general life consciousness made distinctive by its individualization out of an all-encompassing and all-pervasive energy that is collective by nature. Having become individualized out of a collective consciousness, *awareness* possesses the ability to have subjective experience.

In yogic lore, the story of awareness is the story of the soul, a synopsis of which might be expressed as follows:

The birth of a soul is the individualization of awareness out of life's general field of consciousness. Each such soul born thusly is imbibed with an urge to get back to the way it was before it got individualized, but not before it enjoys the subjective experience of all that life has to offer, one piece of that all at a time. When a soul has finished this subjective experience of all that exists, it has not only completed its evolution, it has also recreated all that exists in its own subjective experience.

We share this over-all and long-range *concept* of soul evolution because it is central to one highly respected and traditional yogic perception of *awareness* and *consciousness*. That said, however, we should make it clear that your acceptance or rejection of this concept of the soul as it relates to *awareness* and *consciousness* will have little bearing on your experimentation with practices based on principles presented in this book *up to this point*. Now, back to news we can currently use.

The advantage of getting good at purposely tuning into *each* of the various qualities of *being* (bliss, love, stillness, balance, peace, power, rapture, awareness and more) is that, sooner or later, we will need them all. Not all at once, of course. But separately—as the circumstances of life require.

Depending on where we are in the stress and strain of everyday living, one of these qualities will always be of more assistance to us than the others. And each circumstance of life will signal a need for a different quality until, at some point in our application of yoga in life, all of the qualities of *being* will have been needed and pulled upon so much that our pulling will have become habitual.

Part of what we naturally get good at in this practice of pulling on the qualities of *being* is knowing *which* quality to pull on *when*. If we are feeling panic, for instance, we learn to sense from intuition that seeking out the soul's quality of *balance* is more pragmatically workable in that circumstance than looking for *peace* or *bliss*. If we find ourselves in a negative emotion that we would like to escape, we learn to sense from that same intuition that *awareness* is probably the best soul quality to summon forth since *awareness* is literally born to move.

What intuition wants us to know is: If we find our *self*—which would be our *awareness*—in anger, envy or fear, we do *not* have to stay there—not even for an instant. We can move. We can move our awareness from any negative (or positive) state of mind or emotion into *being* faster than light travels. It *is* possible.

12
Flowing
Moving awareness at will

In this practice, entitled "Flowing," we will be creating and performing two guided meditations designed to help us develop our inborn ability to intentionally move awareness at will. One of these meditations will be designed as a *script*. The other will be designed as a *map*.

As we practice both of these meditations we will be tapping into what we have learned over time from watching the performances of great television, movie and stage actors, who have become—by their natural ability and acquired skill—great movers of awareness.

In preparing our *guided meditation* with *scripting,* we will compose a *script* conveying the enactment of a series of thoughts and emotions that starts negatively and ends positively. In this *script* there will be no dialogue or monologue. Here is an example.

"John enters a room and sits down on a sofa. He is overcome with sadness and grief. Just minutes before, he and his wife, Jane, had argued. This was nothing new. They argued often. This time, however, Jane had stormed out of the house, vowing never to return. Now, the anger John had experienced while he and Jane were yelling at each other turns into anguish. Yet, just as he is about to cry, he remembers exactly what it was Jane said that made him so angry. And again, he becomes upset, this time trembling with rage. In his rage, he begins to mentally chastise Jane for everything he can remember she ever did to upset him. As he reviews all of these bothersome events, however, he sees they were not all generated by Jane. He realizes many of them were of his instigation. In this revelation he feels remorse. Soon enough, *John* is mentally apologizing to Jane for *his* faults. After this cleansing recognition and admission of his own shortcomings, John experiences a curiously uplifting sense of joyful freedom. He understands that in honestly looking at what he did, as well as the person he thought he was while he was doing what he did, he stepped into an ability to see himself as others might see him. In this detachment, he experiences a calm and gentle transcendence of burden."

The meditation portion of this exercise occurs in two stages *after* the *script* has been written. In the first stage, we attempt to live out our *script* in our head as we read it through. In the second stage, we close our eyes to again experience our story line, this time without reading the *script*. A note: Although there is no monologue or dialogue in our *script*, we can have fun creating such imagined talking or conversing on the fly as we inwardly enact our story.

This kind of meditation requires visualization, a remarkable tool for moving awareness creatively. Be prepared to surprise yourself with how powerfully your visualizations can stir quite real emotional reactions and how intensely those emotions can activate quite real physical responses. In the truest sense, visualization is a practical implementation of mind over matter.

A *guided meditation* with *mapping* is similar to a *guided meditation* with *scripting* except that *scripting* is composed of words and *mapping* is composed primarily of pictures. While a *script* is a block of words that gives a somewhat detailed description of a story, a *map* is a collection of images that includes only enough words to convey but a hint of story outline.

The only words on a *map* are in event titles. These titles are placed aesthetically here and there on the *map* page and tied together with directional lines drawn artistically to represent the order of the story's events. In the space left around these titles and connecting lines, drawn or painted imagery depicts the details of the events entitled. Here is an example description of how one such *map* might be drawn:

In the upper left corner of a full blank journal page, we write, "John and Mary argue." We then draw a line from those four words across the top of the page to its upper right corner where we write, "Mary leaves home." Connecting those words to the bottom-right corner of the page with another line, we write, "John is sad." From this title, we draw a line half way across the bottom of the page and write, "John is angry." From there we draw a line to the bottom left corner of the page to write, "John gets critical." From that lower left corner we draw a line about half way up the left side of the page and write, "John has an insight." Finally, we draw a line from "John has an insight" rightward to the center of the page where we write, "John experiences a curious transcendence." Having now completed a briefly worded contour of our story's journey, we go back and fill in the remaining blank space on the page with simple or complex illustrations depicting our story's events in visual detail.

As with our *script* practice, the meditation portion of this *map* exercise occurs in two stages *after* the *map* has been drawn. In the first stage, we live out our *map* in our head, as we are looking at it with our eyes open. In the second stage, we close our eyes to again inwardly enact our *map*, this time without looking at it.

In life as in yoga, these *scripting* and *mapping* meditations can be used as tools for moving awareness whenever we feel the focus of that awareness getting stuck or locked in thoughts or emotions we would like to leave. The example story lines above, for instance, could just as well have been *scripts* or *maps* conceived to methodically move ourselves—our awareness—up and out of unpleasant psychological conditions we have been experiencing, perhaps for years.

The workability of these meditations hinges upon our understanding and acceptance of the principle that each of us is a point of awareness free to travel in the mind as we wish and will. This practice of "Flowing" is designed to provide us with some experience that might generate this understanding and acceptance.

One final note: The words of the *scripts* and *maps* you create should be written in the third person rather than in the first person. In the above example, for instance, it is written, "John and Mary argue," rather than, "My wife and I argue."

This depersonalizing makes the application of *scripting* and *mapping* more beneficial for two reasons: 1. It provides objectivity. 2. It de-emphasizes an implication we *are* the life roles we play (by eliminating the use of the pronoun, "I.")

Now, let us be the awareness we are and flow.

Flowing

• In the top right corner of the next available page in your journal, write the date and time of this practice you are now beginning. In the top left corner of this page, write "My Flow Script." Under that title, compose your *script*.

A note: The "flow script" you compose will be most meaningful to you if it begins with a negative event that you have actually experienced. This will mean the first one, two or three events of your *script* will have already happened, while the remaining events of that *script* will have not yet occurred. In structuring these events that have not yet occurred, you will have an opportunity to intuit a movement of awareness that rises up and out of the negative state of mind you were in when you were experiencing the first event or events you recorded in your *script*.

- When you have completed your *script*, sit in *sukhasana*, initiate an *ujjayi* breath control and perform your *flow-control meditation* on the *script* you have just written—first, while reading your *script* with your eyes open; then, while remembering that *script* with your eyes closed.

- When you have completed your meditation, lie back in *shavasana* and continue an *ujjayi* breath control as you enjoy the aftermath of your *script meditation*.

- When you are ready to move on, sit up and turn to the next available page in your journal (you will need a full page for this) and write "My Flow Map." Under that title, compose your *map*.

A note: Your *map* can be a picture version of the *script* that you have just written, or it can be different. If it begins with and is based upon another event, work as you did with your *script* to compose a *map* that will end on a high note and leave you in a positive state of mind.

- Once you have drawn your *map*, continue sitting in *sukhasana*, initiate an *ujjayi* breath control and perform your *flow-control meditation* on the *map* you have just drawn—first, while looking at your *map* with your eyes open; then, while visualizing that *map* with your eyes closed.

- When you have completed your meditation, lie back in *shavasana* and continue your *ujjayi* breath control as you enjoy the aftermath of the practice you have just completed.

- After about ten minutes or when you are ready, sit up, open your journal and write "My Ever Moving Awareness." Under that title, record your reflections upon your experience of creating and performing your *scripting* and *mapping* meditations. As you reflect, keep in mind this practice of "Flowing" was designed to provide you with an opportunity to acknowledge and exercise your inherent ability to intentionally move awareness at will from a negative to a positive state of mind.

13
Breath
Life of body, leader of mind

Have you ever noticed that your breathing slows and occasionally stops when you concentrate deeply, and your concentration diffuses out of focus when you breathe deeply? Awareness literally moves on breath. For awareness to be still, breath must decelerate and occasionally pause. For awareness to move, breath must become active.

Practices built on a recognition of this connection between *breath* and *awareness* are designed to help develop what is often referred to as "mind control," but might more appropriately be called *awareness control*. The working principle here is that *awareness*, which is *not* physical, can be controlled through the skillful manipulation of *breath*, which *is* physical. This is a most practical teaching. It states that, if we find our awareness fixed in a place we do not want it to be, we can unfix it by simply breathing deeply. Conversely, if we like where our awareness is, we can keep it fixed there by calming the breath into stillness.

The first practitioners of yoga thought of breath as life. Hence, their term for *breath control* was *pranayama*, literally "the control of life force." As those early yogis and yoginis worked with this life control, they learned that *pranayama* could boost physical health by enhancing the exchange of oxygen and carbon dioxide in the physical body. They also learned that *pranayama* could bring an element of transcendent control to both yoga and life. There are a great many *pranayamas*. Thus far, we have worked with four. Throughout the remaining 95 of the 108 chapters of this book, we will explore more.

The *pranayama*s we have covered so far are: the *complete breath*, which centers awareness in *being* as it maximizes oxygen intake and carbon dioxide release; the *cleansing breath*, which moves awareness into a sense of blissful rejuvenation as it increases the elimination of toxins from the blood; the *sigh breath,* which releases awareness from negative emotion as it eases health-harming stress in the physical body; and the *ujjayi breath,* which allows awareness a greater freedom of movement in thought and emotion as it brings a sense of stability, grace, and wellbeing into physical action.

All *pranayamas* are significantly strengthened when they are performed rhythmically. A *rhythmic pranayama* is a breath control that is measured with a counting that is felt as a pulse. *Rhythm* brings hypnotic cadence to breath control and makes it enjoyably sustainable. It also awakens a powerful mysticism.

From a mystical perspective, rhythm is a trance-building pulsation of *doing* interspersed with *being*—each pulse is a *do*; the space between each pulse is a *be*—that can yield, in any action performed rhythmically, nearly limitless power. Such a marvelous potential is too often left sleeping in life, but not in yoga. In yoga, rhythm is extolled for all its worth.

During the practice described in the following chapter, we will work to isolate, appreciate and unleash the real power of *pranayama* by using *rhythm* to enhance our experience of the four breath controls we have learned thus far.

14
Rhythmizing
Using rhythm to vitalize breath control

Anyone can feel *rhythm*. Those who think they can't just haven't tried—not really. Dancers and drummers are good at feeling *rhythm* because it is a necessary part of what they do. But that does not mean they "have *rhythm*" and the rest of us don't. Everybody has *rhythm* just like everybody has a heartbeat. And feeling *rhythm* is like feeling the heartbeat. At first, it doesn't seem like it's there. Then all of a sudden—aha!—we've got it. This fun practice, entitled "Rhythmizing," is all about feeling *rhythm*—especially in the practice of *pranayama*.

Rhythmizing

• In the top right corner of the next available page in your journal, write the date and time of this practice you are now beginning. In the top left corner of this page, write "Breath Dancing to Music."

• Select a rhythmic piece of music that you really like. It can be fast or slow. Rock and roll. Bach or blues. Only you can choose what you like. But please like it. That will make a big difference. Once you have decided upon your one selection of music, play it. Loudly! Or at least as loudly as you can stand. Tap your feet to it. Snap your fingers. Move a little. Have some fun.

• When the song finishes, play it again. This time, get up and dance. Never mind your steps. Just move. Any way you want—any way you can. It does not matter what you do, or how you do it. The only important thing is that you allow the rhythm of the song to move you. This is not a hard thing to do, because it is not done. It is allowed.

• When the songs finishes, play it again. This time, stand still and feel the beat without moving to it. Allow your breath to become coordinated with the rhythm of the song. You know what that rhythm is. You've just danced to it. Now you are allowing that rhythm to enter your breath. When you feel you are breathing rhythmically, balance that rhythmic breath by equalizing the count of its inhalation with the count of its exhalation. If your song is slow, your breathing may fall into a 4/4 count (four counts in, four counts out). If it is fast, it may follow an 8/8 count.

• When the songs finishes, play it four more times. During each of these four repetitions, maintain the balanced rhythmic count you have just established, yet specify your breath control in the following way: During the first repetition of the song, perform the *complete breath*. (If you feel inspired to, add in the physical movement of the *full wing flight*.) During the second repetition, perform the *cleansing breath*. During the third repetition, perform the *sigh breath*. And during the fourth repetition, perform the *ujjayi breath*. (If you feel light-headed during any of these practices, pause for a few moments. Then continue.)

• When you are finished, lie back in *shavasana* and enjoy the aftermath of your "Rhythmizing." After about ten minutes or when you are ready, sit up, open your journal and, under your title, "Breath Dancing to Music," record your reflections upon rhythmizing your practice of the *complete breath*, the *cleansing breath*, the *sigh breath* and the *ujjayi breath*.

15
Wisdom
Insight applied in the fulfillment of need

Thought usually moves in one of three ways. It wanders aimlessly, circles repetitively or plods from point to point. Although these three ways of thinking vary greatly, they share one common factor. They are all processes. Intuition is not a process. It is a freestanding occurrence of direct perception.

Before we proceed too deeply into an investigation of thought and intuition as these faculties relate to yoga, it would be helpful to lay out the gist of the Eastern mystical perspective—composed of thought, inspired by intuition—that forms the backbone of most introspective yoga practices. In summary, that gist is this:

Truth is relative and absolute. A relative truth is only real in the world of manifestation—a world that exists relative to and because of its unmanifest source. The relative truth of the manifest world is revealed in experience. Because experience can only occur if there is an experiencer, the unmanifest Self must manifest as awareness to be that experiencer.

Because awareness can only be aware by becoming what it is aware of, it suffers a propensity for getting stuck in its experience. As awareness gets stuck in and thus wrongly identified with its experience, it loses track of its one, true and essential identity as Self.

In a loss of even a sense of its Self, awareness falls prey to fear and desire. Prodded on by fear and lured on by desire, this lost experiencer—now a pilgrim-on-the-run—has no choice but to take on many transient identities as it works its way back toward a conscious reunion with its one true identity after having experienced all the manifest world has to offer, one piece of that all at a time.

From a perspective like this, the manifest world looks like a precariously shifting existence that does not function according to truths that remain fixed. The statement, "you should wear warm clothes," for instance, would be true during a cold winter but false during a hot summer. Or the statement, "you should do as your father does," would be true if your father was a kind and wise man but false if he was a psychopathic killer.

Yet, we can also sense from this perspective that there is a one unchanging truth that stands behind the very existence of the ever-shifting world we live in as well as that world's ever-changing truths. We sense this one unchanging truth as an ultimate essence that cannot be seen, heard, smelled, touched or tasted because it is timeless, spaceless, formless, causeless and thus obviously indefinable. This one-and-only, behind-the-scenes, off-the-grid ultimate truth is what some yogis refer to as the "absolute truth" or the "unchanging truth" to distinguish it from all those many changing truths that are relative and temporary.

For the most part, our most frequent access to this absolute truth occurs indirectly and incompletely as we strive to solve day-to-day problems in the manifest world of relative reality. In these down-to-earth efforts, we perceive gleanings of this truth absolute in bits and pieces, as it gets filtered through into news we can use. If we are good at this down-to-earth accessing of permanent truth in a practical context, we are said to have "common sense." In this grounded state of clarity, the one and only, unchanging, absolute reality lines up with our personal, ever-shifting and relative needs to reveal pragmatic wisdom on the fly.

Now, back to thought and intuition.

Thought can either help or harm our access to common sense, for thought precedes our physical actions with decisions that either do or do not accentuate that practical knowing. Even if thought is endorsing common sense and trying to accommodate it, it can jam itself up with its own excessive processing. In this way, thought—even well intended thought—can form a screen that even intuition can't pierce.

From a yogic perspective, thought is perceived as a describer and an explainer that lives in its own world. Because that world of thought is fortified by its own filtering of bliss, those who live there in it do not want to leave it and strive to stay there by thinking just for the bliss of it and nothing else.

In yoga, we work to use thought not as a toy but as a tool for deciding our way through life toward life's essence. With this end in mind, we first use thought to exert a control over our instinctive nature by making decisions that allow our will to work positively toward a transmutation of our lower urges into higher aspirations.

And as we use thought in this way, we find that, if the thought we employ in making daily decisions is of the aimlessly wandering sort, or if it flies in circles, it will be far less effective than if it plods from point to point. Yet we also find that, if our daily thought is *none* of these three, but instead is of a more open sort of mentality that ushers in and fortifies even a little bit of intuition, *that thought just could be brilliant.*

Although logic is a magnificent thing and deserves all the respect it receives, it should best be carefully considered during any sort of important decision-making, for it is a double-edged sword that can work with or against our intuitive inspiration. If logic is set to reveal and support intuition, that intuition can be made manifest and beautifully expressed. Yet if that logic gets set to block intuition, there is nothing intuition can do to get through. It must wait.

There are two ways to deal with logic when it is blocking intuition. One way works. The other one doesn't. The way that works is the way of allowing. The way that doesn't work is the way of warring.

If we choose to war with logic, logic will antagonize every surfacing of intuition and disparage its very existence. If we choose to allow logic to do what it does, it will work its way willingly toward intuition to eventually see right through it to its source.

To *allow* logic is to let logic play itself out. Once logic has drained its arsenal of memories into thought and has worked that thought through until thought itself is no longer fascinating, it will gladly trade what could have been a fight for what one famous yogi used to call "the third-eyed sight of insight."

There is one catch here. If memory—the reservoir of information that logic needs for its functioning—keeps getting restocked, it will never drain.

It is upon this point of committing new information to memory that logicians and yogis part ways. While logicians assume their logic will suffer if they don't remember enough, yogis assume their meditations will suffer if they remember too much.

Not surprisingly, once yogis have set themselves on a clear path of practice, they curtail their intake of outside information and focus upon processing the data they are already holding. In this effort, they read a little less and meditate a little more, ask fewer questions than ever before. And through all their careful sifting, they throw out what they do not need and keep just what they do as they slowly clear a window they can see right through. Soon enough, they are enjoying a controlled and consistent flow of intuition.

Once this regular surfacing of intuition gets established, it needs to be made useful. To be made useful it must be assimilated into thought and expressed in words. Since this assimilation and expression may not occur flawlessly because of the limitations of thought, thought itself must be used to double-check itself in its amalgamation with intuition. This is where a cooperative logic is most helpful.

Yet even when an intuitive break-through has been fully assimilated into thought, expressed in words and double-checked with logic, it must still be put to work in a fulfillment of need to finally don its crown of wisdom, for wisdom not needed is not wisdom at all.

Here is an example of wisdom in action: A woman who has, for many years, intuited she is not a mortal body but is instead an imperishable soul, receives unexpected news that she has terminal cancer. While her family and friends are overcome with grief and sadness, she is amazingly calm and serene in a sense of knowing that now rises up to cradle her in an assurance that the intuition she has felt for years is correct— She is a soul that cannot die.

Although all of this rumination about thought, intuition and wisdom offers obvious guidance for living and moving in the world of manifestation, it is really only an introduction to the deeper thrust of yoga, which is to focus upon the "I" that does the living and moving. In this more essential yoga, we dismantle manifest life back into its unmanifest source by relentlessly investigating the experiencer of experience.

The final goal of an investigation like this is, as has been mentioned, *to realize life's fullest potential by merging with life's ultimate essence*. Yet most serious yogis who are committed to this pursuit simply see themselves *doing* what it has now finally come their time *do* and *being* what it has now finally come their time to *be*. Having left unnecessary thought behind and having established a conscious experience of *being* as the highest priority of their lives, these yogis live as *awareness*, the closest "I" to Self.

There are many ways we can approach living as *awareness*. One of these is through the practice *of intentionally becoming absorbed*. In this practice, we allow awareness to do what it is naturally inclined to do—which is to become what it is aware of—with the stipulation that this becoming occurs under conscious supervision. The yogic effort here is to consciously *control* a basic function of life that usually occurs unconsciously and *without control*.

As we begin this practice of *intentionally becoming absorbed*, we are an *observer* who is *observing* an *observed*. As this practice progresses, that *observer* gradually becomes so absorbed in *observing* that it becomes its *observed* to the extent the "I" that *observer* perceived itself to be no longer exists—at least for the duration of that *state of being absorbed*. Example: A surfer becomes so intentionally absorbed in riding a wave he becomes the wave.

When *awareness* gets designated as the *observed* and the observer becomes absorbed in *that*, only awareness exists. If awareness, which is an extension of Self, can remain absorbed in itself and resist the urge to surge out into manifestation to get absorbed into something else, it can eventually withdraw back to the "the brink of the Absolute" and from there merge back into its Self—the essence of all.

Early on in this practice *of intentionally becoming absorbed*, we discover we can easily become one with something we are interested in, but have great difficulty in finding that same level of integration with something we couldn't care less about.

At this point, we might wonder if we are ready for a deeper practice of yoga, for we can see that yoga demands an *interest* in becoming *absorbed* in *awareness*. Yet, as soon as we figure out that awareness comes with bliss and we have worked it out within ourselves that it's okay to enjoy bliss, which is something everyone really wants, suddenly we can accept that we might just be able to develop the sort of *interest* that would make a deeper yoga practice possible.

Soon enough, however, we also come to the sober realization that awareness, unlike surfing, is illusively subtle, and that attempting to grab and hold anything illusively subtle is like "trying to catch the wind in a paper bag."

Those who follow their yoga past this point of realizing a simple pursuit is not always an easy pursuit usually get at least a little humble. The good news here is that, although getting humble is not always fun—especially if it is arrived at though humiliation—it's always a blessing, for there is nothing that humility can't help, especially in yoga.

In the self-effacement of genuine humility, our yoga of working with awareness gets softened, our character becomes pliable and our life adjusts smoothly to change. Through all of this, we cannot help but see that, from the perspective of pure *awareness*, the many "I's" of the world are fragile and forever morphing, and in that morphing forever homing in on Self. The delight of this insight inspires us to make our daily decisions from the inside-out as *a soul in a body* rather than from the outside-in as *a body with a soul*.

Next to the needs of the body, the needs of the soul don't feel like needs at all, for they aren't infiltrated with that desperate, fear-of-death clutching that comes with physical existence. All the soul needs is the exercise of its intuition to derive wisdom from experience.

16

Wait Watching

Catching distraction

In this practice, entitled "Wait Watching," we will develop a healthy respect for the surreptitious power of distraction as we strive to catch that distraction in the moment of its seduction of our awareness.

Wait Watching

• In the top right corner of the next available page in your journal, write the date and time of this practice you are now beginning. In the top left corner of this page, write "On my Watch."

• Lie back in *shavasana* and perform a *rhythmic ujjayi* in a count that is the same for both the inhalation and the exhalation. As you perform this breath control, let your "I" be the watcher. And let that watcher wait for distraction.

A note: A good way to initiate this practice is to attempt a visualization of emptiness. Certainly, you can be aware of an emptiness devoid of things, thoughts and emotions, but can you be aware of a complete emptiness? Isn't it true that the one thing you cannot empty out of your emptiness is the feeling of *being*?

When we discover that *being* is forever present, though sometimes not obviously so, it becomes apparent that purposely sitting in a conscious awareness of *being* is a good place to hunker down while waiting and watching for distraction.

• When you catch yourself in the midst of a distraction that has somehow crept in to distort your sense of *being*, stop your *rhythmic ujjayi*, perform three *sigh breaths*, and focus upon tracing that distraction's sequential story line backwards to the moment it stole your awareness away. Once you have located that moment of capture, return to *being* to wait and watch.

A Note: In this waiting in and watching from within *being*, your objective is to catch distractions as close to their point of origin as possible. As you work to perform this surprisingly difficult task, you will find yourself somehow moving from *not being distracted* to *being distracted* with no awareness of how or when that transition occurred. It is because pinpointing the beginning of this transition is so innately illusive that a good portion of this exercise will consist of tracing distractions backwards from the time you catch them consciously to the point they caught you, your awareness, to take you over.

Example: In the midst of your contented waiting and watching you suddenly find yourself working out the details of repairing a leak in the roof of your home. As you trace the story line of this distraction backwards toward its source, you realize that right before you were mentally repairing that leak you were speculating how easy it would be for professional carpenters to take advantage of unsuspecting clients. And before that, you were lamenting that you had some financial problems. And before that you were reflecting that you should be saving more money for retirement. And before that you were thinking that money concerns cause stress. And before that you were sitting contentedly in *being*, waiting but apparently not watching all that closely for distraction.

As you finish up this backwards tracing, you feel empowered as you realize how effective simply becoming observantly aware of the sequential structure of a distraction can be in awakening an alertness within you that will not so easily allow such a distraction to so blatantly overtake you again.

- After about 20 minutes (or longer if you like), remain in *shavasana* to enjoy the aftermath of this practice. Then sit up, open your journal and—under your title, "On my Watch"—record your reflections after having performed this *countering* exercise of *Wait Watching*. As you reflect, try to specify the degree of your settling into watcher awareness. Your sense of calm, the stillness of your breath, the intensity of your bliss and the relaxation of your body will provide helpful clues as you make this assessment.

17
Needs
Useful aims of desire

Even best friends could not convince us of the importance of a thing or a thought or a feeling for which we could sense no apparent need. But what we do not need today we might need tomorrow, for our needs evolve with the unstoppable changes of our life.

Our initial perception of this coordinated evolution of need and life stimulates a general feeling that we are undergoing some sort of large-scale, long-range development through bodily existence. We cannot quite determine what we are developing toward or why. All we know for sure is we are in the middle of a forward motion we can't escape. Not surprisingly, all of this not-knowing-for-sure leaves us feeling insecure.

Since the intent of all our yogic *countering* exercises is to cancel out *doing* with *doing* to *be*, and since a feeling of insecurity is simply a result of externalized thinking due to a lack of intuition, which is an inherent quality of *being*, it should come as no surprise that finding *being* through the yoking of yoga eliminates insecurity.

Through our own experimentation with yoga principles and practices, we can see for ourselves how insecurity is a product of externalized thinking—externalized thinking that could become internalized if thought were allowed to align with intuition. From this we can learn that externalized thinking is thought minus intuition, and internalized thinking is thought plus intuition—the psychological basis for a deeply rooted sense of security.

In addition to eradicating insecurity, intuitive thought can eliminate angst, confusion, frustration, depression, despair, pessimism, grief, impatience, anger, hatred, worry and much more. Yet it does not give back, all at once, the opposite of all these, as logic might expect. What it gives back instead is insight—as in *inner sight*. Through this inner sight of insight, we know what we need to know when we need to know it in the moment. Again, *need* is the key and *now* is the time.

That insight fulfills only the need of the *now* does not mean it is frugal. Quite the contrary. Insight is always abundant. If we find ourselves in a state of confusion, for instance, insight can most happily supply us with a considerable variety of options for solving practical problems in practical ways. If we are feeling pessimistic, insight can fill us to the brim with a great sense of hope spiced with a bountiful anticipation of a bright future full of infinite possibility. Truly, the insight of inner sight is, in every way, perfect and plentiful in its providing.

Since a lot of our discontent stems from wanting what we think we need but don't, simply understanding what we actually do need can provide us with a great sense of contentment all by itself. Yet before we can understand what we do need as opposed to what we don't need, we must understand *need* in relationship to *desire* and *will*.

A *need* is a circumstance of necessity while a *desire* is a force of wanting that seeks fulfillment by *will*. Because *need* requires *desire*, and *desire* requires *will*, these three—*need, will* and *desire*—are necessarily interdependent. Over time their mutual function and development might occur something like this: As *will* fortifies *desire* to override *need* in the gratification of instinctive impulses, our experience of the consequence of this early activation of *need*, *will* and *desire* eventually teaches us to control *will* to restrain *desire* within the confines of *need*.

When we are eating a meal, for instance, there is a point when our *need* is fulfilled and our *will* either restrains our *desire* to eat more then we *need* or fortifies our *desire* to ignore *need* and keep on eating. To cognize the kind of aggressive impulsiveness that can blur even our perception of that critical stop-or-go point is to understand the nature of *desire* and *will* as they work together to either heed or override *need*.

If becoming an adult includes cultivating an awareness of needs associated with bodily survival in the physical world, then growing up must include mastering the use of *desire* and *will* for the responsible fulfillment of our *needs* more than the gratification of our senses.

Although physical needs are as real as physical life and should be attended to, they can generate an erroneous conviction that we *are* the physical body we live in. This misconception leaves awareness stuck in a three-way hold imposed by a desire for life, a fear of death and the burden of physical needs.

Even a little meditation can alleviate this crowding pressure of desire, fear and need, at least enough for our sense of "I" to temporarily reorient itself to a deeper place and, by that adjustment, allow the revelatory insight that stepping out of a sense of identity with the physical body actually *helps our function within the physical body*.

Once we have proved to ourselves, through our own experience, that detachment can actually benefit our involvement with the challenges of everyday life, we become more willing to perceive our daily existence as a matrix for the creation and resolution of karma.

The word *karma*, which literally means "action," is the principle of action-and-reaction or cause-and-effect that requires us to learn *from life* by enduring the consequences of our actions *in life*. When we refer to "a karma," we are generally indicating a specific action/reaction that has not yet been resolved with understanding.

As we come to appreciate the law of karma by living under its rule, we see physical life not only as a greenhouse for the evolution of karma but also as an environment for the maturation of the soul we might now be willing to perceive ourselves to be. Once we have developed this kind of healthy respect for life on earth, our needs expand beyond the physical into the blissful realms of spirit.

18
Needalizing
Identifying needs

In this practice, entitled "Needalizing," we will be establishing useful aims of desire by identifying physical and psychological needs.

Needalizing

• In the top right corner of the next available page in your journal, write the date and time of this practice you are now beginning. In the top left corner, write "My Needs." Under this title, draw one long line down the center of the remainder of your page to create two vertical columns of equal width. At the top of the first column, write "Physical Needs." At the top of the second column, write "Psychological Needs."

• After you have become comfortably settled in a seated position with your journal in your lap, and a pen in your hand, casually reflect upon your life in an easy-going way to identify and group your needs into physical and psychological categories. As these needs occur to you, write them down in their appropriate column.

A note: To isolate only what we *do* need reveals by contrast what we *do not* need. This categorization alone stimulates great perceptual clarity. Such clarity frees intuition to guide awareness into a *now* that feels no need at all, for in *now awareness* there is a detachment from mind and body—the only two places that needs can exist. From within the detachment of *now awareness*, we can be—like a parent to its children—the optimal judge of what our mind and body actually require.

- When your list is as complete as you think you can make it with easy effort, perform the *full wing flight* three times, followed by three rounds of the *cleansing breath*. In the pleasant aftermath of these practices, lie back in *shavasana*. Once you are settled, try to imagine life without the needs you have listed. Ask yourself, "If these needs did not exist, would I? If so, who would I be?" Then wait with an open feeling of receptivity for clues to answers.

- After about ten minutes or when you feel the time is right, sit up and open your journal. In the top left corner of the next available page in that journal, write "Free Writing 2." Then close your eyes. Visualize a vacant space in front of your face. Allow that vacant space to be filled with whatever comes. Whatever comes, open your eyes and write it down.

19
Experience
The means by which we know

Experience teaches us that experience *is* knowledge, which is to say we only know with certainty what we have experienced. Although we might conjecture from this that we—whoever we perceive ourselves to be—evolve by *knowing* through *experiencing* the *all* of existence, one piece of that *all* at a time, we could not deny this is but speculation. All we really know, with a certainty that can only come from experience, is we cannot have an experience that does not teach us something, for it is undeniably true we learn from every experience we have, whether that experience is deemed "good" or "bad."

Yet, even as we approach life with a reverence for experience, there is often a crumbling of that reverence *while* we are enduring experiences that are painful. *After* such encounters with pain, our respect for experience gets reestablished and perhaps fortified as we more deeply come to appreciate the lessons of life those painful experiences had to offer us and thus lament to ourselves something like, "What is pain and why is it of concern, when it is obviously both temporary and necessary in a continuum of experience that is forever changing, and in that changing, forever moving forward?"

What experience would like us to know *about* pain is that the instant we recognize we are no longer *in* pain, we have moved forward *out* of pain into another experience in another *now*. And in that new experience in a new *now*, we are able to see that our perception of pain and pleasure, like our perception of good and bad, is forever changing, and in that changing, forever moving forward.

Experience also has much to teach us about fear and desire, for it is from experience that we realize how these two powerful forces are such major motivators of progressive change anywhere their impact is felt. Because fears and desires are also always changing, and in that changing, forever moving forward, their influence is all the more a catalyst for change in our lives as well as all they affect.

From our own experience of fear and desire, we can see, as our fears pull us back and our desires lure us forward, how we kindle a desperate need for security. Yet the instant we think we have found that security, we lose it as our fears and desires change yet again to shift us into dealing with a whole new set of insecurities brought on by a whole new set of fears and desires. All of this perception is coming to us from our experience—not our speculation.

Although understanding life as an experiential metamorphosis might not completely eliminate the feeling of insecurity, a deepening of our experience will. When awareness plunges in to deep mystical experience, it moves from the insecurity of external life to the security of internal life where there is a powerful sensing of certain fixed truths providing existence with a cosmic law and order of sorts. What intuition wants us to know about these fixed truths is that the only specific understanding we can have *of them* will be in accordance with what we need to know *from them* right *now*.

One way to gain a more functional comprehension of how these fixed truths work in our lives is to observe them as principles playing themselves out in repeating patterns of experience. Take, for instance, the experiential pattern of *pulling back in fear and lurching forward in desire*. This is a pattern *of* experience we understand *from* experience. Yet it is a pattern representing principles we do not completely understand because we do not *need* that complete understanding *now*.

After we have encountered a lot of fear and desire, we can understand through insight based on experience that, in principle, *fear and desire perform a positive function in our lives and have much to offer us through our experience of them*. What we can then learn from this little bit of insight applied through more experience is that *a wise fear is a prudent caution, and a wise desire is a loving urge to serve*.

That which we do unto others gets done unto us. This is another experiential pattern based on a principle we cannot understand completely but have named "karma" anyway. All we can really know about karma is what we need to know from its pattern of experience played out right *now*, which is *we should be careful to act with forethought*.

Although this intuitive understanding and appreciation of consequence is forever awaiting us in the *now*, we usually have to go through quite a bit of experience before we can catch and value its fullest significance in practical application. Yet whatever experience we have to have to get to that *living respect for the law of karma* can do nothing but move us forward in the growth of understanding that can only occur through accumulating experience.

20

Facing

Confronting fear and desire

In this practice, entitled "Facing," we will brave an honest look at some of our more prominent fears and desires. Because fears and desires are often embarrassing, they can be a little more difficult to identify then needs. Certainly, this is understandable since we generally perceive our fears and desires to be weaknesses that either make us a person we don't think we should be or keep us from becoming a person we think we could be. Revealing and facing such weaknesses is *not* going to be something we will naturally feel inclined to do. Yet *doing just that*—revealing and facing these weaknesses—changes us for the better by stimulating a release of those fear-and-desire-based shortcomings out into the open scrutiny of intuition functioning through awareness, detached.

Facing

- In the top right corner of the next available page in your journal, write the date and time of this practice you are now beginning. In the top left corner, write "My Current Fears and Desires." Under this title, draw one long vertical line right down the center of the remainder of your page to create two vertical columns of equal width. At the top of the first column, write "Fears." At the top of the second column, write "Desires."

- After you have become comfortably seated with your journal in your lap and a pen in your hand, reflect upon the feeling of fear. This will bring up memories of fearful experiences. As these memories surface, look for repetitions—certain, recurring, oh-my-god-here-we-go-again experiences stimulated by the same or similar fears. Under your title, "Fears," summarize these dreaded experiences in one or two-word descriptions like: "competition," "heights" or "public speaking."

- When you feel you are ready, reflect upon the feeling of desire. Again, this will bring up memories of experiences driven by desire. As before, look for repetitions—certain, recurring experiences of comfort or pleasure stimulated by the same or similar desires. Then, under your title, "Desires," summarize those comfortable or pleasurable experiences in one or two-word descriptions like: "shopping," "eating" or "hanging out."

A note: It is pure awareness and intuition that we are working with here as we strive to simply see and list our fears and desires. Although pure awareness is a powerful tool all by itself, it is never by itself when it is aware of something other than itself. Then it is working with intuition, and intuition will never miss the gist of that which falls before its gaze.

- When your list is as complete as you think you can make it, perform the *full wing flight* three times, followed by three rounds of the *cleansing breath.* In the aftermath of these practices, lie back in *shavasana* and enjoy the bliss of *being.*

• Once you are settled, try to imagine life without fear or desire. Ask yourself, "If these fears and desires did not exist, would I? If so, who would I be?" and wait with an open feeling of receptivity for your answers. Spend about ten minutes with this.

• Then, remaining in *shavasana,* reflect upon the statement: "I am," as you allow your intuition to guide you into that *being* that knows nothing of fear and desire.

• After about ten minutes or when you feel the time is right, sit up and open your journal. In the top left corner of the next available page, write "Free Writing 3."

As in the previous free-writing exercises, close your eyes, visualize a vacant space in front of your face, and allow that vacant space to be filled with whatever comes. Whatever comes, open your eyes and write it down. When you are done, don't read what you've written right away. Let some time pass—maybe a day. When you *do* read it back, compare it with what you have written during the previous two free-writing exercises.

21
Opposites
The parameters of thought

We have all heard the phrase, "dead center." In the *New Oxford American Dictionary,* "dead center" is defined as "the position of a crank when it is in line with the connecting rod and not exerting torque," like a steering wheel of a car turned neither left nor right.

Being is like that unturned steering wheel. When *being* gets turned left or right, it becomes a *doing* that sparks the manifestation of a dormant potential. Once a dormant potential becomes manifest, it is never quite balanced for becoming balanced would mean returning to dormancy. So, the current state of any physical, emotional, mental or spiritual manifestation of dormancy exists at some point off "dead center," somewhere between two polar opposites.

The breaking light of dawn and the dying light of dusk, for instance, are physical conditions that exist somewhere between the two polar opposites of noon and midnight.

Although opposites are easier to specify when they are physical, they can at least be generally acknowledged when they are not physical. Take "happy" and "sad," for instance. Even though we could rightly assert ten different people will have ten different perceptions of what it is to be "happy" or "sad," anyone would have to agree that any degree of gloom or cheer would have to exist somewhere between some assessment of "happy" and "sad."

When intuition leaves *the world of being* to get applied in *the world of doing*, it becomes thought, for to think intuitively is to take intuition and *do* something with it. Once intuition becomes thought, however, it is no longer a simple, clear and direct perception of an absolute. Suddenly it is a concept subject to the laws of the slippery, tug-of-war world of opposites like right and wrong, good and bad, smart and dumb, pure and impure and so on. To further complicate matters, these opposites of this ever-shifting world are specified differently by each person who perceives them.

Because the old yoga masters fully understood the propensity for thought to muddle its own most important function of implementing intuition, they worked to keep their thinking minimal. Yet in all their thrift of thought, they never considered *not* escorting intuition *into* thought and double-checking its positioning there *with* thought.

Of course, it was never their contention that intuition needed double-checking. They knew intuition was *never wrong*. What they conceded *could* use some review was the clarity of their own perception of that intuition, as well as their thought and expression of it.

Because intuition must pass through thought to get used, it only makes sense the thought it passes through should be not only logical but also open. As a type of reflection that makes a priority of not misusing its power to fortify a limited point of view, open thought focuses on remaining centered and equitable as it adjusts quickly and smoothly to the constant change of a never-static world in which even polarities are not fixed. Since such sophisticated thought does not just happen, it needs to be cultivated like a skill needs to be developed.

In the cultivation of this kind of thought, we strive to think logically while feeling intuitively. Happily, these two functions are not as contradictory as they might seem to be and actually work quite well together when given a chance to do so.

22
Luminating
Leading thought with intuition

In this practice, entitled "Luminating," we will work to translate intuitive feeling into useful thought that is both open and logical—then put that thought into words on paper.

Luminating

• In the top right corner of the next available page in your journal, write the date and time of this practice you are now beginning. In the top left corner, write "My Intuitive Thoughts."

• Lie back in *shavasana*. Take three *sigh breaths* and ask yourself a question about anything that is really important to you. Examples: "Why can't I get along with mom?" "How can I make more money?" "Why am I not more popular at work?" or "Does God really exist?"

• As you hold your question lightly poised before an open mind, perform *rhythmic ujjayi,* tune into *being* and wonder what the answer to your question might be.

A note: Keeping in mind that one who *wonders much* becomes *wonder-full*, let your wondering be an end in itself as you hold it focused upon your question and, as a consequence of that focus, feel it tilting in perhaps unanticipated directions.

If the question is, "Does God really exist?" for instance, you might feel yourself wondering how life might be different if there was a definitive answer to this question. If your question is, "Why can't I get along with mom?" you might feel yourself wondering what it is that stimulates anger.

Sustaining a sense of *being* during this kind of discipline can be especially challenging when you have posed a question concerning an issue that might ordinarily compel you to react negatively. Since such negative "issues" are almost always the source of your most sincere questions, you might find the real work of this exercise is in *holding being* in *rhythmic ujjayi* as your more difficult inquires pull you out toward negative emotional reaction.

As you work to hold an open mind in *being* while focusing on your question, you will observe a multitude of partial answers flashing spontaneously before you. While this flashing is happening, it is best to refrain from analytical thought, for any attempt you make to purposely understand and organize those flashes as they occur will simply pull you out of *being*. Rest assured those flashing puzzle parts will be there waiting for you when you are ready to assemble them into your question's answer in the next step of this exercise.

Because the "art of waiting," as this detached wondering is sometimes called, is so central to a non-intellectual cultivation of mysticism, it is highly respected in yoga.

- After about ten minutes of this "waiting" for an answer to your question, sit up and get yourself situated comfortably with your journal in your lap, pen in hand. Then ask your question again. This time, think out your answer. Think as you would normally think about anything. When you are ready, write your thoughts down. Make a special effort to express those thoughts logically.

A note: Having preceded this thought and writing with some "waiting" in *being*, you have established intuition as the leader of thought. As you will discover, this can yield some unusual results. You might find, for instance, that—contrary to the impulse of logic when left to its own devices—logic led by intuition might unexpectedly address what your question is actually trying to get at by stating and answering a different question instead—or eliminating your question altogether.

If you are asking, for instance, "How can I make more money?" your intuition might motivate you to ask instead: "How do I want to spend the rest of my life?" or if you are asking, "Why am I not more popular at work?" you might find, as you are sitting there in the bliss of *being* asking this question, you don't really care whether you're popular at work or not.

- When you have reached what seems like a natural conclusion to your thinking and writing, read each sentence you have written and let yourself feel if it seems right. Then, sentence by sentence, rewrite your answer, according to your feeling. If you sense it is necessary, repeat this editing again.

A note: To think, write and edit, following a yogic preparation, is a good example of yogic *sequencing*. The principle behind this yogic science of *sequencing* is *no single action stands alone*. Each and very action is greatly affected by the action that precedes it. Because we want our action of thinking, writing and editing an answer to our question to yield a mystical result, we precede that action with some mystical *sequencing—pranayama* and "waiting."

- When you have completed this entire process with one question, repeat it with another, and another—as many as you like. When you are done, stand up, stretch and perform three rounds of the *full wing flight*, followed by three rounds of the *cleansing breath*. Then lie back down in *shavasana* and enjoy the pleasant aftermath of this entire practice.

- After about ten minutes, sit up and open your journal. In the top left corner of the next available page, write "Free Writing 4." As in the previous free-writing exercises, close your eyes, visualize a vacant space in front of your face, and allow that vacant space to be filled with whatever comes. Then, whatever comes, open your eyes and write it down. After some time has passed, compare what you have just written with what you wrote during the previous three free-writing exercises.

23
Thought
The middleman in the pecking order of power

From a yogic point of view, the phrase, "mind over matter," does not point to the mind's capacity to control matter as much as it indicates matter blooms from mind, which blooms from *being,* which blooms from *Self.* Since yoga extols *Self* over *being, being* over *mind* and *mind* over *matter*, our yogic practices reveal to us where mind stands in life's pecking order of power.

The word "mind" is a general term used in a variety of ways. It can mean *consciousness,* "There is a mass mind;" *intellect,* "She has a developed mind;" or *attention,* "I have my mind on you." In our use of the word "mind" here, we are referring to the part of us that thinks. Yet where there is thought, there is also emotion, for thought and emotion are like brother and sister. Thought triggers emotion and emotion triggers thought.

Some thoughts and emotions are useful and some are not. Some useful thoughts and emotions are needed and some are not. For needed thoughts and emotions to be accurately determined, thought must be allowed to lead emotion so that intuition can lead thought.

Once we have established a habit of spending at least a little bit of time every day tuning into *being,* this hierarchy of intuition-over-thought-over-emotion establishes itself of its own accord and easily allows our truly needed thoughts and emotions to become apparent. This daily dipping into *being* also allows thinking and emoting to be controlled *without force* through intuitive understanding, rather than *with force* through suppression.

Nothing blocks intuition like suppression. A suppression is an intentional subduing of a fear or desire that is unpleasant because it is not understood and not understood because it is unpleasant. A repeated suppression creates a repression. A repression is a fear or desire that has been so deeply suppressed in our subconscious we only know it's there when it pops up in the events of our life, usually unexpectedly. The deeper a repression gets embedded, the harder it is to find, much less intentionally express or confess.

No such suppression or repression can exist if intuition is often allowed substantial access to thought. The implied warning here is the delicate trickle-down of wisdom from intuition to thought to emotion and into action is most likely to get blocked at the level of thought where suppression occurs.

One of the tasks of yoga, therefore, is to tactfully coax thought into allowing and accepting the influence of intuition. Since intuition is always striving to work its way into thought, this yogic coaxing is a stepping-up of a natural process—a quickening of sorts.

A "quickening" like this can be helpful when a "natural process" appears to be moving too slowly, which is what can seem to be occurring once we have developed a keen interest in moving more intensely into our exploration of intuition through a practice like yoga.

Too often fortified by a fierce independence born of a bloated sense of self-importance, thought can be stubbornly slow in accepting intuition. Because it is just sure it does not need any help doing what it does, thought uninfluenced by intuition happily works alone doing what it pleases until it is eventually driven to its knees by its own mistakes. In the humiliation of failure, it is finally willing to acknowledge a need for help and consider the assistance of intuition. Yet, even then, its full acceptance of intuition is slowed by doubt.

This is when and where yoga can accelerate the elimination of thought's resistance to intuition by stimulating thought to resolve itself with more thought—to think itself on through into its own demise. In this capacity, yoga is a "quickening" of a mental wrangling *that cannot be avoided*. The product of this thought resolution is a *clear mind* that is free, open and available to serve as a vehicle for intuition. Although this "clear mind" is usually a later development in yoga, the mere wanting of it is what drives many ardent aspirants into the practice of yoga in the first place.

If we are dealing with basic survival needs without the help of a clear mind, and those needs are not being easily met, life can seem to stop. Like the gaping mouths of children who never get enough to eat, those needs can seem to stand obstinately in the middle of our path, not letting us pass, forcing us to focus only on them.

At such times we feel trapped—cut off from what we perceive to be positive and smothered by what we perceive to be negative. Without the assistance of a clear mind, we gain some solace from using thought to draw a line of protection between ourselves and others. Then, using more thought, we place the blame for our circumstance on the other side of that line. The little bit of solace that we gain from this inspires us to draw more lines. All of this breeds and feeds a tendency to analyze, categorize and criticize.

Soon enough we are drawing lines between good and bad, right and wrong, smart and dumb, passive and aggressive, in and out, up and down, black and white—on and on, just about indefinitely—until we start hearing back from friends and relatives that our presence is no longer enjoyable because we have become so "judgmental."

We are shocked. We are hurt. We feel misunderstood. "How could this be?" we ask ourselves. We were only trying to "put things in order." Tormented by doubt and confusion, we draw even more lines. Intuition wants to help but it can't—it's on the other side of a line.

As we persist in this business of dividing off and stacking up justifications for all of our various apparent inadequacies and become more and more antagonistically abrasive in the process, our friends and relatives continue to retreat until we are all but completely alone.

In this self-imposed exile we are forced to admit that not only has all that line drawing failed to improve the quality of our lives it has actually deteriorated that quality by leaving us deeply unhappy and isolated. Worst of all, we are now feeling compelled to recognize and acknowledge that we just cannot seem to stop drawing those lines. In our lonely solitude, lined off from intuition, trapped by habit, and humbled by failure, we are as ready as we ever will be for the yoking of yoga.

24
Redoing Doubt
Moving from doubt to faith

The *New Oxford American Dictionary* defines *doubt* as "a feeling of uncertainty or lack of conviction," *faith* as "complete trust or confidence in someone or something" and *an open mind* as "an unprejudiced willingness to consider new ideas." In our practice of an introspective yoga, we want to dissolve *doubt* into a *faith* that is not blind because it has been developed through an intelligently *open mind*.

Through a mind intelligently open to new input, we discover we often *resist* understanding if we live our lives in *doubt* alone; and we often *miss* understanding if we live our lives in *faith* alone. What we also discover through an intelligently open mind is that *doubt* can be transformed up into intelligent questioning, and *faith* can be grounded down in intuitive knowing.

In this practice, entitled "Redoing Doubt," we will modify doubts into questions. Then, as we work to answer those questions, we will mold a grounded faith in a wisdom intuited from experience.

Redoing Doubt

- In the top right corner of the next available page in your journal, write the date and time of this practice you are now beginning. In the top left corner, write "Some Doubts, Questions and Answers." Under that title write down five doubts of your own choosing. These doubts can be about anything. Examples: "I doubt God exists." "I doubt I can make a million dollars in five years." "I doubt I can lose twenty pounds."

- Under your five doubts, create and record five questions from those doubts by replacing the "I doubt" of each doubt with "Is it possible." Examples: "Is it possible God exists?" "Is it possible I can make a million dollars in five years?" "Is it possible I can lose twenty pounds?"

- Lie back in *shavasana*. Once you are settled, take three *sigh breaths* and tune into *being*. When you are ready, ask yourself each of the questions you have just written down. As you open up to answers, allow yourself to mentally converse with yourself as you draw forth intuitive understanding from within yourself based upon experiences you have had rather than concepts you have learned.

A note: As you begin to piece together answers, you might find your intuition leading you to other questions. If, for instance, you are considering the question: "Is it possible that I can make a million dollars in five years?" your budding answer (partially comprised of other questions) might look something like this: "Yes, it is certainly possible that I can make a million dollars in five years. It is a fact that countless others have done this. But is it *probable*? From my own experience, I can see I have always achieved what I really wanted to achieve, sooner or later. This being true, the question then becomes: Do I have the necessary desire to do what it takes to make a million dollars in five years? Here again, I know from my own experience that where there is a desire there is a will; where there is a will, there is a way; and where there is a way, there is usually a positive attitude toward following that way. Yet if there is *not* the necessary desire, will, way and attitude, how can I *not* doubt my capacity to make a million dollars in five years?"

- When you are ready to formalize your thoughts, sit up, open your journal and write down your five answers to your five questions.

- Finally, write down one last title: "Reflections upon doubt, faith and an open mind." Under that title, record any insights you might be having now that you have submitted to this exercise of building faith in your own intuition by consulting your own experience to answer intelligent questions sprung forth from your own doubts.

25
Intuition
The sage behind the scenes

The shape of the life we live is determined by the decisions we make. Although we must abide by the law of karma and by that law must live out the consequences of all that we do, we hold the power to decide what we do, and with that power have some degree of control over our destiny. Understanding this, we respect why good decision-making is crucial in life and one of many practical skills worth developing through an exploration of yoga.

At first we make our everyday decisions from within our instinctive nature where we follow bodily impulses and emotional whims to learn, by the law of karma, that a life shaped this way is a difficult life to live for long.

During this period, we have practically none of that self-control that would spawn a life-control that could save us from existing at the mercy of the people and circumstance surrounding us. In the blindness of this reactionary survival, we live like animals on the run with no inclination to consider even the possibility of experiencing a better life. None of this is a mistake. It is all progress in process, derived from experience. We are learning and growing as we experience the totality of our lower instinctive nature.

When we finally catch a glimpse of a hope for a better existence and decide in that hope to generate some self-discipline, we undertake a more or less aggressive development of our mental faculties, thinking thought will give us the control we need to reign in the animal side of our nature. And for a while, thought seems to do just that—provide a control born of reason. While we are establishing this reasoned control, and developing our ability to think in the process, we become orderly and rational people living orderly and rational lives.

For a good stretch of time we are content with this approach to living and a little proud of it too. Then doubt comes in. We don't know why. All we know is that not knowing why only exacerbates the doubt.

After dealing with doubt for as long as we can with reason alone, we finally hand over the development of thought to intuition where our thinking becomes more introspective and our everyday decision-making becomes more refined.

Now firmly seated in intuition, we can clearly see that it is with intuition that thought works best, that it is actually the inherent nature of thought to work with intuition, and that the primary function and service of thought merging with intuition to become intuitive thought is to provide us with a more powerful steering device for deciding our way through the experiences of our life.

From within this intuitive perspective, we are able to sense we possess an inherent spirituality. And we are able to sense we have a fundamental responsibility to flow in obedience to rather than defiance of this spirituality's "voice of conscience."

When we make life decisions from within intuitive thought and from that perspective choose to live in harmony with our inherent spiritual nature, our lives become anchored in *being*. In the world of *being*, wisdom is the only rigid rule. Since intuition—a quality of *being*—is the harbinger of that wisdom, it is also the spokesperson for its rule.

One effective yoga practice for consciously maintaining an intuitive perspective is to think of thoughts as living, breathing beings. Although this approach might seem like a mental exercise, it's really not, for thoughts—referred to as "thought forms" by occultists—are actually astral entities that get born, live and die in lives lasting as long as the energy they are given can sustain them. If they get more energy along the way, they keep on living and growing.

Take the thought of "love" for instance. That love-thought is quite plump and getting plumper by the minute as it keeps getting fed by everyone who thinks it. And everyone thinks it sooner or later. Although this love-thought has been around for who-knows-how-long, it probably has little to do with the love-experience. But who would know what that love-experience is without having it?

The "God" thought is another rather stout mental structure—probably one of the few thoughts better fed than the thought called "love." More than the love-thought, this God-thought usually points to the actual God-experience more by contrast than by resemblance.

To meditate on a thought is to grow that thought into maturity by infusing it with intuition, for a mature thought is an intuitive thought that reflects truth. Although a reflection is but a hint, it's a hint that points toward an experience—a truth in itself—which can be ours to have if we should decide to want it.

The meditative development of an non-intuitive thought, consisting of all its many disparate impressions, into an intuitive thought, consisting only of that which *reflects* the truth upon which it is built, is a slimming process, for the form of an intuitive thought is a svelte and beautiful thing to behold—and an easy thing to read.

26

Inneracting
Personifying thought-forms

In this practice, entitled "Inneracting," we will be refining thought through a meditation of a role-playing sort. In this role-playing meditation, we will think of thoughts as people who can speak for themselves through us.

This meditation exercise will be similar to the "scripting" practice in Chapter 12, entitled "Flowing." This time, however, instead of enacting a script after having written it, we will record a script that spontaneously unfolds as we become the character speaking. So our script will be a monologue and our speaker will be a thought we have chosen to personify.

Inneracting

• In the top right corner of the next available page in your journal, write the date and time of this practice you are now beginning. Then think of a concept you want to more deeply understand and give that concept a personal name like—"Little Moe Patience," for instance. Once you have named your thought, compose that name into a monologue title in the top left corner of the page. That title might read something like: "Little Moe Patience's Soliloquy."

- In preparation for this role-playing meditation, lie back in *shavasana*, take three *sigh breaths*, establish *ujjayi* breath control and tune into *being*. After about ten minutes or when you feel the time is right, sit up, get comfortable with your journal and prepare to shift identities.

- Like an actor on stage, try to become the concept you have chosen to personify. If that concept is *compassion*, for instance, and you have named *compassion* "Mr. Goodheart," simply allow yourself to be Mr. Goodheart. Then write down in your journal what you hear Mr. Goodheart saying about himself while talking to a person like you.

    Here is another more specific example. If your chosen concept is *intuition* whom you have named "Ms. I. B. Knowing," your script for Ms. Knowing's monologue might read something like this:

Hello there. I'm so very happy to have been given this opportunity to introduce myself in this somewhat fun fashion, even though there was never a time when I wasn't with you, since what I am is a depth of you that's hard to pen down at first, but gets easier as you admit what I say is true, when you be true to you.

I am also the sister of thought. When we get along, I make him look good, although you'll never hear him say that. He is a bit proud, you see, and not so duly inclined to concede that he and I were meant to be not apart but together, as were we three: him, you and me. Hence, I thank you for letting this trio be—this trio of him, you and me.

- When you are done, stand up, stretch and perform three rounds of the *full wing flight*, followed by three rounds of the *cleansing breath*. Then lie back in *shavasana* and tune into *being*.

- When you feel the time is right, sit up, grab your pen and on the next available page in your journal, write "Free Writing 5." As in the previous four free-writing exercises, close your eyes, visualize a vacant space in front of your face, and allow that vacant space to be filled with whatever comes. Whatever comes, open your eyes and write it down. As before, let some time pass before you compare what you have just written with the content of your previous four free-writing exercises.

27
Now
The only experience of time

A mother thinks, "My children must study today for a test they'll take tomorrow." A gardener thinks, "Because it rained yesterday, my flowers are happy today." Although thoughts like these reference a past, present and future, they can only occur *now*.

Even *thoughts about time* ("time passes by," or "time marches on,") or *perceptions of time* ("time is a succession of events in space") can also only occur *now*, for no thought or experience of any sort, anywhere in manifest existence, can occur otherwise.

The New Oxford American Dictionary defines *time* as, "the indefinite continued progress of existence and events in the past, present, and future regarded as a whole." A baby just out of the womb knows nothing of a *time* like this, yet it knows of the *now* as much as anyone does. *Now* needs no thought to exist. *Time* does. *Time is a concept. Now is an experience.*

That there is only *now,* however, does not mean that concepts of *time* and the structure these concepts bring to thought do not have worth. Obviously, such concepts and their practical use in our daily decision-making are of great value.

As we cognize the nature of thought through our yoga practice, we see time as a conceptual perspective superimposed upon the *now*. When we leave concept in our deeper yoga practice, we also leave time (which is a concept) to become absorbed in *now awareness*.

In *now awareness*, we are so immersed in our current experience we have little sense of being an experiencer. This is a wondrous place to be since a *total* absorption of experiencer into experience is the ultimate attainment of yoga. Thus, while living in the *now* is an unavoidable matter of *fact*, living in *now awareness* is a resplendent manner of *being*.

In Self, there is no experience, because there is no separate experiencer. In *being*, there is an intuitive sensing of Self. In *doing,* there is a propensity to lose track of that sensing of Self as we lose track of *being*. The deeper we go into the practice of yoga, the more we realize yoga as a means of withdrawal, a way of yoking *doing* back into *being* and *being* back into *Self*, a path of *Self-absorption* in which the sentence of life on Earth gets truncated from "I am a person" to "I am That" to "I am" to "I." In the aftermath of the non-experience of Self, there is a retrospective acknowledgement of having just merged with Self. This looking back upon a non-experience is more accurately what the title, Self Realization, is meant to name.

In the last stretch of yoga's backtracking journey to source, *now awareness* in *being* indicates the final closing of duality's gap. At this point our journey snowballs as all of our yoga practices finally begin to yield their fullest potential through the power of habit.

When yoga practices get repeated enough to become yoga habits, their "benefits" increase exponentially. As yoga habits get fed by even more repeated practice, their effects continue to grow in the domain of our unconscious life until they eventually touch the entirety of our existence, culminating in a complete transformation of our nature.

Because the ill effects of repeated harmful practices can grow by this same power of habit, even a mention of this principle should serve as both an inspiration and a warning, even though bad habits also yield forward motion *through difficulty* on life's path of discovery and growth *through experience*.

Yoga adepts who are said to be continually meditating have simply become habitual meditators. They have developed the habit of living meditatively—or as we might say another way, "living in *now awareness*." In their own easy, inner manner, these ardent practitioners of yoga live life making better decisions and fewer "mistakes" even as they hasten their attainment of yoga's "end of ends."

Practices worth repeating for the habitual enjoyment of *now awareness* could include any well-founded yogic exercises aimed at directly experiencing any of *being's* qualities of *bliss, love, stillness, balance, peace, power, rapture, intuition, courage, contentment, timelessness* and the rest.

The attainment of any of these qualities is also the attainment of the rest, as well as their home: *now awareness*. In the *timelessness* of *now awareness*, memories take their rightful place as the building blocks of *intuitive thought*; fear and desire transmute into *courage* and *contentment*; karma resolves in the *peace* and *balance* of *stillness*; and *love* is realized as a one life force, felt as *bliss*.

In *now awareness*, we do not gain some special knowledge about the *now* we didn't have before. All we gain is a loss of any sense of time but *now*.

Since *now awareness* is somewhat nebulous as a yoga-practice-destination, it is best allowed to arrive as a natural consequence of other inner disciplines—like striving for the enjoyment of *bliss, love, stillness, balance, peace*. Thus, our yogic effort—and effort it is since countering *doing* with *doing* to *be* requires due diligence—is best spent in the continuing development of those habits that would leave us seated quite effortlessly in the desirelessness of *now awareness*, on the brink of the absolute, face to face with Self.

28
Spiraling
Focusing into now *absorption*

There is a significant difference between a yogic *practice* and a yogic *attainment*. A yogic *practice* is an *act of doing* in which there is a sense of passing *time*. A yogic *attainment* is an experience of *being* sweetly poised in *now awareness*.

As an *act of doing in time*, a yoga *practice* is an exercise designed in the *past* and performed *now* for the sake of achieving a specific result in the *future*. This is as it should be. Yet the *attainment* of that yoga practice will bear no sense of achievement nor any feeling of having been caused by goal-based action. It will simply be a state of *now absorption* in which we "lose track of time."

Look at *concentration* and *meditation*. *Concentration* is a *practice* in *doing*. *Meditation* is an *attainment* in *being*. In concentration, minutes may seem like hours as we laboriously haul awareness back from distraction again and again and again. Yet, slowly, through this most arduous effort of awareness retrieval, we eventually *become* the object of our focus. In this becoming, we forget all of our previous effort, and all of our previous distraction, as we lose ourselves in the enjoyment of our *attainment* of meditation.

Though we may or may not gain a great sense of accomplishment from our *practice*, that sense or its lack will become irrelevant in our *attainment*. A yogic *attainment* should stand on its own in *now awareness*—causeless, independent and complete within itself. If it does not, it is not an *attainment*.

In the following practice, we will be "spiraling" awareness within as we lengthen the span of our concentration and tighten the focus of our awareness into the absorption of meditation. In particular, this practice of "Spiraling" accommodates the natural tendency of awareness to move by *requiring* it to move until it slows and stops of its own accord.

Spiraling

• In the top right corner of the next available page in your journal, write the date and time of this practice you are now beginning. In the top left corner write, "A Spiraling Map."

• In the middle of the page draw a red dot. Around this dot, draw a circle. (The circle diameter should be about half the width of your journal page.) Then draw twelve points around the outside of that circle, equidistant apart, as on a clock.

Starting at the first point to the right of top center, write the following descriptions of each of the twelve points: 1. Mr. Dee Light, 2. Ms. D. Votion All, 3. Mr. Con Cord, 4. Ms. Trang Quil, 5. Mr. Calm Ness, 6. Ms. Powa O'Life, 7. Mr. Elay Shawn, 8. Ms. Joy Full, 9. Mr. No Ing, 10. Ms. Ever Plucky, 11. Mr. Ku Head, 12. Ms. B. Now.

• Get comfortable in *sukhasana*. Place your *Spiraling Map* where you can see it easily (preferably just below eye level about three feet away, perhaps on a small table). Take three *sigh breaths*, establish *ujjayi* breath control, and let your eyes rest in *trataka* (as described on page 15) on the red dot at the center of your *Spiraling Map*.

• When you feel the time is right, begin your "spiraling" as follows. Chant the *Aum* three times audibly. Then move your *trataka* gaze from the red dot center of your circle to "1. Mr. Dee Light." Holding *trataka* there, become Mr. Dee Light. Feel as he would feel. Be him.

A note: This exercise should not be laborious. In personifying concepts —as in perceiving the concept of "delight" in the person of "Mr. Dee Light," and the concept of "devotion" in the person of "Ms. D. Votion"— we are allowing awareness to work with thought as a child would work with thought.

Unlike thought, which can get heavy, intuition is always light and easy—almost playful. *To allow* is the key here. *Allow* intuition to lead. She will take you right into Mr. Dee Light. Your only job will be to delight in the experience.

- After about a minute, move your *trataka* gaze back to the red dot at the center of your *Spiraling Map*, and again, chant *Aum* three times. Then, move your *trataka* gaze to "2. Ms. D. Votion." Holding *trataka* there, become Ms. D. Votion. After having merged with the personification of devotion, continue moving around the clock of your *Spiraling Map* to become the other entities listed.

A note: Remember to repeat *Aum* three times as you gaze upon the red dot at the center of your circle before you proceed on to a meeting and merging with your next personified concept. This centering upon *Aum* will clear your *slate of consciousness* so your awareness can be free to become completely absorbed in a new experience.

Also, be sure to keep your eyes open and focused in *trataka* throughout this entire exercise. Remember, your eyes are a physical version of your awareness. Holding them open and fixed upon a one physical spot will assist you in focusing your non-physical awareness.

- Merge your way around the clock of your *Spiraling Map* at least two more times.

A note: As you repeatedly move around this cycle of twelve "people," you can expect a lengthening of the time you spend merging with each "person." This lengthening will indicate a deepening of your concentration into meditation brought on by your gradual absorption into a oneness with your points of focus.

- When you feel the time is right, sit up. On the next available page in your journal, write "My Twelve Friends." Under this title compose a brief description of each of those twelve entities you have just come to know so intimately. Try to write at least two or three sentences about each one. Finally, record your reflections upon the efficacy of "Spiraling" as a means of moving through concentration into the *now absorption* of meditation.

PART TWO
THE DEEP AND WIDE

29
God

An unfixed concept of a fixed reality

So far on this journey we have shared, we have eased our way into a general understanding and practice of yoga. Yet we have traveled only 28 of 108 steps. Now, we must—here at step 29—prepare our thinking mind for what it might find at step 109, one ventured pace beyond our journey's end where there is no path but the path each one of us makes and takes alone.

This conceptual preparation for what is to come is important because, as we have learned, thought can help or hinder our deepest experience of yoga. We want it to help.

Realizing that thinking cannot give us truth, yet can block it, we dare not ask thought to presuppose what will occur during the remainder of this yogic trek we have only just begun—or what might come to be once this trek is done. All we want thought to do at this point on our mystic quest is to patiently hold itself open and receptive to new ideas as it ponders an old set of yoga-friendly concepts.

With this brief introduction, we now ask you to consider the following philosophical premise designed by sages of antiquity to set and hold the mind in a state of unobtrusive transparency so as to allow yoga's deepest experimentation. It is only one premise among many. Yet among those many, it is ancient and well respected. Here it is.

God is both personal and impersonal. As the impersonal, unmanifest source of manifestation, It is the timeless, formless and spaceless Self. Yet as the pure force of life flowing through all form, and as the uncreated, ever-existent primal soul, He/She is also immanently and eminently personal.

As souls who are God as Self in essence, we are immortal. Yet we falsely presume ourselves to be mortal because we live in physical bodies that get born and die, and in those bodies assume many false identities that seem to be real while they last.

The realization of our one, true and essential identity as Self is illusive because, through all of our various false identities, we become immersed in the creation and resolution of karma, which in turn manifests and dissolves the physical, emotional, mental and spiritual worlds that we live in and are mesmerized by.

This venerable thought structure is as old as the *Vedas* (composed 1500 BCE) and predates Hinduism as it is known and practiced today. It is by no means infallibly correct. No philosophy or theology ever is or could be. But it is a way of thinking that both allows and inspires unlimited experimentation in the mystical pursuit of truth absolute.

In any yoga that focuses upon the attainment of Self Realization, the subject of God must be addressed, for if we cannot *think* of God as our Self, we will most assuredly have great difficulty allowing ourselves to *realize* God as our Self. With respect for the power of mind to blind, we must acknowledge we can hold ourselves away from the ultimate yoking of yoga with one simple thought: "I am *not* That." Yet with another thought just as simple, "maybe I *am* That," we can break that hold to make a window of a wall. Just that "maybe" is enough.

30
Questioning
Opening the mind to change

In this practice entitled "Questioning," we will ask and answer three questions after we have warmed up with some yogic sequencing. The purpose of this exercise is to identify and possibly modify or perhaps even eliminate those of our concepts of God we feel might bar our deepest awakening of the deepest yoking yoga has to offer.

Questioning

- In the top right corner of the next available page in your journal, write the date and time of this practice you are now beginning. Then sit in *sukhasana* and chant *Aum* nine times. Be sure to chant slowly and audibly so you can feel the "aa" vibrating within the chest, the "oo" vibrating in the throat and the "mm" vibrating in the head. When you are finished, lie back in *shavasana*, establish *ujjayi* breath control and enjoy *being*.

- After about ten minutes or when you feel the time is right, sit up in *sukhasana* and write, "My Teachers," in the top left corner of your journal. Then draw a line down the center of the remainder of your page to create two columns. At the top of the first column write "People." At the top of the second column write "Events." Once you have set up your page, identify and record under the appropriate heading which *people* and *events* have been your most influential teachers about *anything*.

Example: In the category of *people*, your list of influential teachers might include ministers, priests, secular educators, bosses, co-workers, coaches, trainers, family members, friends, book and magazine authors, television and movie stars, or political and social personalities. In the category of *events*, your list might include experiences like "my first date," "my last day a school," "my 25th marriage anniversary," or "my nine-day water fast."

A Note: In composing these lists, you might find it helpful to dive back as far into childhood as you can recall and chronologically remember forward to the present. Or you might prefer to follow this same procedure in reverse. Start from the present and remember backwards.

Please keep in mind you are only listing your *most influential* teachers. These would be teachers who stand out in your mind now for some particular reason. Out of the eight teachers that guided your secular education while you were attending elementary school, for instance, perhaps only your second grade teacher impressed you deeply.

- Once you have your general lists of *people* and *event* teachers assembled, put a check mark by each of the teachers that influenced your perception of God.

A note: Out of thirty people-teachers, perhaps only your priest, your mother, a college professor, two friends and the author of a book you read profoundly influenced your perception of God. Out of thirty event-teachers, maybe only "a nine-day water fast," "the death of a friend" and "a car accident" impacted your concept of God.

- When you are ready, write down your first question: "1. How have I been influenced to perceive God?" Then compose your answer to this question as you review what your "checked-off" teachers taught you about God.

A note: We have all been influenced to perceive God in some way, even if only through exposure to simple statements like, "God only knows," "Good God almighty," "God willing" or "God be with you."

- When you have finished answering the first question, write "2. What do I think about how I have been influenced to perceive God?" As you prepare to compose your answer, consider whether your initial "gut reaction" to the sum of these influences is negative or positive? Then let that initial response set the tone for the rest of your evaluation. Be sure to include a determination of whether or not what you have been taught is logical.

A note: You remember a teacher telling you, "If you sin, God will condemn you to hell and eternal damnation." Perhaps now, as you recall this statement, you sense it just doesn't *feel right*. "Not only that," you think to yourself, "It *doesn't even make sense*. Why would God create man, give him the ability to sin, and then punish him for sinning?"

By contrast, as you remember your mother telling you, "God helps those who help themselves," you sense now how this statement feels right and also seems logical—and helpfully applicable in everyday life. "It only makes sense," you think to yourself, "that a positive industriousness should attract inspired assistance."

Then you realize this statement could also be understood another way—as a license to be selfish. And you wonder to yourself, "What did my mother mean by that?" As you strive to look into your mother's mind, you think to yourself, "whatever she meant, I can now make a choice to perceive that statement any way I want."

Such feeling and thought combinations, with regard to how you have been influenced to perceive God, are what you want to process into words in response to this question.

- When you have finished answering the second question, write "3. Do I believe in God?—and if I do, who or what do I perceive God to be?"

As you prepare to answer this last question, review your answers to the first two. As you do, please include—with no special preference—a consideration of the "yoga premise" presented in Chapter 29 (Page 73) and note it offers three broad ways to know God: as Self, as pure life force, and as the primal soul.

A note: In composing your response to this question, keep in mind that one of the several truths this exercise is meant to reveal is that *what* we think is not as important as *seeing* what we think, for thoughts we can *see* cannot bind us.

Although being able to see thoughts objectively offers a certain control over thought, this control should not be perceived as an ability to alter thought in any way, for thought does not need altering. What we can and should want to control *in* thought is our movement of awareness *through* thought, our choosing of which thoughts to think. If we choose, for instance, to stop thinking, "I hate politics," the thought, "I hate politics," will not change or go away just because we no longer think it. It will still be there—just as it is—to be thought by someone else.

When we can navigate awareness through thought into intuition, intuition will help us choose to think those thoughts that will help our full experience and realization of our divinity within.

31
Soul

An unfixed concept of a changing entity

From the same open-mindedness that allows us to realize the *Self* as *God*, we can perceive a *soul* to be that Self's first assumed identity. Since we can know from Self Realization what it is like to come out of *the Self* into *a self* of individualized awareness, we can see how that first sense of separation from Self might look like the birth of a soul.

Although referring to this entity with an assumed identity as a "soul" says something about what that entity is, it does not completely describe it. To get anchored in a more workable authenticity, this entity must be perceived as something more than just a ball of individualized awareness. It must have a form—a vehicle, shall we say. Hence, a better description of this entity needing a more substantial identity might be stated: "The individualized soul is an immortal and spiritual *body* of light, the essence of which is God as Self."

All of this pigeonholing of the very idea of a soul into a nest of words is aimed at dealing with the thinking mind tactfully so thought will not block intuition. Because we want our mind to be our happy, healthy and well-developed friend, we are careful to feed it concepts—especially concepts about God, soul and world—that not only make sense but also reflect the spirit of what we can and will actually experience as we seek from our yoga the best that yoga has to offer.

The *Vedas* state that *anandamaya kosha*, the body of the soul, evolves through reincarnation and beyond to become *Sivamaya kosha*, the body of God. In the time that has passed since the *Vedas* were written, countless qualified sages have bravely asserted a variety of yogic philosophies based upon their intuition this *Vedic* proclamation was conceptually helpful. Since sages are generally expected to have earned what they've learned from a lot of long-term introspection peppered with a lot of real-life experience, it is commonly assumed that whatever they say is of note.

Yet, whether or not what a sage says is of relative significance, isn't it what the listener hears that really counts? And isn't it true a listener might sometimes hear something higher and deeper than what the sage is actually saying? Who then is the sage?

As might be expected, it is the worthiest of sages that say the least, but have the most to say. Yet who could be better judges of the little even these most highly qualified sages say than those listeners who resonate with what is being said while hearing something more as well.

Intuition is the real sage here and she is always teaching, even though we may not always be listening. It is in fact only our lack of listening that engenders our lack of learning, for the teaching of intuition—which is never lacking and is as impartial as the law of karma—is forever and equally available to all.

If we are guided by intuition to accept the *Vedic* idea that we are each an ethereal soul body growing up—like the physical body of a child growing up into the physical body of an adult—we will be more inclined to also accept the idea that working with intuition is integral to growing spiritually. When we experience a stepped-up spiritual growth felt as an energy intensification inspired by intuition, we will know beyond the shadow of a doubt why following intuition is of such central importance in a deeper yoga practice.

That we are this soul body the *Vedas* call *anandamaya kosha*, and that this *anandamaya kosha* is growing up to become *Sivamaya kosha*, the body of God, is venturesome speculation to be sure. Yet if we intuitively sense this speculation to be true, that inner sensing will be an experience from which we can gain faith, just as we have gained faith from all we have learned from all of our experience.

In the life of *Sivamaya kosha* (according to *Vedic* thought) there is no coming or going, no starting or finishing, no moving through processes and arriving at the ends of processes. In God's state everything is perfect—is as it is with no need for improvement.

In the life of *anandamaya kosha* (also according to *Vedic* thought) there *is* coming and going, starting and finishing, moving through processes and arriving at the ends of processes. Since all of this movement intimates growth and growth intimates a developing entity with a form that needs a name, this entity called *anandamaya kosha* can easily be perceived as a being that will develop until it can develop no more, even though it is and always was perfect in essence.

32
Searching
Using the mind to learn

In this practice, entitled "Searching," which will be quite similar to the practice of *Questioning* in Chapter 30, we will ask and answer three questions after some yogic preparation.

As in the "Questioning" practice, the purpose of this exercise is to identify and possibly modify or perhaps even eliminate those concepts of *soul* we feel might bar our deepest awakening of the deepest yoking yoga has to offer.

Searching

- In the top right corner of the next available page in your journal, write the date and time of this practice you are now beginning. Then sit in *sukhasana*, chant *Aum* nine times, lie back in *shavasana*, establish *ujjayi* breath control and enjoy the bliss of *being*.

- After about ten minutes or when you feel the time is right, sit up in *sukhasana* and write, "My Soul Teachers," in the top left corner of your journal. Then draw a line down the center of the remainder of your page to create two columns. At the top of the first column write "People." At the top of the second column write "Events." Once your page is set up, turn back to the general lists of *event* and *people* teachers that you composed during your *Questioning* practice for Chapter 30. From that list bring forward and record here those *people* and *events* that impressed you with ideas about the soul.

- When you are ready, write "1. How have I been influenced to perceive the soul?" Then compose your answer based upon how you feel the *people* and *events* you have listed affected your perception of the *soul*.

A note: As with *God*, we have all been taught *something* about the *soul*, even if only though statements like, "She's a good soul," "That music has a lot of soul," or "You gotta have soul." Hearing and using statements like these affect our perceptions more than we know.

- When you have finished answering the first question, write "2. What do I think about how I have been influenced to perceive the soul?" As you prepare to compose your answer to this question, consider whether your initial "gut reaction" to the sum of all your soul-oriented influences is negative or positive? Then let that first response set the tone for the rest of your evaluation. Include a determination of whether or not what you have been taught is logical.

Example: When you were 14 years old and completing a high school English homework assignment, you stumbled upon a statement made by the ancient Greek philosopher and scientist Aristotle: "The soul cannot think without a picture." Now, as you review this input years later, you find you are still struck by the inspiration of it, as well as its logic.

- When you have finished answering the second question, write "3. Do I believe I am a *soul?*—and if I do, who or what is this soul that I am?"

    As you prepare to answer this last question, review your answers to the first two. As you do, please include a consideration of the following statement from Chapter 31: "The individualized soul is an immortal and spiritual body of light, the essence of which is God as Self," and another: "It is the *anandamaya kosha*, the body of the soul, that evolves through reincarnation and beyond to become *Sivamaya kosha*, the body of God."

A note: The primary aim of this exercise is to provide an opportunity for you to consciously acknowledge the continuity of external influence and internal perception that got you where you are now in your understanding of the *soul*. This conscious acknowledgement is important as a means of positioning your current thoughts about the soul out in front of you so you can decide from a detached point of view which to keep, which to change and which to relinquish.

    Yoga favors no particular understanding of or belief in God or soul. All yoga requests is an open mind pliable to change, for change is yoga's progress.

33
Chakras
Seven centers of power

The *anandamaya kosha* is distinguished by its *ananda* or "bliss," the first feeling the soul encounters as it becomes individualized out of Self. The *Vedas* refer to this feeling of pure bliss as "Satchitananda." In Sanskrit, *Satchitananda* means "existence, consciousness and *bliss*." Although *bliss* is the primary feeling of *Satchitananda*, that feeling *exists* in *consciousness*. Thus, *existence, consciousness* and *bliss* are inseparable and constitute a one experience.

When we pull back out of *doing* into *being* and reside there undistracted, we are experiencing *Satchitananda*. According to the *Upanishads*, that part of the *Vedas* that focuses more specifically upon mystical teachings, this *Satchitananda* is not only the essence of our *anandamaya kosha*, it is also God experienced as the primal force of life flowing in and through all things. Although experiencing God as *Satchitananda* is not realizing God as Self, it is but one step away.

From the *Upanishadic* point of view, it is within the *anandamaya kosha* that the *chakras* exist. A *chakra*, literally translated as "wheel," is a spinning vortex of energy that stimulates and governs the flow of certain instinctive, intellectual or spiritual powers. Although there are many of these vortexes of energy in the body of the soul, seven are primary. Because these seven non-physical force centers in the soul body coexist with seven nerve ganglia along the spinal column of the physical body, yoga teachers will commonly use the physical body as a frame of reference for indicating the location of these chakras.

In this physical frame of reference, the first chakra spins at the base of the spine. This first vortex of energy governs memory and is called *muladhara* in Sanskrit. Through the power generated by the *muladhara chakra,* we learn to live in the physical world with a sense of stability born of habit patterns we establish in memory. These habit patterns ground us in a lifestyle that feels secure.

The second chakra, about six inches below the navel, rules reason and is called *svadhishthana* in Sanskrit. With the power of the *svadhishthana chakra*, we learn to manipulate memory with reason to create plans for fulfilling desires and dealing with fears.

The third chakra in the region of the solar plexus commands willpower and is called *manipura* in Sanskrit. Empowered by the *manipura chakra,* we *will svadhishthana's* plans into manifestation as we learn to defend what we have and get what we want.

It is through real-life situations stimulated by these first three chakras—the *muladhara*, the *svadhishthana* and the *manipura*—that we become immersed in a survivalist's mentality, dodging fears, hounding desires, giving undue credence to the erroneous notion we *are* the physical body and throwing all of our thought and emotion into experiencing the fullest extent of selfishness. The four chakras above these first three stimulate a different kind of energy and a different kind of life.

The fourth chakra in the center of the chest supervises direct cognition. This chakra is called *anahata* in Sanskrit. Through the power generated by this *anahata chakra* we gain more than a periodic access to intuition, and through that access cognize a oneness binding the *all* of manifest life. This sense of oneness blooms into a compassionate sort of love through which we feel what others feel. Exercising this power to feel beyond ourselves pushes our selfishness into selflessness.

The fifth chakra, which is centered in the throat and called *vishuddha* in Sanskrit, inspires an unconditional love. The distinctive love engendered by this *vishuddha chakra* transforms *anahata's* wise compassion up into an impersonal sort of benevolence that seeks only to flood out as blessings to all. Although this chakra is often referred to as a force center of communication, the *real* communication it stimulates is of a one-way emanational sort that need not be intentionally expressed to have its effect. Needless to say, when this communication *is* intentionally expressed in *any* way, its effect is bedazzling.

The powers generated by the sixth and seventh chakras are transcendent and otherworldly. The sixth chakra at the third eye (between the two physical eyes and up about one inch) unfolds "divine sight" and is called *ajna* in Sanskrit. It is through this sixth *ajna chakra* that our psychic abilities are awakened. The seventh chakra at the apex of the skull gives rise to spiritual illumination and is called *sahasrara* in Sanskrit. It is through the unfoldment of this *sahasrara chakra* that Self Realization becomes possible.

These last two chakras, are not so useful in dealing with matters of practical concern, nor are they generally open to random, casual or curious access, for they are—for the most part—*exit force centers* that draw us in, up and out of our involvement with the world of manifestation. As such, these two mystical vortexes are usually of little real interest to us unless that ultimate exit has enticed our desire.

With regard to access, each chakra is most amenable to a full vitalization when it is approached from the chakra below it, for all seven chakras are designed to work in succession from bottom to top.

The first chakra develops the memory that the reasoning second chakra needs to devise plans for chasing desires and escaping fears. Once these plans are made, the will of the third chakra goes to work making those plans manifest. Since these first three chakras churn on selfishness, the mounting karma they create can eventually only be unraveled by the cognition of the fourth chakra, which awakens a little bit of love that blossoms into a whole lot of love through the fifth chakra. That selfless love of the fifth chakra attracts the attention of high souls on deep inner planes of consciousness who then begin to develop a working relationship with us though our sixth chakra. Finally, when the time is right, these higher plane beings help us through the seventh chakra, over the brink of the Absolute and into the Self beyond.

So it is that each of these seven spinning force centers gets awakened by the whirl of the vortex below it. Once a chakra wakes up and starts to spin, the power it generates can and must be developed through use. While the awakening of these spinning vortexes usually occurs in an orderly fashion from the bottom to the top, their development through utilization most often takes place randomly according to the necessity of the moment.

The ascension of awareness up through the spinning of the chakras tells its own story of desire's slow transmutation, fear's incremental release and the soul's meticulous assimilation of life's lessons. As we begin to see from the transformation of our own fears and desires how this story might be our story and how the unfoldment of our story registers in our nervous system as a growing intensity we can actually feel, we begin to intuit beyond faith a great sense of ultimate destiny.

34
Ascending
Moving awareness up

In this practice, entitled "Ascending," we will be working to sense our way into an experiential understanding of the seven chakras. In this sensing effort, our first focus will be on the four upper chakras of *being*. We are taking this approach because the lower three of these energy centers are rooted in *doing*. Because, in yoga, we want to *be* before we *do*, we will first *be*, then *see* — *see* the *doing* of our lower three chakras from the *being* of our higher four chakras.

Being in and *seeing* through the unique energy of each of the higher four chakras requires becoming centered in the power of the spine. Recognizing that breath control induces mind-control—as in awareness-control—and acknowledging that such mind/awareness control is what we need to orient our consciousness within the spine, we will now learn and use a new *pranayama* specifically designed to bring about this balance we seek. This *pranayama* is called *anuloma viloma pranayama* in Sanskrit and "alternate nostril breathing" in English.

Anuloma viloma pranayama (*anuloma* means "with flow" and *viloma* means "against flow") centers awareness in the power of the spine through a control of breath that equalizes the flow of air through the left and right nostrils.

The right nostril is governed by the sympathetic nervous system and corresponds to the left, masculine-aggressive, heating and "thinking" side of the brain. The left nostril is governed by the parasympathetic nervous system and corresponds to the right, feminine-passive, cooling and "feeling" side of the brain.

The sympathetic nervous system is that part of the autonomic nervous system that mobilizes the body's resources under stress. It consists of nerves stemming from ganglia near the middle part of the spinal cord. The parasympathetic nervous system is that part of the autonomic nervous system that aids the body in its ability to rest and recuperate. It consists of nerves stemming from the brain and the lower end of the spinal cord. When the sympathetic and parasympathetic nervous systems are allowed to work in close cooperation, the equilibrium that signifies the yoking of yoga through the balancing of masculine and feminine nerve currents gets established as a foundation for the ascension of our awareness up through the seven great force centers of our soul body.

One of the greatest yoga practices for harmonizing these two contrasting nervous systems is *anuloma viloma pranayama*. Here are instructions for performing this breath control (See figure 6):

1. Sitting in *sukhasana,* rest your left hand on your left knee in any fashion that is comfortable for you. Then, close your eyes and curl the first (index) and second (middle) fingers of your right hand down the inside of your right thumb until the nails of those fingers rest against the base of that thumb.

Figure 6: *The hand positions for breathing through the left and right nostrils during the alternate nostril breath control known as* anuloma viloma pranayama *in Sanskrit*

2. Squeeze your left nostril shut with your ring finger as you breathe in slowly through your right nostril. At the peak of a full inhalation, release your ring-finger block of the left nostril and close your right nostril with your thumb as you breathe out slowly through your left nostril.

3. In a reverse of step 2, keep your right nostril closed with your thumb as you breathe in slowly and deeply through your left nostril. At the peak of this inhalation, release your thumb block of the right nostril and close your left nostril with your ring finger as you breathe out slowly through your right nostril.

These three steps performed in sequence constitute one complete round of *anuloma viloma pranayama,* which may be repeated.

Ascending

- In the top right corner of the next available page in your journal, write the date and time of this practice you are now beginning. In the top left corner, write "A Rise."

- After you have become comfortable in *sukhasana*, perform three rounds of *anuloma viloma pranayama*.

- Remaining in *sukhasana*, practice *ujjayi* breath control as you enjoy the aftermath of your *anuloma viloma pranayama*. Once you have become balanced in this enjoyment, feel in the center of your chest for the vortex of power that is your fourth chakra.

    As soon as you have caught this feeling, visualize energy flooding into that chakra from the outside of you as you inhale. Then, visualize energy flooding out from that chakra as you exhale. Perform this *pranayama*-visualization until you feel an inclination to rest in peace.

A note: Once you have induced the feeling that you are actually doing what you are visualizing, you will discover visualization can bring about super-physical effects if it is not forced to obey physical laws (which it need not be).

- After having caught the feeling of moving energy in to and out from the center of the chest, move energy in to and out from the throat, the "third eye" and the apex of the skull. When you have completed this practice with the upper four chakras, look down into the lower three chakras just long enough to feel their presence, one after another—one, two, three.

- After having caught the feeling of the lower three chakras, perform the following breath control and visualization: On the in-breath, visualize yourself successively gathering up the energy of each of the seven chakras, one after another, from the bottom first to the top seventh. On the out-breath, flood your gathered energy up and out through the top of your head.

A note: This exercise cannot be performed badly. Even a meager attempt will bring about surprisingly noticeable effects. For best results, however, work to feel what you are visualizing.

• When you sense the time is right, open your journal and under your title, "A Rise," record your reflections on "Ascending."

35
Bodies
The five sheaths of the soul

The mystical idea that a soul grows through the development of its ethereal body of light makes more sense if we understand what the *Vedas* call "the five bodies."

According to the *Vedas*, *anandamaya kosha*, the "body of bliss," is but one of these five bodies. The other four are *vijnanamaya kosha*, the "body of cognition;" *manomaya kosha*, the "body of thought, will and wish;" *pranamaya kosha*, the "body of vital force;" and *annamaya kosha*, the "body of food."

Of these five bodies, *anandamaya kosha* is both primary and essential. It is primary because it is the first body created. And it is essential because without it the other four bodies would have no reason to exist. It is this *anandamaya kosha* that cannot die. And it is upon this *anandamaya kosha* the other four bodies fit like clothes or "sheaths."

Although the *Vedas* state all five bodies are sheaths of the soul, their description of how these bodies actually work indicates it is the *soul body* getting sheathed. In this functional description, there are two central ideas to understand: 1. The soul cannot exist apart from its body of light. 2. The soul body needs the other bodies to experience the totality of manifest life.

Here follows a condensed summation of how the outer four bodies are perceived by the *Vedas* to function in serving the soul body:

The *vijnanamaya kosha* allows the soul to enter a realm in which intuition mingles with high thought. Naturally, from a perspective that sees souls as evolving entities, this "mental body" would be expected to develop late in soul evolution. When this *vijnanamaya kosha* becomes powerful, it is sometimes referred to as the "mystic body" or the "psychic body."

The *manomaya kosha* gives the soul access to a domain in which desires are fulfilled by intentional will. It is in this body, often referred to as the "emotional body" or the "instinctive body," the soul experiences and expresses fundamental urges and feelings.

The *pranamaya kosha* lets the soul delve into the vitality of the physical body. This body, sometimes called the "pranic body," "health body," or "vital body," lives closely in sync with the physical body and is said to hold the vital life force of physicality.

The *annamaya kosha* is the physical body in which the soul has an opportunity to physically express all of the potential it has generated through its utilization of the other bodies—then, by the law of karma, endure the repercussions of that expression.

Thus it is that a primary function of all these four bodies is to provide the soul body they serve with a means for moving through different spheres of existence and consciousness. Although there are many of these spheres, each of them has its place somewhere in one of three vast worlds of manifest life: the physical world, the astral world or the spiritual world.

In the *Vedas*, the physical world is called *Bhuloka,* "the world of Earth;" the astral world is called *Antarloka*, "the world of the in-between;" and the spiritual world is called *Brahmaloka*, "the world of heaven." The *Antarloka's* "world of the in-between" includes an upper region called the *Devaloka* and a lower region called the *Naraka*.

According to the *Vedas*, "great souls," sometimes referred to as *mahadevas* or gods, live in the *Brahmaloka*; "high souls," sometimes called *devas* or angels, live in the *Devaloka*; "low souls," sometimes referred to as *asuras* or demons, live in the *Naraka*; and "embodied souls," human beings, live in the *Bhuloka*.

From this *Vedic* perspective, no entity lives anywhere permanently and all entities are forever graduating up. What this means in practical terms is, at any given point in our own soul development, each of us has explored or will explore every nook and cranny of all these worlds. This exploring gets done as we follow our desire to its ultimate fulfillment in desirelessness through a vast potpourri of experience. During all of this experience, we live in five bodies most expertly designed to deal with the challenges of the worlds in which they exist.

When we are awake, we are experiencing the physical world from within the physical body. When we are asleep and dreaming—or when we are emoting and thinking—we are, in accordance with the nature of our thought and feeling, experiencing either the lower or higher astral world from within either our emotional or mental body. And when we are immersed in otherworldly visions or deep meditation—or even when we're simply enjoying a moment of insight—we are experiencing the spiritual world from within our soul body.

When we die and leave the physical body and its physical world, according to the *Vedas*, we take up primary residence in the inner world and body to which we most often retreated during emotions, thoughts, dreams and meditations we nurtured while we were "alive." There in that place, we either hanker after another birth in a physical body so we can fully express and thus manifest what we are brewing in our "in-between," or we relish the bliss of release from mortal toil and hanker after nothing but an enjoyment of our own deepest nature.

Including an open-minded consideration of this *Vedic* perception of bodies and worlds in our understanding of manifest life can inspire us to view living as a learning and growing that occurs on many levels of existence at the same time. Such a view cultivates the deep and wide conceptual foundation we need to make motives worth acting upon in a mystic quest aimed at the end of ends.

36
Internalizing
Moving awareness in

In this practice, entitled "Internalizing," we will go *in* through the five bodies like we went *up* through the seven chakras in the practice described in Chapter 34, entitled "Ascending."

Internalizing

- In the top right corner of the next available page in your journal, write the date and time of this practice you are now beginning. In the top left corner, write "My In."

- Lie down flat-back and perform three rounds of *jackknife* as described in Chapter 8, entitled "Blessing." Following this invigorating exercise of the physical body (*annamaya kosha*), lie back in *shavasana* and relax into the bliss you can now feel filtering through your pranic body (*pranamaya kosha*).

A note: The word, "prana," is used to describe the primal life force when it is vitalizing the physical. When we work within the physical or the pranic body to unblock that force, we open our access to the innate bliss of the soul body. Because all of our five bodies are so intimately connected, a sensation in one of them gets felt through all of them. So it is that the tension/release of the physical jackknife sets off a chain reaction of relaxation that gets felt right through to the soul body where it leaves our innate bliss fully exposed.

- After about ten minutes or when you feel the time is right, sit up in *sukhasana* and perform three full rounds of *anuloma viloma pranayama* as described in Chapter 34, entitled "Ascending." Following this exercise and invigoration of the pranic body, simply linger in *sukhasana* to enjoy the poised and blissful centeredness that *anuloma viloma pranayama* leaves.

A note: It is this centeredness, born of the balancing of *prana*, that will fortify you for that which awaits you next as you encounter the emotional body of *manomaya kosha*.

- Remaining in *sukhasana*, hold the focus of your awareness centered in the bliss you are now feeling. When your first distraction comes—perhaps as a thought or an emotion associated with a "good" or "bad" memory—make it your new point of focus. As you train your awareness upon that distraction, strive to maintain watcher awareness.

A note: As we have already discovered, to hold watcher awareness is to simply observe something—*anything*—from within the blissful detachment of *being*. Intentionally maintained watcher awareness will naturally invoke the power and presence of your *vijnanamaya kosha*—variously referred to as the "mental body," "mystic body," or "psychic body"—when distraction arises to steal your concentration.

This *vijnanamaya kosha* is the body that actually gets developed as it works to resolve and dissolve that which stands before it as distraction. The development of this body in its dealing with distraction is key in the practice of yoga, for that which distraction holds, *wrong perception* and *unresolved memory*, forms the greatest barrier to the yoking of yoga. In this context, *wrong perception* refers to thought that is not intuitive and *unresolved memory* refers to a past that stimulates a negative emotional reaction when it is remembered.

• When intuitive flashes begin to occur within the *vijnanamaya kosha*, let those flashes hook themselves together into wisdom.

A note: Here we are working with three bodies at once. We are calling upon the *mental body* to meld its thought with the intuition of the *soul body* to relieve the *emotional body* of its confusion.

Aside from focusing awareness, our primary ambition in this process should be to dial back the intensity of our discontent into the bliss of *being* enough for us to be able to face our inherently difficult-to-face *wrong perception* and *unresolved memory* with the detachment necessary for understanding.

• Keep enjoying your gathering of insight until that insight means less to you than the bliss of *being* you feel behind it. When bliss overpowers insight, simply enjoy the bliss.

A note: When your continued focus of awareness naturally withdraws awareness from insight to the bliss of *being* behind insight, you will find yourself relishing the experience of *satchitananda*—existence, consciousness and bliss. This enjoyment of *satchitananda* is your exercise of your deepest soul body, *anandamaya kosha*.

- When you feel the time is right, open your journal. Under your title, "My In," record your reflections after having experienced this practice of "Internalizing."

37
Motive
A desire voiced as a reason for action

A motive is a desire voiced as a reason for action. Example: "I want money. So I will get a job." By itself, "I want money" is simply a desire. When "so I will get a job" gets added, "I want money" becomes a motive for getting a job.

A desire and the motive for the fulfillment of that desire will always be worded in the same way. In the above example, "I want money," states both a desire and a motive. Therefore, if we have a desire we can state in words, we also have a motive for that desire's fulfillment.

To pursue the fulfillment of a desire with a motive invites forethought. To pursue the fulfillment of a desire with no motive invites impulsiveness. The former generates wisdom. The latter does not.

When a desire cannot be worded, there can be no motive for its fulfillment because a motive must be preceded by a worded desire. A desire will be difficult to word if we are disinclined to acknowledge we are feeling the power of its pull. We will be thusly disinclined if that desire is amoral or harmful. Our intuition decides the relative quality of a desire. Our voice of conscience relays that intuitive decision to us through a simple sense of "yes" or "no."

If we are sensing an intuitive "yes," we can happily and easily acknowledge, define and pursue our desire with a powerful motive. Example: If we want to do work that helps others yet provides us with plenty of money for a happy life free of worry, our voice of conscience will readily condone that desire. With this blessing of conscience, we will be inspired to define and pursue that desire with a motive.

If we are sensing an intuitive "no" about a desire we are feeling but modify (transmute) that desire up until we can sense a "yes" about it, we can also easily acknowledge, define and pursue that desire with a powerful motive. Example: If we want to have sex but modify that wanting up into a desire to fall in love, our voice of conscience will bless that transmuted desire with a "yes" and help its successful fulfillment.

Yet, if we are sensing an intuitive "no" about a desire we are feeling but follow that desire anyway, we will find it difficult to acknowledge and define that desire. Since a desire *not* acknowledged and defined can have no motive, such a desire can only be expressed impulsively in ways we will likely regret later.

If we are living under the influence of a desire we intuitively know to be amoral or harmful, we might quite flatly refuse to admit we are feeling that influence. Such a refusal is a conscious act of denial. A denial of desire causes a suppression of desire. Suppressing a desire does not eradicate it. It simply shoves it out of view. That suppressed desire still exists as strongly as ever. It just doesn't enjoy our conscious acknowledgment, definition and pursuit. If, every time that desire is aroused, it is denied and suppressed, it becomes a repression.

Repressed desires still seek fulfillment. They just do so erratically and unpredictably. Because repressed desires are not allowed free expression, they build an explosive power that endows them with an amplified capacity to disrupt order when they finally break out into expression. Example: If we have been indoctrinated with the idea that sex is "bad" and because of that indoctrination suppress into repression our urge to have sex rather than allow that urge to be expressed in ways our "voice of conscience" would condone, we might find what has come to be known as our usual prudent lifestyle will occasionally be disrupted with intense episodes of uncharacteristically lecherous behavior.

If a happily admitted desire is not expressed impulsively and is allowed to become a motive for a purposeful and methodical action, that motive will trigger a need for a plan requiring thought. The thinking that then must necessarily commence to produce that plan can be either logical or logically intuitive. If it is logically intuitive, it will be influenced by our "voice of conscience" and will likely produce a plan that is not only insightfully efficient but also morally balanced.

Although it is true a healthy and admitted desire can *also* be expressed impulsively, such impulsiveness will more likely be caused, in such cases, by an easily correctable tendency to be impetuous or impatient, rather than a blunt and stubborn refusal to even acknowledge the very existence of that desire in the first place.

Impulsively expressing repressed desires leaves us living at the mercy of the law of karma rather than working wisely with it—forever learning from hindsight rather than foresight. Also, the very fact repressed desires cannot be acknowledged makes their transmutation impossible, at least while they are not being acknowledged. Repeatedly acting upon these unacknowledged desires piles up negative karma in dire need of resolution.

Such double-barreled mishandling of desire generates a pattern of living that looks something like a dog chasing its tail. In the spin of a life cycle like this, we are victims of circumstances propelled by forces we won't acknowledge through events we can't understand in a repetition of experiences that is forever leaving us feeling like we're trapped in a nightmare we cannot seem to avoid reliving again and again.

Although in a spiritual sense there *is* progress even in a predicament like this, that progress is barely recognizable. The good news here is that escalating such minimal forward motion is not as difficult as it might seem. All it takes is an admission of a repressed desire.

Admitting a repressed desire can actually embarrass us into wanting to upgrade that desire at least a little bit. Once expressed in words, a fresh, new desire to upgrade an old desire can establish a new motive—something like "I want to improve," or "I want to be a better person." Depending upon the quality of the decisions this new motive inspires, the actions resulting from those decisions can significantly develop our character. And character development is both an indication and a proof of transmuted desire.

38
Motivation Evaluation
Inviting forethought

In this practice, entitled "Motivation Evaluation," we will recollect portions of our past for the purpose of seeing how we have done in working with motive to pursue desire with forethought.

Motivation Evaluation

- In the top right corner of the next available page in your journal, write the date and time of this practice you are now beginning. In the top left corner write "A Statement of Desire."

- To calm mind, body and emotions for clear recollection and honest self-reflection, stand up, stretch and perform three rounds of the *full wing flight*, followed by three rounds of the *cleansing breath*. Then lie back in *shavasana* for a few minutes to enjoy the bliss of *being*.

- When you feel ready, sit up in *sukhasana*, open your journal and prepare to write. As you relax into your seated position for meditation, try to recall exactly what you wanted out of this book when you first began to read it. Once you have that desire identified, put it in writing under your title, "A Statement of Desire."

- Now, think of what you have just written not as a statement of desire but as a statement of motive. Then try to recollect whether or not you had that motive in mind when you began your experience of this book. If you did *not* begin your experience of this book with that motive—this is common—ask: "Did I have a motive at all?" or: "Did I have a motive that I would have stated differently than I stated my desire?" If you had a motive, but it was a motive that you would have stated differently than you stated your desire, write that motive down under your stated desire.

- When you have finished writing, lie back in *shavasana* to again enjoy the bliss of *being*. When you are ready, sit up in *sukhasana* and open your journal. Under your statement of desire (and your statement of motive if it is different)—write down a new title: "Reflections."

- Read the three options below (A, B and C) and choose the one that pertains to you. Under your title, "Reflections," record your reflections after following the instructions posed in the option you have chosen.

A. If you had a conscious motive for beginning the study of this book and that motive could be worded like you worded the desire you just noted in your journal, seek to understand how having that motive has affected your experience of this book thus far? As you proceeded through this book, did your desire/motive change? If so, how?

B. If you had no conscious motive for initiating your study of this book, seek to understand how your experience of this book might have been different if you began with a consciously established motive.

C. If you began your experience of this book with a motive that you felt you had to word differently than you worded your desire to read this book, seek to understand why you felt that wording had to be different. Then try to come up with a one wording that would describe both your desire and your motive.

A note: When a desire and a motive are worded differently, the wording of the motive usually turns out to be what the wording of the desire should have been. This is because a motive worded differently than its source desire usually brings that desire down to earth by setting commonsense parameters for its fulfillment. When a proposal for actualizing that motive gets created, that motive's source desire gets tested for its strength to endure what must occur for its fulfillment.

Example: In coordination with a desire worded: "I want to be more attractive," a commonsense motive for the fulfillment of that desire might get worded, "I want to lose weight and be a nicer person." When a logical course of action for the implementation of this motive turns out to be exercising more and complaining less, the original desire gets grounded in a "reality check" that may or may not inspire its immediate fulfillment. The good news here is that, having gone through the process of establishing a motive that can be worded like the desire behind it, a seed that assures an eventual fulfillment of the original desire, or a transmutation of it, gets planted.

- In this last step of this exercise in self-reflection, we would like to ask you to think of your most embarrassing desire. Then, *not in your journal* but on a separate piece of paper, express that desire in writing. Then burn the paper it is written upon.

39
Yogas
Variations on a theme

There is yoga and there are yogas. To be more specific, it could be said of yoga, and the family of yogas it has become, what might be said of anything made manifest: "First there was one; then there was more than one." Such proliferation could not really be dubbed beneficial or not any more than a cell dividing or a couple having children could be considered helpful or not. It's simply a natural consequence of the life of something—*anything*—doing what it does, which is (among other things) to bloom out of innate simplicity into manifest complexity.

Known history maintains that yoga was officially codified as a practice by a man named Patanjali who lived about 200 BCE. Although the *Vedic Upanishads* indicate yoga was practiced at least a thousand years before Patanjali was born, Patanjali has been given credit for getting yoga established in an official way because he was apparently the first person to write down a coherent description of it.

In his terse handbook, the *Yoga Sutras,* Patanjali laid out a set of disciplines he called *ashtanga yoga*, "the yoga of eight limbs." This *ashtanga yoga* came to be known as *raja yoga*, "the king of yogas."

The "eight limbs" or progressive steps of *ashtanga yoga* are *yamas* (restraints), *niyamas* (observances), *asana* (posture), *pranayama* (breath control), *pratyahara* (withdrawal), *dharana* (concentration), *dhyana* (meditation) and *Samadhi* (mystic oneness).

Although *ashtanga yoga* was originally conceived as a one system, parts of it have been separated out to become yogas in themselves. Prominent among these are *hatha yoga*, highlighting body development; *kriya yoga*, emphasizing breath control; and *jnana yoga*, featuring introspection. Knowledgeable yogis also assert that *karma yoga*, focusing upon selfless service, and *bhakti yoga,* focusing upon devotion, were derived from the *yamas* and *niyamas* of Patanjali's *ashtanga yoga*.

The spawning of these first spin-off yogas inspired the development of other yogas out of Pantajali's original *ashtanga yoga*. These included *japa yoga, nada yoga,* and *kundalini yoga*. Through the passage of time, even more yogas came—many of them named after their teachers or the places they were originally taught. This snowballing multiplication of yogas continues today. But it all started with Patanjali and his *ashtanga yoga*.

The greatest good that has come from the proliferation of yoga into yogas has been its extensive development through specialization. The basic *pranayama* of *raja yoga*, for instance, which originally offered only a simple means of preparing for meditation by controlling breath to calm body, mind and emotions, got sophisticated into *kriya yoga*. *Kriya yoga* is a system of breathing exercises so elaborate and complete within itself it offers a path to God Realization through breath control alone.

The greatest harm that has come from yoga's proliferation has been its frequent forfeit of original intent. Since the literal meaning of the word *yoga* is "to bind back," as in binding back to source, it should not seem unreasonable that a practice *called* yoga should *be* yoga in the truest sense of the word. Yet, many of the specialized yogas that have developed out of *raja yoga* are not binding back to source as much as they are bounding forward toward some end or ideal within their own area of expertise. *Hatha yoga*, for instance, is often taught only as physical exercise for physical health.

The most intriguing evolution of *raja yoga* from its inception to the present has been its successful absorption back into itself of that which blossomed out of it into specialization. When this amalgamation of developed-new back into stable-old is allowed to occur wisely, which usually means under the guidance of a qualified teacher, those developed parts getting merged back do not change the original structure of that from whence they came as much as they support and enhance that structure. Thus, it may be said, in best-case scenarios, today's *raja yoga* has not lost the house it built but has instead gained for that house a constructive reinforcement.

In yoga as in life, knowledge is power. Because this is true, we can be sure the foundational knowledge we bring to any yoga we practice will most certainly increase that yoga's benefits tremendously. Yet, to maximize these benefits, we must assimilate this knowledge we bring with the desire we have. As of now, 39 steps into our journey, we have a fairly healthy stockpile of knowledge. What we might be lacking, however, is a clear and honest perception of exactly what we want out of our yoga practice right now.

It is not so important that we want yoga's ultimate "binding back" right from the start of our practice. Higher desires cannot be forced. But they can be enticed. Yoga—however it is practiced and for whatever purpose—entices the high through an overall overhaul of the low.

40
Innerrelating
Using yogas together

Although it could be said all of the practices we have utilized so far on this book's journey have come from what we are calling a *one* "tempered" *raja yoga*, it could also be said—in accordance with the way yoga is often taught today—they have come from *many* yogas. However we classify these practices intellectually, our own experience of them will reveal they always work well together in whatever way they are combined. In this practice, entitled "Innerrelating," we will prove this truth out experientially by combining yoga exercises *simultaneously* as well as *sequentially*.

Innerrelating

• In the top right corner of the next available page in your journal, write the date and time of this practice. In the top left corner of this page, write "My Inner Relationships."

• From a cross-legged seated position, pull the heel of your right foot into your groin, straighten your left leg out in front of you and lean forward to touch the toes of your left foot with the fingers of both hands (see figure 7). If you cannot touch your foot without bending your extended leg, focus on keeping your back straight as you reach your hands as far forward as you can comfortably. This *hatha yoga* position is called *janu shirshasana* in Sanskrit.

Although you will not be able to breathe deeply in the forward-bending of *janu shirshasana*, apply the *ujjayi* breath control anyway. As you equalize the length of your inhalation with the length of your exhalation, visualize a pure, bright, rich orange color. Let yourself become sensitive to the unique vibration of this unadulterated orange and allow that vibration to permeate your entire nervous system.

A pure orange is supposed to consist of red, the color of vital physical health, and yellow, the color of vital mental health. Is this how orange feels to you? How orange feels to you is what is true for you.

Take note of how this mystical effort of visualizing a color while sensing a vibration translates into a physical experience. Also note how this physical experience is affected by the simultaneous application of *janu shirshasana* and *ujjayi*.

A note: If visualization is new for you, the first thing to understand is that seeing with your imagination—which *is* visualization—is a non-physical activity you are probably much better at than you think you are. To test out your natural knack for this, see and feel the color orange by recalling orange things you know—like orange oranges, orange flowers, orange balloons and orange sunsets. Then visualize all of these usually orange sights in unlikely colors: as in purple oranges, black flowers, grey balloons and green sunsets.

Once you have caught the vibration of the color orange perceived *in context* as it contrasts with the vibrations of other colors perceived *out of context,* you will be able to appreciate how different colors consist of different vibrations that can be sensed from within *being*.

• After about three minutes or when you feel the time is right, move into a second version of *janu shirshasana* by pulling the heel of your left foot into your groin, straightening your right leg out in front of you and leaning forward to touch the toes of your right foot with the fingers of both hands (see figure 7).

After about three minutes in this *janu shirshasana*, shift into a position called *paschimottanasana* by moving your left foot forward so both of your legs are extended in front of you and you can touch the toes of both feet with the fingers of both hands (see figure 7).

In both of these positions, maintain your visualization of the color orange.

- When you are ready, pull out of *paschimottanasana* and prepare to experience a new set of three *hatha yoga* postures.

To assume the first of these three new postures, called "cobra" in English and *bhujangasana* in Sanskrit, lie on the floor on your stomach with your hands positioned not directly under your shoulders but forward about six inches. Then, raise your head so that you are looking straightforward at a point about three feet away and about three feet up off the ground.

In this position, inhale deeply through your nose. Then, as you exhale long and slow, also through your nose, push your upper torso up with your arms until your elbows are almost but not quite locked. In this position your feet, legs and pelvis should be on the floor with your lower back arched and your head tilted back so you are looking straight up (see figure 8). While you are holding this posture for as long as you can comfortably, which may be less than a minute, perform a slow *ujjayi* breath control and visualize a bright blue light.

Also while you are in this swayback position, pinpoint the exact location of your greatest physical tension. Is it in the small of your back where one might logically expect it to be? Maybe not. Perhaps it is between your shoulder blades—or in the nape your neck. Wherever that tension is, flood that place with the blue light you are visualizing.

When you are ready, slowly lower your torso to the ground.

A note: By holding awareness fixed upon a point of physical tension, two events occur simultaneously and in equal measure: the tension relaxes and the focus of awareness internalizes. Each of these triggers the other in a one synchronized experience. Both of these can be accentuated with color visualization.

Light blue is supposed to vibrate as exhilarating upliftment. Dark blue is supposed to vibrate as devotion. How do the blues feel to you?

- In preparation for the second of these three positions, position yourself on the floor facedown as you did in preparation for assuming the "cobra" *(bhujangasana)*. From this position, bend your knees and raise your feet until you can reach back with both hands and clasp both ankles—left hand to left ankle and right hand to right ankle. Then, looking up, arch upward by pushing your ankles back and away from your head, thus

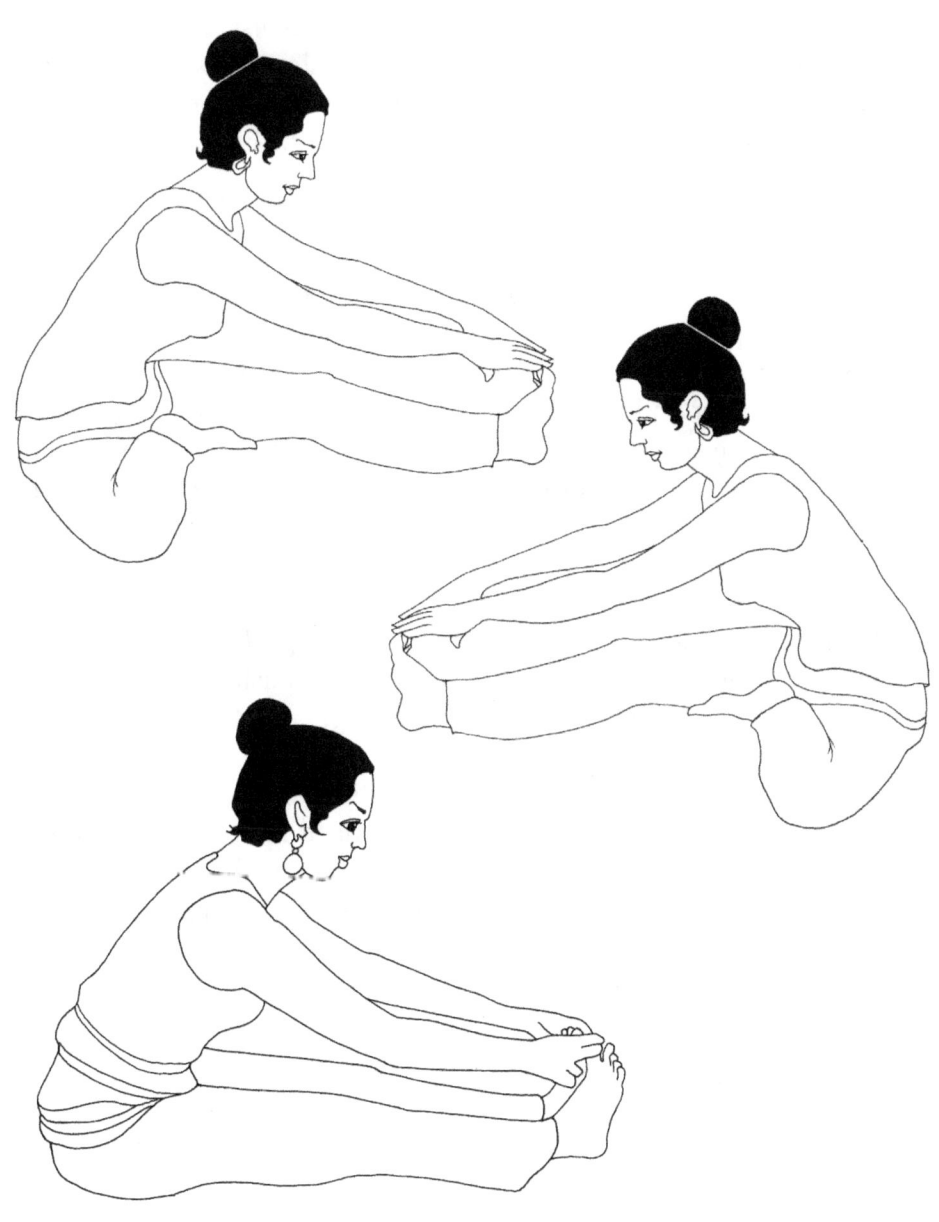

Figure 7: *Top, the two versions of* janu shirshasana. *Bottom,* paschimottanasana.

pulling your head and shoulders up (see figure 8). This *hatha yoga* position is called "bow" in English, *dhanurasana* in Sanskrit.

As you hold *dhanurasana* for about a minute or so, apply *ujjayi* breath control and hold the focus of your awareness upon your greatest physical tension as you flood that tension with blue light. When you are ready, slowly lower your torso to the ground.

• The third position in this last set of three *hatha yoga* postures is called *panchanga pranamasana* in Sanskrit. In this position you counter the back bending of the previous two postures of this set by sitting on your heels in a kneeling position to lean forward until your upper forehead touches the floor and your arms, with the palms of your hands joined together in prayer formation, are stretched as far in front of you as you can reach (see figure 8). In this position there should be no tension to flood with colored light—only the vibration of blue enjoyed from within the bliss of *being*.

• When you are ready, sit up, take three deep *sigh breaths*, open your journal and under your title, "My Inner Relationships," record your reflections, having experienced "Innerrelating."

A note: By adding concentration and visualization into *hatha yoga* posturing, we are working all five bodies at once as we simultaneously release physical tension, unblock *prana*, calm emotions, focus awareness (through concentrated visualization) and enjoy *being* in a practice that is in sync with the spirit of *ashtanga yoga*.

41
Yoga
Yoking awareness back to source

Many spiritual seekers with no shortage of sincerity inch their way into yoga slowly and cautiously only because they are not quite sure what they are getting into. This is understandable. As has been mentioned, "there is no one system of yoga, as yoga is taught today, and no one fixed

Figure 8: *Above, the "cobra" known as* bhujangasana *in Sanskrit. At center, the "bow" known as* dhanurasana *in Sanskrit. Below, a forward-bending posture of relaxation known as* panchanga pranamasana *in Sanskrit.*

Two additional postures:
Above, an advanced version of "cobra" known as "king cobra." Below, a posture called "up dog" or urdhva mukha svanasana *in Sanskrit. The "up dog" is similar to and often confused with the "cobra." While in the "up dog" the hands are placed directly under the shoulders to create a strength-building isometric tension in the arms and core of the body, the positioning of the hands in the "cobra" is about six inches forward from a vertical alignment with the shoulders. The purpose of this latter hand placement is to create a more severe arch in the back. If strength and flexibility allow, the "king cobra" and the "up dog" may be performed in addition to the "cobra" and the "bow."*

criterion by which the relative quality and authenticity of any of today's many yoga systems might be evaluated."

Of all the many yogas that have blossomed out of *raja yoga*, *hatha yoga* is the most popular. It is also the one taught most similarly by different teachers. Because it is primarily physical and therefore conveniently tangible, *hatha yoga* can yield easily recognizable and measurable results, especially in dealing with down-to-earth problems like anxiety, stress, depression, weight-gain, high blood pressure, poor circulation, bad digestion, inflexibility and much more. Yet all of these issues are but surface symptoms of deeper imbalances that can only be more profoundly corrected through the combined application of many yogas, or as the old masters might have said in reference to the one original *raja yoga*: the one application of the one yoga for the one purpose of God Realization.

If we are newcomers to yoga, arriving with an intense desire to "bind back" to source, there are at least two good reasons why we might not be inclined to freely leap into the deeper more introspective yoga practices: 1. *We don't have faith.* 2. *We don't have guidance.* In putting these two reasons together, we might say: *We don't have faith to leap because we don't have guidance to follow.*

When we are externalized, good guidance with regard to any deep mystical pursuit dodges direct acquisition when we are seeking it and deft apprehension when we have found it. This makes its attainment as illusive as the faith it takes to follow it.

When faith and guidance are illusive, they can seem to arrive out of nowhere and in their own timing—like two fingers on the right of God come to fetch us after we have stumbled and humbled ourselves so much we can't go on without a touch of grace. And grace these two can seem to be as they materialize in our lives more like gifts given than awards won.

From an internalized perspective, however, where life is a little less convoluted, faith and guidance are more likely to be viewed simply as endowments of intuition. We have already met intuition. She stands beside *bliss, love, stillness, balance, peace, power, awareness* and all those other wonderful qualities of *being*.

This brings us to the subject of the guru.

In India, *guru* just means teacher—that's all. A teacher of math is a math guru. A teacher of music is a music guru. And a teacher of spirituality is a spiritual guru. Yet there in India, an important distinction is made between a spiritual teacher who conveys spiritual information—often called a pundit—and a spiritual teacher who actually leads or pushes students into spiritual experience.

If this latter version of a spiritual teacher is really good at what he does, he is referred to as a *Sat Guru*. *Sat* means "pure being or existence." Thus, a *Sat Guru* is a purified spiritual preceptor who has realized God as Self and is therefore qualified to help others move toward that same attainment. He does this by pulling or pushing them into their own intuition, for it was through intuition deep in the core of life's fruition that he finally attained what his students must now claim as their rightful and most essential spiritual heritage.

42
Tuning the Body
Preparing for meditation

At the end of this practice called "Tuning the Body," we will be pulling forth from within ourselves a better understanding of *faith* and *following*. First, however, we are going to spend enough time with *hatha yoga* to discover how this aspect of a tempered *raja yoga* is not as completely physical as it might appear to be.

Hatha literally means "sun/moon." *Ha*, "sun," refers to a subtle nerve current in the soul body called the *pingala nadi*. This nerve current is masculine in nature. *Tha*, "moon," refers to a similar nerve current in the soul body that is feminine in nature and is called the *ida nadi*. The practices of *hatha yoga* include manipulating the body and controlling the breath to calm and harmonize the *ida* and *pingala nadis* so the *sushumna nadi* can be activated and the *kundalini* can rise. The *sushumna nadi* is the central psychic nerve current of the soul body that coexists with the spine in the physical body.

We encompass *hatha yoga* into a tempered *raja yoga for* five primary reasons: 1. To invigorate the physical body so it will not distract us with inordinate discomfort during a deeper practice of yoga, 2. To strengthen the nerve system of the physical body so it can sustain the building intensity of energy released during a deeper practice of yoga, 3. To optimize the interrelationship of the physical body with the inner bodies so the physical body can reflect the growing vibrancy of those inner bodies as they bloom during a deeper practice of yoga, 4. To calm and balance thought and emotion by calming and balancing the physical body in preparation for a deeper practice of yoga. 5. To aid in the release of those subconscious repressions that tense the physical body and inhibit introspection.

In this practice, entitled "Tuning the Body," we will be practicing a little bit of *hatha yoga* for all of these five reasons. The postures we will be assuming are known in Sanskrit as *virasana, paryankasana, sarvangasana* and *halasana* (see figure 9).

To perform *virasana,* we kneel and spread our feet apart so that we can sit with our buttocks touching the floor between our ankles. In this position, also known as the "hero," we place our hands together in prayer formation at the level of the heart.

To perform *paryankasana,* we must first assume *virasana.* From *virasana,* we move into *paryankasana,* also known as the "couch," by arching back until the top or back of our head touches the ground. In this posture, the palms of our hands are held together in prayer position over our chest.

To perform *sarvangasana,* also known as the "shoulder stand," we lie on the ground flat-back and face-up, then throw our hips and straightened legs up vertically to be caught and held by our hands, palms placed to mid-back for support.

To perform *halasana,* also known as the "plough," we must first assume *sarvangasana.* From *sarvangasana,* we move into *halasana* by lowering our straightened legs slowly over our head until our toes are touching the ground. If this position cannot be achieved or sustained with the legs held straight, the knees can be slightly bent.

Tuning the Body

• In the top right corner of the next available page in your journal, write the date and time of this practice you are now beginning. In the top left corner, write: "Reflections on Faith and Following."

Figure 9: *Clockwise from top:* virasana *known as "hero,"* paryankasana, *known as "couch,"* halasana, *known as "plough" and* sarvangasana, *known as "shoulder stand."*

- As you perform *ujjayi* breath control, assume the *hatha yoga* positions just described in the following manner:

    First get comfortably seated in *virasana* (the hero pose). After about three minutes or when you are ready, move into *paryankasana* (the couch pose). When you sense your nervous system has adjusted to *paryankasana,* assume *sarvangasana* (the shoulder stand) for about five minutes, followed by *halasana* (the plough pose) for about three minutes. Finally, relax back into *shavasana.*

- When you are ready, sit up in *sukhasana*, open your journal and — under your title: "Reflections on Faith and Following" — record your insights on *faith, following,* the *Sat Guru* and *intuition*. Please include in this record, your reflections on how a *hatha yoga* preparation affected your access to insight.

43
Sat Guru
A spiritual teacher

From an externalized point of view, the Sat Guru is perceived as a physical person. From an internalized point of view, the Sat Guru is perceived as wisdom — wisdom revealed through a live person, a life experience or direct intuition. Intuitively, we discover this wisdom through introspection. Personally, we find it with the help of a physical teacher. Experientially, we locate it in the sometimes-difficult experiences of life.

When this wisdom that is the Sat Guru comes indirectly — which would be through a physical person or the experiences of life — it guides us toward direct perception through intuition. Yet intuition is not the Sat Guru's truest identity. That identity would be as it is for us — the Self God within.

From this sequential joining of truths, we can catch the whole crux of a one practice of a one yoga for a one purpose of God realization: that God, Self and Sat Guru are not separate. They are one. As such, these three in one constitute our ultimate identity and destiny.

For those who might assert that telling a beginning yoga student he or she *is* God, Self and Sat Guru might be recklessly unwise, we would reply, "How far wrong can such a teaching go that it couldn't be caught and corrected by the *life* or *live* Sat Guru?"

The *life* Sat Guru—the experiential teacher—misses no opportunity to feed us lessons we earn and learn through the infallible law of karma. Although these lessons come from this *life* Sat Guru, they are derived from experiences we have set in motion of our own volition. Thus, the responsibility for the direction our training takes in the arena of life governed by action and reaction lies with us and not with our teacher. Knowing this, we perceive this neither wrathful nor merciful *life* teacher as an unbiased messenger of that karmic law we all must honor and obey.

It is, in fact, only because of the *life* Sat Guru's perfect impartiality that the law of karma can function as it does, throwing back upon us the kind of education that can only occur through our experience of the consequence of nothing more or less than precisely what we ourselves have done.

Although the *life* Sat Guru is with us throughout embodied existence, the *live* Sat Guru usually makes his or her appearance only after we have experienced most of all the *life* Sat Guru has to offer. Yet when that *live* Guru finally does come, the *life* Guru does not go away. Where there is *life*, there is the *life* teacher. The *live* teacher only doubles the *life* teacher's strength to more powerfully usher in the influence of that more deeply inner teacher that works directly through intuition.

When the influence of the Sat Guru becomes triply strong by working uniformly through all three of its channels, it becomes impossible to ignore. Fortunately, this full-blown preceptor of threefold power cannot force itself upon us before we are primed and ready. Love holds it back until love can hold it no more, which is when its love becomes our love and there is no separation between us.

In our deeper understanding of karma, wisdom, love and such, it becomes apparent why the Sat Guru's full story can only be told one chapter at a time, like the play of life can only be experienced one act at a time, and the journey of yoga can only be walked one step at a time.

44
Appreciating
Taking the best and leaving the rest

Since the Sat Guru has worked with us indirectly through our experience and directly through our intuition from the day we were born and before, we cannot claim we are strangers to his influence. What we *can* claim, however—if we are willing—is that we have almost certainly not always been fully appreciative of that influence. Therefore, in this practice called "Appreciating," we will be focusing upon recognizing, acknowledging and respecting some of the gifts of wisdom we have already received from this grand teacher who is forever accessible to us through our experience and intuition.

Before we make this introspective effort, however, we will perform a bit of *hatha yoga* sequencing for the balancing of mind through the balancing of body. Although all of the postures we will be assuming have already been introduced, we will state them here with truncated descriptions for easy reference. (Their fuller descriptions are provided in chapters 40 and 42.)

Appreciating

- In the top right corner of the next available page in your journal, write the date and time of this practice you are now beginning. In the top left corner, write "Taking the Best and Leaving the Rest."

- In preparation for appreciating, perform *ujjayi* breath control as you spend two or three minutes becoming settled into each of the following *hatha yoga asanas*. For best results, assume these postures in the order they are listed:

Janu shirshasana: From a seated position on the floor, straighten your right leg out in front of you, pull your left foot into your groin, lean forward and (ideally) touch the toes of your right foot with the fingers of both hands. Then assume this same posture with your left leg extended and your right foot pulled in.

Paschimottanasana: From a seated position on the floor, straighten both legs, lean forward and (ideally) touch the toes of both feet with the fingers of both hands.

Bhujangasana: From a prone position facedown, push the upper torso up with the arms while holding the feet, legs and pelvis to the floor. Make sure your hands are placed *not* right below your shoulders but forward about six inches.

Dhanurasana: From a prone position facedown, reach back, clasp both ankles with both hands and slightly straighten the legs to pull and arch the upper torso up and back.

Panchanga pranamasana: From a kneeling position, lean forward, forehead to the floor, arms to front and palms together in prayer formation.

Virasana: Kneel with feet spread apart, buttocks to the floor.

Paryankasana: From within *virasana*, lean your upper body back until the top or back of your head is touching the floor. In this posture, the palms of your hands are together in prayer position over your chest. Coming out of this position, raise your upper body to a vertical position and bend forward until your forehead touches the floor in front of you while your buttocks is still touching the floor between your ankles.

Sarvangasana: From a face-up, prone position, raise your lower torso and straightened legs up until your body from the neck down is vertical, with your hands placed mid-back for support.

Halasana: From *sarvangasana*, lower straightened legs over your head until your toes touch the floor behind you.

- Relax in *shavasana*. In the blissful aftermath of your *hatha yoga*, look back into your past to one experiential example of each of the four following life scenarios:

A. A sad event
B. A fearful event
C. A humiliating event
D. A challenging event

Once you have located these memories, strive to observe them objectively, making a special effort to fearlessly face the unpleasant as well as the pleasant.

• When you feel you have concluded this retrospective observation, sit up in *sukhasana*, open your journal and—under your title: "Taking the Best and Leaving the Rest"—put into words your perception of the wisdom each one of those experiences had to offer.

Example: Wisdom gained from a humiliating event might be described as follows: "When I got fired on the first night I ever worked as a waiter, I learned that being a good waiter includes understanding how to remain calm, observant, humble, friendly, patient and forbearing while dealing with difficult circumstances and unhappy people."

• Now, consult your powers of recall again. This time, seek out memories of four inspiring experiences you feel occurred because you made decisions with forethought. As you identify these "good" memories, observe them from within and record what you feel they taught you.

A note: If we feel we have neither learned nor benefited from a certain past experience, we can be sure we have missed something, for every experience we have offers some gift of wisdom from the *life* Sat Guru. If we are not receiving that gift, it is not because it is not being given.

    Although it is true that our past will *generally* repeat itself through the natural cycles of life, it is most assuredly also true that a certain portion of our past will *specifically* repeat itself through experiences designed to provide a wisdom we were previously offered but could not perceive, acknowledge or accept.

45
Virtue
Being good

Wise is the *live* Sat Guru who leads an aspirant through a tempered *raja yoga* that the aspirant himself validates every step of the way as he listens to the inner Sat Guru of intuition and learns from the Sat Guru who is life itself.

If we approach the practice of yoga as Patanjali would like us to, we must come to grips with his contention—as represented in the *yamas* (restraints) and *niyamas* (observances) of his *ashtanga yoga*—that to reap the greatest benefit of a deeper yoga practice, we must be "good" rather than "bad." Although logic might wonder what being good has to do with realizing the Self beyond time, form and space, experience reveals that the purity of goodness is a way station of simplicity not far from yoga's ultimate end.

Our first discovery of a respect for goodness occurs after we have endured the painful consequences of living badly, or as we might say another way: living unskillfully due to ignorance. From the perspective this discovery establishes, goodness looks like wisdom, wisdom looks like experience and experience looks like the teacher of the world stimulating the teacher within to say, among a great many other things, "What you do unto others, you do unto yourself. So—be good."

With regard to *ashtanga yoga*, this general respect for goodness is given specific expression in the *yamas* and *niyamas*.

The literal meaning of *ahimsa*, the name of the first *yama*, is "non-violence."

As we listen to the Sat Guru speak through wisdom, world and man, we come to understand that non-violence is the opposite of violence and violence is an unavoidable fact of life. "Life feeds on life," He says. "For one thing to live and flourish, another thing must suffer or die. Animals kill to eat. Man fights to survive."

"So how are we to be non-violent?" we ask.

"Live in a love that sees no separation," He says, "a love in which there is respect and consideration for all, even in a world where suffering and death occur as they must."

Although *satya*, the name of the second *yama*, literally means "truth," this *yama* refers more specifically to *not being untruthful.*

As we listen to the Sat Guru speak through wisdom, world and man, we come to understand that—apart from truth absolute—*untruth* is the opposite of *truth* in a world where *truth* is relative. "Beyond time, form and space, *truth* is absolute," He says. "In thought, *truth* is wisdom. In the world, *truth* is an honest provision of clarity when such clarity is useful and helpful."

"So, how are we to provide such well-timed, honest and helpful clarity?" we ask.

"Live in a love that sees no separation," He says. "See clearly. Think deeply. Then, in accordance with the needs of the *now*, honestly and fearlessly say what you see and think."

The literal meaning of *asteya*, the name of the third *yama*, is "non-stealing."

As we listen to the Sat Guru speak through wisdom, world and man, we come to understand that non-stealing is the opposite of stealing and stealing is a desperate act of ignorance blind to love. "Forgive those who steal," He says, "for they know not what they do. They clutch at life in fear of death in search of prey like you."

"Oh no, we're not *that*," we say.

"Have you not stolen attention, recognition, control, respect and opportunity?" He asks.

"Okay, okay," we say. "How may we cultivate non-stealing?"

"Live in a love that sees no separation," He says. "Give a little more than you take and take just what you need. Then let your left-over giving leave a good-will seed."

Although *brahmacharya*, the name of the forth *yama*, literally means "walking with God," this *yama* refers more specifically to refraining from promiscuous sex.

As we listen to the Sat Guru speak through wisdom, world and man, we come to understand that not walking is the opposite of walking, walking is living, living is life and life retained is power gained when man's base urges are restrained. "Refraining is abstaining from a loss of power," He says, "a loss of life before its flower."

"Okay," we say. "In what way can we keep this flower power?"

"Live in a love that sees no separation," He says. "But don't give in a love that spawns dissipation. Love the body but keep it leashed, for it's the animal of you. To do the work that you must do, use the body, don't abuse it—and don't confuse these two."

The literal meaning of *Aparigraha*, the name of the fifth *yama*, is "non-selfishness."

As we listen to the Sat Guru speak through wisdom, world and man, we come to understand that, although selfishness is self-obsessed and quite a mess indeed, selfishness will be selfless when greed thins out to need. "Who is this selfish 'I' you think you are?" He asks. "Who is this 'you' that you appease? Let self be Self, then be selfless, as selfless as you please."

"Easier said than done," we say. "How can we do *that*?"

"Live in a love that sees no separation," He says. "See others as yourself and be selfish just for them. Let their concerns be yours. Then let this selfish be as selfish is in a bliss a lack of self assures."

These five *yamas* just conveyed in rhythm and rhyme are *nots*—stuff we try *not* to do. Although *not* following an urge might seem like a *non-action*, it's not, for an urge is a powerful force that can only be controlled or restrained by a counter-action of some sort. Yet wisdom trumps power in mind-over-matter where motives for action are made. Thus, motives made in wisdom from the substance of the *niyamas*, induce action in which the power of the urges named in the *yamas* gets redirected in and up.

The *niyamas* naturally engender the *yamas* because *not doing* one thing is most easily accomplished by *doing* something else instead. In accordance with this principle, the *niyamas* are what we are asked to *do* instead of acting upon the urges the *yamas* ask us to restrain.

Shaucha, the first *niyama*, means "purity." *Santosha*, the second *niyama*, means "contentment." *Tapas*, the third *niyama*, means "austerity" or "self-discipline." *Svadhyaya*, the forth *niyama*, means "self-reflection." *Ishvara pranidhana*, the fifth *niyama*, means "devotion to a personal Lord." All of these dignified "do's" are natural inclinations of the soul that wisdom will always inspire us to nurture through the concrete action of practice.

In nurturing these soul inclinations, we can benefit from a tempered *raja yoga's* incorporation of *bhakti* and *karma yoga*. *Bhakti yoga*, which means "union through devotion," awakens love. *Karma yoga*, which means "union through action," awakens service. Love and service fade a hardened "I."

It is this "I" that grows vividly powerful as we pursue the urges of man named in the *yamas*. And it is this "I" that fades as we—through the practices of *bhakti* and *karma yoga*—become absorbed in the soul qualities the *niyamas* name.

In *bhakti yoga*, we *worship* God as the creator of all living things. In *karma yoga*, we *serve* God as the life flowing through all living things. In *raja yoga*, we realize God as the Self of all living things. What we give up in worship is an "I." What we forget in service is an "I." What we release in realization is an "I." Most certainly, dealing with these "I's" in some manner of relinquishment is the common denominator of all our yoga practice.

The devotion of *Ishvara Pranidhana* is the very essence of *bhakti yoga* and the *impetus* for *karma yoga*. As a result of giving up our "I's" through the practice of *bhakti* and *karma yoga*, we are left relieved of a burden in the purity of *shaucha*, and the contentment of *santosha*. In this purity and contentment, our austerity of *tapas* is effortless and our *self-reflection* of *svadhyaya* is fearlessly honest.

Although the *yamas* and *niyamas* are positioned as the first two of *ashtanga yoga's* eight steps, their fullest development awaits us one step beyond that yoga's end. Thus, we will meet these restraints and observances again and again from here on in and up, for their flowering will indicate our empowering of a mystic life within.

46
Gauging Good
Assessing a degree of virtue

In this practice, entitled "Gauging Good," we will be evaluating the goodness of the lives we lead toward a yoga freed of misdeeds and the karmic baggage those misdeeds accrue.

In our preparation for this gauging exercise, we will be learning two new breath controls. One is called *surya bedha pranayama*; the other, *chandra bedha pranayama*. *Surya bedha pranayama* (*surya* means "sun") stimulates the left, masculine-aggressive, heating and "thinking" side of the brain, which is coordinated with the right side of the body. *Chandra bedha pranayama* (*chandra* means "moon") stimulates the right, feminine-passive, cooling and "feeling" side of the brain, which is coordinated with the left side of the body. When these two breath controls are put together, they form the *anuloma viloma pranayama*.

Instructions for the practice of *surya bedha pranayama* and *chandra bedha pranayama* begin like instructions for the practice of *anuloma viloma pranayama:*

Sitting in *sukhasana,* rest your left hand on your left knee in any fashion that is comfortable for you. Then close your eyes and curl the first (index) and second (middle) fingers of your right hand down the inside of your right thumb until the nails of those fingers rest against the base of that thumb.

After this preparation, the practice instructions for *surya* and *chandra pranayamas* are diametrically opposed:

In *surya bedha pranayama,* squeeze your left nostril shut with your ring finger as you breathe in slowly and deeply through your right nostril. Then, at the peak of a full inhalation, release your ring-finger block of the left nostril and close your right nostril with your thumb as you breathe out slowly through your left nostril.

In *chandra bedha pranayama*, squeeze your right nostril closed with your thumb as you breathe in slowly and deeply through your left nostril. Then, at the peak of this inhalation, release your thumb block of the right nostril and close your left nostril with your ring finger as you breathe out slowly through your right nostril.

In this following practice entitled "Gauging Good," we will be using these two breath controls in conjunction with *anuloma viloma pranayama* to balance body, mind and emotions in preparation for some honest self-facing and plan-making.

Gauging Good

• In the top right corner of the next available page in your journal, write the date and time of this practice you are now beginning. In the top left corner, write "My Goodness."

- When you are ready to begin, listen to your body. Feel what it needs. Then choose from the *hatha yoga* postures you have learned (from this book or elsewhere) those postures you feel will bring balance, harmony and bliss to your physical body in accordance with its current state of relative imbalance.

A note: Now, you are being called upon to consult your own intuition even for the sequencing you do in preparation for your practice of a specific meditation or yoga exercise. Through this effort applied in *hatha yoga*, be like a cat, stretching this way and that, realizing you are the one that knows precisely what you need to do to ready your body for deep introspection.

- Once you feel physically prepared for a contemplative yoga practice, sit in *sukhasana* and become aware of your breathing. Practice one round of *anuloma viloma pranayama* to discern which nostril has the freer flow of air. (Usually, one of your nostrils will be at least slightly blocked.) If the left nostril is blocked as compared with the right, perform *surya bedha pranayama* until the left nostril opens. If the right nostril is blocked as compared with the left, perform *chandra bedha pranayama* until the right nostril opens.

    If the left nostril is completely blocked, lie down on your right side until that nostril begins to clear and before you practice *surya bedha pranayama*. Conversely, if the right nostril is completely blocked, lie down on your left side until that nostril begins to clear and before you practice *chandra bedha pranayama*.

- When you feel the flow of air through both nostrils is fairly even, practice three to five rounds of *anuloma viloma pranayama*. Then lie back in *shavasana* to enjoy the blissful sense of balance these breath controls have helped establish.

- After about ten minutes or when you feel the time is right, sit up, open your journal and prepare to record your answers (under your title: "My Goodness") to the five questions listed below.

    Before you begin writing, however, read all five questions through quickly to see that not one of them can be answered with an unequivocal "yes." For this reason each one of your answers must necessarily begin with a "no," followed by an honest assessment of where you think you stand with a plan for moving toward a "yes."

1. Do I live in a love that sees no separation, a love in which there is respect and consideration for all, even in a world where suffering and death occur as they must?

2. Do I see clearly, think deeply, and—in accordance with the needs of the moment—honestly and fearlessly express what I see and think?

3. Do I give a little more than I take, and take just what I need—and let my left-over giving leave a good-will seed?

4. Do I use the body and not abuse it—and not confuse these two?

5. Do I see others as myself, letting their concerns be mine, letting such selfish be as selfish is in a bliss a lack of self assures?

Example: One possible answer to the first question: "No, I don't live in a love that sees no separation—not always. I also don't always have the kind of respect and consideration for others that I know I should have. All of this, I admit. I also admit I have given myself permission to live without this love, respect and consideration because I see other people living this way—or so it seems to me. Yet I can see that living this way and giving myself permission to live this way can't possibly be helpful. So, my plan now is to be a better person and let other people be."

47
Three Realms
The physical, mental and spiritual

As we begin to intuit the sweeping variety of energies at play between the urges Patanjali would like us to restrain in the *yamas* and the dignities he wants us to observe in the *niyamas*, we can begin to gain a greater respect for the forces that must be dealt with through life and yoga in the *world of manifestation*. This "world of manifestation," as it is commonly perceived in mystical thought, is comprised of a physical realm, a mental realm and a spiritual realm.

In the *physical realm*, we live in a physical body that is governed primarily by the *instinctive mind*. Although this instinctive mind operates automatically to control physical functions like food digestion and blood circulation, it also operates reactively to generate emotion and desire. This instinctive mind is as much with the animal as it is with us, for our physical bodies *are* animals.

In the *mental realm*, we humans are alone. There, in that brainy place, we do the one thing animals cannot. We think conceptually. As we think in this manner, we develop an *intellectual mind*, which operates creatively according to thoughts we choose to use.

The *spiritual realm* is the inner matrix for the physical and mental realms. In this spiritual realm we function through the *intuitive mind*. As this intuitive mind gets put to work in practical application, it merges with conceptual thought to become useful wisdom. Although each of us has equal access to this intuitive mind, the way we each think intuition through into practical application is unique.

Because our first use of conceptual thought in the mental realm occurs while we are living mainly at the mercy of instinctive forces in the physical realm, our first conceptual thinking is often of the cunning sort that can actually take us down below rather than up above our animal nature. In this seemingly back-stepping use of our mental faculty, we think to connive our way toward fulfilling our lower urges in ways the animals quite literally could not even imagine. In so doing, we create our most confusing muddles and our heaviest karmas in a hell of our own making, which—mystically speaking—is the only hell there is. In that hell, we form a desperate desire to rise.

Out of this desire to rise, we learn to lean on conceptual thought to first understand the predicaments we've gotten ourselves into, then make plans for extricating ourselves from those predicaments. Although this use of thought represents a positive development of mental acuity, it still leaves us living in reaction to life rather than in control of it.

When we have finally had enough of living-in-reaction, we use conceptual thinking to move from hindsight to foresight. In this commonsense application of intelligence, we gain some semblance of a useful control over our daily life. This is about when a program like living the *yamas* by following the *niyamas* starts to make sense.

Once we have become somewhat accustomed to using thought-control for life-control, we discover thought can be a great source of enjoyment. More specifically, we find a filtering of bliss in the mental realm that makes the intellectual mind an attractive place to be, especially if we set up shop there and begin to think of ourselves as an intellectual person of distinction.

Eventually, we come to realize intellectual bliss is stimulated by temporary fascinations that are ultimately unfulfilling. When we are finally ready to move on beyond our enjoyment of thought, we discover, as wonderfully captivating as the intellect is when we are in it, it can be confusingly distracting when we want to go beyond it.

As it becomes apparent to us the pull of the intellect can baffle our path to spirit, we feel stuck between two desires—a fading desire to follow thought for fun and a growing desire to follow spirit for bliss. As we sit there stopped in our feeling of being stuck, all we can do is look at our situation. Yet in this looking, we stumble upon a great spiritual truth: *observation is the first awakening of the intuitive mind.*

To observe is to see with a calm and open mind that is free of preconception and attachment. Although this kind of clear seeing can and should be cultivated, it often occurs naturally at turning points in our life when we are not sure which way to go or what to do next. At such turning points, we can look in and out at the same time—out at our problems and in to their solutions. If our observation is keen and our seeing is clear, solutions to our problems can look like answers obviously and inseparably connected to the questions that precede them.

When a fascination with the intellect is seen clearly through observation, it looks like a fluttering bird caught in a net—a mental stimulation stuck in thought's limitation. As observation inspires in us a growing respect for an economy of thought, it also reveals to us that an unnecessary ramification of thought almost always occurs only when thinking is allowed to flap and flicker unbridled for its own sake and for its own pleasure.

48
Clarifying
Assessing a level of living

In this practice, entitled "Clarifying," we will be evaluating the lives we live with regard to the degree of our involvement in the physical, mental and spiritual realms of manifest life through our instinctive, intellectual and intuitive perception.

Clarifying

• In the top right corner of the next available page in your journal, write the date and time of this practice you are now beginning. In the top left corner, write "Realms of Mine."

• As you did in preparation for the practice outlined in Chapter 46, entitled "Gauging Good," lead yourself through the *hatha yoga* postures you sense will be helpful in balancing the way you feel right now.

• Once your physical body feels balanced, get comfortable in *sukhasana* and practice one round of *anuloma viloma pranayama* to see which nostril has the freer flow of air. As in your preparation for the practice described in Chapter 46, perform *surya bedha pranayama* if the left nostril is more blocked than the right, or *chandra bedha pranayama* if the right nostril is more blocked than the left.

• When you feel the flow of air through both your nostrils has become sufficiently equalized, practice *anuloma viloma pranayama*. When it becomes apparent that your *pranayama* practice has reached its natural culmination — sensed as an inclination to be still — lie back in *shavasana* and enjoy the bliss revealed.

• After about ten minutes or when you are ready, sit up in *sukhasana* and allow yourself to sense the vibration of your instinctive mind as it functions in the physical realm, your intellectual mind as it functions in the mental realm and your intuitive mind as it functions in the spiritual realm. When you feel the time is right, open your journal. Under your title, "Realms of Mine," respond in writing to the following questions:

1. What percentage of a typical, 16-hour, waking day do you spend in: a. the instinctive mind of the physical realm; b. the intellectual mind of the mental realm; and c. the intuitive mind of the spiritual realm?

A note: The a/b/c percentage numbers that would form your answer might look something like this: 80/30/20—80 percent for "a," 30 percent for "b," and 20 percent for "c." (Since these minds and realms often function concurrently, these numbers do not have to add up to 100.)

2. How did you arrive at your evaluation of your involvement with the minds and realms?

Example answer: "I gave myself 80 for 'a,' because I'm a pretty basic guy. Most of my waking day gets absorbed into doing whatever I have to do to deal with people and circumstance. Although I don't think I really overindulge my instincts all that much, I do occasionally eat and drink what I shouldn't, talk more than I should and watch more TV than I need to.

"I gave myself 30 for 'b,' because I'm just not a very intellectual person. To be honest, I just think when I have to. For the most part, the little thinking I do is dedicated to handling fairly mundane problems.

"I gave myself 20 for 'c,' only because I have recently taken up the practice of yoga. If it were not for that, this number might be something like 10 at best."

3. Are you content with the degree of your involvement (during a typical day) with the instinctive mind in the physical realm, the intellectual mind in the mental realm and the intuitive mind in the spiritual realm? If your answer is "no," what would have to happen in your life for that answer to become a "yes?"

49
Three States
The outer, inner and deeper within

From a mystical point of view, our experience of the three realms of manifest life occurs from within *conscious*, *subconscious* or *superconscious* states of mind.

We are in a *conscious* state of mind when we are awake in a physical body and aware in the physical realm. In this most externalized state of consciousness, we are vitalized by gut instinct, memory, emotion and information received from external forms of communication like newspapers, magazines, radio, television, telephone and the Internet. If we are not artistically, philosophically, religiously or mystically inclined, we can live in the misconception that this conscious state of mind is the only reality.

The *subconscious* state of mind is an internalized and largely unrecognized level of consciousness that works behind the scenes of our life in two ways: 1. It functions like a meticulous recording device to document every detail of every experience we have regardless of that experience's perceived value. 2. It functions like a psychogenic computer to subliminally process that which it records into either storage or practical application. In practical application, it serves as an unconscious support for our conscious activity.

The *superconscious* state of mind is a deeply internalized level of consciousness sometimes referred to as "the divinity of the soul." It is from within this deep state of mind that we experience the bliss of *Satchitananda*. And it is from deep within *Satchitananda* that we realize the Self beyond time, form and space.

Understanding these *three states* of mind separately, together and as they relate to the *three realms* of manifest life, forms a large-scale grid we can use for mapping the movement of our awareness through consciousness. A grid like this is useful because, to effectively navigate from one place to another in the playing out of our desires, we need a ground upon which we can grip "one place" and "another."

Once we have allowed ourselves to acknowledge that desire—until it plays itself out—is a fact and force of life, and we have become smart enough to work *with* that desire rather than *against* it, we can learn to harness, aim and use its formidable power in a positive way to achieve worthy goals in accordance with a deepening understanding of the *states* of mind and *realms* of manifestation.

From a mystical perspective, a goal is a destination point set by the thinking mind in response to an urge felt coming from the physical realm, the mental realm or the spiritual realm. But a destination point can only exist in relationship to a starting point.

If we can see our point of origin, *where we are*, as clearly as we can see our destination point, *where we want to be*, our intuition can fill in the space between those two points with an appropriate course of action for goal achievement.

Intuition is always on our side. If it can get through, it will unfailingly help us in any way it can. But it needs an empty space to fill—like pouring water needs an empty cup to catch it. In our case here, that empty space exists between a clear perception of *where we are* and *where we want to be*.

In applying this desire-based map-making to problem solving, we would start by quickly identifying a problem as we first see it. We might say, for instance, "I don't have a job." Having stated this problem immediately and simply, we have objectified it enough to see it apart from a fear stimulated by the insecurity of not having a job.

This greater clarity then allows us to grasp our problem more completely—perhaps like this: "Although this no-job predicament exists primarily as a physical circumstance, it has the potential to churn up negative thoughts and emotions. I can see I'm going to have a hard time maintaining a positive attitude toward finding a job if I'm thinking and feeling negatively. I can also see how a lack of a positive attitude will inhibit the attainment of any positive goal."

This broader and deeper assessment of our problem allows intuition to more precisely define what that problem actually is, which might get stated something like this: "I don't have a job. And not having a job is shaking my self-confidence, which is making it hard for me to maintain a positive attitude while I'm looking for a job."

This clearer problem statement firmly establishes our *where-we-are* point of origin as it frees us to see clearly and function positively in solving our problem.

With our map's origin now more clearly defined, our next step would be to establish a destination point. To accomplish this, we might ask ourselves something like, "What job will I have?" Then, based on a reasonable assessment of our skills and talents as they relate to our need-based desire, we would state *in the present tense* precisely what we sense that job will be—perhaps something like this: "I am working from home as a marketing consultant making $150,000 a year, dealing with good, positive people in happy working relationships."

Once this well defined destination point has been set and we know exactly where we are coming from—our point of origin—our subconscious can go to work ushering superconsciousness through intuition into our conscious mind to develop an initial plan for the achievement of our specified destination.

If, as we proceed in life according to that initial plan, our subconscious does not overly resist our conscious efforts and we are able to allow our plan to be flexibly modified in accordance with our intuitive sense of need in the *now*, we should be able to experience a relatively effortless achievement of our specified objective.

50
Planning
Using the mind to fulfill a need

In this practice, entitled "Planning," we will devise a strategy for using the conscious, subconscious and superconscious states of mind to achieve the fulfillment of a desire that has been whittled down to need.

Planning

- In the top right corner of the next available page in your journal, write the date and time of this practice you are now beginning. In the top left corner, write "My Plan."

- As you did in preparation for the practices outlined in both Chapter 46, entitled "Gauging Good," and Chapter 48, entitled "Clarifying," lead yourself through those *hatha yoga* postures you sense will be helpful in balancing the way you feel right now. After you have completed your chosen *hatha yoga*, get comfortable in *sukhasana* and adjust the centeredness of your breathing with either (the masculine) *surya bedha pranayama* or (the feminine) *chandra bedha pranayama*. Then perform *anuloma viloma pranayama* (alternate breathing).

• When you are ready, pick a desire—any desire. Observe that desire first from within the conscious state of mind, then from within the subconscious state of mind, and finally from within the superconscious state of mind. As you observe, let each of these mind states respond. Then, let those responses help you understand your desire from three different perspectives. If your conscious, subconscious and superconscious states of mind all agree your chosen desire is worthy of pursuit, prepare to plan that desire's fulfillment. If even one of these three states of mind withholds its sanction, modify your desire until you have a full conscious, subconscious and superconscious blessing to proceed toward your desire's fulfillment.

Example: The desire you have chosen is a desire to be rich.

Your conscious state of mind likes this choice and thinks, "Fulfilling this desire to be rich will allow me to fulfill other desires, for money is a power in physical life." From this you can see that your conscious state of mind understands your desire for wealth to be a necessary prerequisite for the fulfillment of other desires.

Your subconscious also reacts favorably thinking, "Being rich might provide a sense of security and relieve me of some of my worries and fears." From this you can see your subconscious perceives your desire for wealth as being a need for security.

Although your superconscious does not desire, it can help you work with your conscious and subconscious desires by intuiting their value and—if they are perceived to *have* value—designing an expeditious plan for their fulfillment.

With regard to a desire to be rich, your superconscious might intuit, "Like power, money will not be problematic if it is used wisely. And in the fulfillment of big and worthy plans, making a lot of money can be a genuine need." From this, you can sense the superconscious views the relative value of any desire in the light of the law of karma, and gives its blessings to this specific desire to be rich, with the stipulation the wealth obtained be used wisely.

• When you feel the time is right, open your journal. Under your title, "My Plan," use a full page to devise your strategy as follows:

1. Mark a dot in the upper left corner of the page, right under your title: "My Plan." Beside that dot, write a description of your "point of origin." If your chosen desire is to be rich, for instance, your description of your origin point might include your current age, the amount of money you have now saved, the quality of life you are currently experiencing and an honest assessment of your talents, skills and professional aspirations. This description should also include your intuitive perception of any mental or emotional negativity you might be experiencing—such as, for instance, thoughts and feelings that might be voiced: "I don't deserve to be rich." or "Rich people are usually shysters."

2. Let your destination point be indicated by a dot placed toward the bottom left of the page. Beside that dot, describe your destination in the present tense. If your chosen desire is to be rich, for instance, your description of your destination should include the amount of money you see yourself having saved by the time you are a certain age—say 65—as well as the job you see yourself performing and the lifestyle you see yourself living at that time.

3. Allow your intuition to assist you in filling in the blank page between your points of origin and destination with an initial plan loosely developed as a series of goal-based steps.

Example: If your desire is be rich and your aspirations are unselfish, your (initial) map might look something like this:
   • Point of origin: I am 22 years of age. I have $25,000 saved. I have been well trained in accounting and have a job working at a starting position in a well-established accounting firm. I am currently making $55,000 a year. Although I enjoy the sense of security that comes from working in the accounting field, I can't spend lavishly on

my current salary, even though I live alone in a small apartment. I can see that my biggest obstacle is a fear of failing. Already, I can see myself creating excuses for failure. • Eight years later: I am 30. I am married to a wonderful lady. We live in a house we have just purchased. I have used $250,000 of the $500,000 I have saved from salary, raises, benefits, bonuses and wise investments to start my own accounting firm, which is now quite successful. Having made a significant amount of money, my confidence is strong and my attitude is positive. • Ten years later: I am forty. My wife and I have three children. I have one million dollars saved. I sell my business and make another million dollars. I feel wholesome about the honest money I have earned and want to help others. I write a book on how to build wealth from nothing. That book becomes a best seller. I am happy. • Ten years later: I am fifty. I have five million dollars. Now, my money is making money. I am using my wealth to help others and enjoying life. • Destination point: I'm 65 and I have ten million dollars. I am now focusing on setting up trusts and endowments to help good people and organizations. Our three children have families of their own and are well settled in life. With the extra time my wife and I now have, we enjoy a powerful spiritual life.

PART THREE
THE RELATIVE

51

The Conscious State
The waking level of mind

If we position awareness in the physical body and the physical realm, and we spend all our waking hours in that conscious state of mind, naturally we are going to identify with that body, that realm and that state.

When we practice a deeper yoga that focuses on breaking out of this three-faceted sense of false identity, we find ourselves stepping back and detaching into a watcher awareness, observing the physical body, the physical realm and the conscious state of mind.

At first, this watcher awareness is faint because it has arisen inadvertently as an unanticipated consequence of a general yoga practice. Yet, as we catch the idea this state of detached observation is worthy of intentional pursuit, we begin to cultivate watcher awareness as a yoga in itself.

Working to hold watcher awareness, we find we can study the power of our instinctive nature from a distance where we can feel its magnetism just beginning to pull us into all-encompassing experiences of seeing, hearing, feeling, smelling and tasting in the physical realm. We also find we can investigate just how this involvement with the physical realm through the instincts of the physical body can trigger emotions that urge us to seek solace in the intellect. Finally, we find we can examine the intellect to see how its development begins with a manipulation of remembered information rather than truly original thinking.

All of this and more we can learn about the conscious state of mind by simply being that watcher that can only see what it sees because it is separate enough from what it sees to see it clearly. From this we can also sense that, when we are the watcher, we are not in an externalized state of consciousness at all. We are outside externalization—or to put it more precisely, we are inside externalization, looking out at it.

If everyone suddenly pulled back into watcher awareness, the conscious state of mind would not be what it is at all, for it is what it is only because of the externalization of those consumed enough in an awareness of it to be caught by it. "Externalization" here refers to a state of mind in which nothing beyond a world perceivable through the five senses is acknowledged as having substantial existence.

Because the conscious state of mind is a product of awareness consumed in the physical realm, it is also a product of awareness preoccupied with physical *things* to want and have. Since blind ignorance is the common ground of awareness bound in this conscious state of mind, no one caught there knows that no *thing* can yield happiness. Thus, most everyone caught there seeks happiness by seeking *things*.

Additionally, since being caught in the conscious mind also means identifying with the physical body, those thus caught also seek happiness by thrilling, clothing and feeding the body—and by making a lot of money to do more of the same. Such stuck-in-the-body living is like treadmill-running after a satisfaction that is forever advancing ahead of us, just out of reach.

When we feel trapped in this most externalized state of consciousness, we experience a stark variety of fear that can only arise when we are so completely cut off from our own intuition we have lost even the faintest sense that we are actually an immortal entity impervious to harm. As might be expected, it is when we find ourselves so fully at the mercy of a fear like this that we are so understandably inclined to cobble together whatever externalized security we can derive from name, fame, fortune, and the like.

Though we could be in any of many places besides this outer condition of consciousness, we will not be anywhere but there so long as we remain unknowingly addicted to the lure of our own fascination with novelty. Drawn into the conscious mind by intrigue, curiosity and desire, and hounded there by fear, we seek a seeming safety in a fortress we build around a false sense of "I." Although this hard-walled stronghold of wrong identity makes us insensitive and tough, we perpetuate it at all costs—even when it begins to cost more than the sense of security it was created to nurture and protect.

Thus it is that a primary objective of yoga is to withdraw from the conscious state of mind—when we are ready, of course, for how could such withdrawal occur otherwise? When we *are* finally ready and withdrawal *does* finally occur, the conscious state of mind becomes an object of study and a point of focus for internalizing rather than externalizing awareness.

52

Observing

Watching the conscious mind

In this practice, entitled "Observing," we will be working to study the conscious state of mind from the detachment of watcher awareness.

Before we begin this practice, a foundational statement:

We create and perpetuate the very existence of the conscious state of mind by continually arousing it into manifestation through our own fascination, curiosity and desire.

If we can accept this conceptual statement enough to experiment with it in practice, we will have positioned ourselves well enough to enjoy the watcher awareness this exercise is meant to cultivate.

Although it *is* in the nature of awareness to temporarily *become* what it is aware of, it is *not* in the nature of awareness to permanently *identify* with what it is aware of. Such identification exemplifies yoga's view of ignorance: "to perceive the unreal as real and the real as unreal." In this perception, ignorance is *not* bliss. It is open access to pain.

In watcher awareness there is no suffering of pain; there is only an observation of it. What the watcher feels in the background of its watching is the bliss of *being*. This bliss, continually magnetizing awareness back into the watcher, keeps awareness from forging needless bonds of identification with what it is aware of. Not surprisingly, it is the cultivated enjoyment of this bliss that reveals the validity and stability of watcher awareness.

We can immediately stimulate and enter a blissful watcher awareness by simply allowing intuition to zero in on the statement: "I am not what I am aware of." It is not even necessary to successively repeat this statement as in the practice of affirmations (See Chapters 71 and 72). All we need to do is say it once: "I am not what I am aware of." Then wait. Wait for awareness to respond by retreating back into that *being* that need not be told it's not what it is aware of. Then, as thought and emotions again begin to move in (as they invariably will), just say again, "I am not what I am aware of." And again, wait.

Now, let's find the watcher and watch.

Observing

- In the top right corner of the next available page in your journal, write the date and time of this practice you are now beginning. In the top left corner, write "The Day That Was."

- After you have become comfortable in *sukhasana,* initiate the practice of *trataka* as it was described in Chapter 6, entitled "Encountering." Once your eyes have become fixed upon a physical point, pull awareness back into the bliss of *being* as deeply as you can without allowing your eyes to close or lose their designated point of focus.

A note: What you are working to achieve here is a state of consciousness in which awareness is healthily divided. In this meditative state, a minimal portion of your awareness is focused out through the eyes on something physical while the rest of your awareness is focused in toward an enjoyment of the bliss of *being*. Respected by yogis as a discipline that can be performed even amidst the intensity of everyday life, this inward/outward gazing provides a means of "being *in* the world but not *of* it."

- After about fifteen minutes, relax your *trataka*-based internalizing of awareness and close your eyes. In the blissful heady energy you will then most certainly be feeling, say to yourself: "I am not what I am aware of," and watch how quickly your intuition lets you actually feel you are not what you are aware of. Once you have caught this very real feeling of not identifying with the object of your awareness, say to yourself: "I am," as you allow awareness to sink back into a full experience of pure *being*. Finally, from within the centered security of *being*, say to yourself: "I am the watcher," as you let awareness come *out* of *being* just a little bit—just enough to watch. When you sense yourself losing watcher awareness to the invasion of thought and emotion, go back to the beginning. Say to yourself: "I am not what I am aware of." When you can feel that, say: "I am." When you can feel that, say: "I am the watcher." Then watch.

A note: We are skipping our usual body-and-breath sequencing in the first portion of this practice to emphasize that we can get into watcher awareness without going through a lot of extensive preparation, even during our working day when we have only a few minutes to spare.

Once we have become accustomed to focusing our eyes *out*, and our awareness *in*, we will be able to move deeply into the bliss of *being* and from there slightly *out* to a state of watcher awareness in just a matter of seconds. It is this state of watcher awareness arising out of *being* that we want to achieve in preparation for our practice of "Observing."

• When you feel balanced in watcher awareness, open your journal and prepare to write. Then, remember backwards through your yesterday from the time you went to bed to the time you woke up. Under your title, "The Day That Was," list each event you can recall. Once your list is composed, underline the events that were dominated by fear or desire.

A note: Fearful events can be indicated by feelings that are infrequent but intense like fright, terror, panic and horror; or feelings that are more frequent but less intense like worry, concern, stress, anxiety and dread. Even anger is a fear-driven emotion—a turbulence aroused by a fearful defensiveness that seeks to protect an externalized *thing* we value or an externalized *person* we think we are.

Events motivated by desire can be indicated by higher-minded feelings of creativity, ingenuity, originality, inspiration and enthusiasm; or lower-minded feelings of infatuation, yearning, craving, coveting, longing and lusting. Blocked or unfulfilled desire—especially if it is of a lower type—can manifest as envy, jealousy, spite and depression.

• When you have finished your backwards description of your yesterday and you have underlined its fear and desire driven moments, lay back in *shavasana* and take a break. Just take a break. Let go. Allow your mind to go off duty so you can become rejuvenated from within.

• After about ten minutes or when you feel the time is right, sit up and again open your journal. Write down a new title, "The Day that Could Have Been." Under that title, rewrite your *day that was* as a *day that could have been*. And let that new day be devoid of fear and desire.

53
The Subconscious State
The subliminal level of mind

Our computer-like subconscious is a remarkable state of our mind. Long before we become aware of it, or even if we *never* become aware of it, that subconscious is there thanklessly handling all of the basic and crucial functions of our physical body like blood circulation, food digestion and muscle coordination. And while it is doing all this, it is also recording, categorizing and processing every single experience we have in our conscious state of mind, even as it creates from those experiences elaborate programs for the automatic implementation of skills like typing, driving and speaking a language. Thanks to this marvelously self-contained and self-reliant part of us just beneath the range of our conscious perception, we are free to focus our surface awareness upon exploring and learning through new experience.

As marvelous as this apparently free-standing and independent subconscious state of mind might seem to be, it *can* be inhibited by us. More than we know, we can inadvertently block our subconscious reception of superconsciousness.

When, due to an impure and/or a selfish lifestyle, our subconscious receives more negative input than it can process immediately, it becomes overloaded with *wrong perception* and *unresolved memory*. A backup into a backlog of this gloomy mind-matter is "negative karma." Fortunately, there is no limit to the amount of negative karma the subconscious can hold. Unfortunately, however, as these negative karmas mount, they thicken their block of the very superconscious influence that would insure their resolution.

As we begin to realize we are more than a body and a mind with fears and desires, we start to sense we really don't have to live life in the shadow of excess negative karma. We also begin to sense—and this sensing is a result of our superconsciousness getting through to us any way it can—we can help our subconscious better its collaboration with our superconscious to more efficiently handle our backlog of *wrong perception* and *unresolved memory*.

At this point we start living life on the high side of our conscious mind by trying *to do good and be good* so as not to burden our subconscious with more low-level problems than it can handle with a minimum expenditure of energy. Such intentionally positive living leaves impressions in the subconscious that don't need to be "fixed" later. This smart creation of "positive karma" frees the subconscious to expeditiously work on its backlog of "negative karma."

In yoga, we "do good and be good" by tailoring our lives around the *yamas* and *niyamas*. Maintaining these restraints and observances dissolves our blocks to the superconscious by adjusting our negative attitudes, demagnetizing our personality conflicts and allowing the flowering of spiritual qualities like humility, patience, forbearance and fortitude. All of this intentional adjustment opens a wide window for the light of superconsciousness to shine through our subconscious into our conscious mind.

To further assist our subconscious in working efficiently with superconsciousness, we can make special efforts to remain detached as we deal with past and present experience. Such detachment invites the assistance of intuition—our direct connection to superconsciousness.

When awareness is detached, it is not identified with thought and emotion. This detachment gives awareness unblocked access to intuition. When awareness is not detached, but instead allows itself to become magnetized into an identification with thought and emotion, it partially or completely loses its functional connection with intuition.

When we habitually and thus frequently allow awareness to become identified with thought and emotion, we live life personally. In this personal living, we have no choice but to see life through the eyes of an identity caught and stuck in a physical body that was born, is alive and will die. From this point of view, we are not looking at life intuitively because intuition is not personal; it is impersonal.

From experience, we know the non-reaction of detachment can only arise from an intuitive perception that we are Self. We also know we do not have to *realize* the Self to sense that the Self *does* exist and is our essential identity. Sensing we are the source of the body we live in is easy. It's even *logical*. But if we cannot manage to *let this sensing be*, we *will not* be detached and we *will* react to life personally.

To perceive the experiences of life in detachment without reaction is to see those experiences impersonally. Seeing the experiences of life impersonally leans us toward a creation of positive karma, as well as an expeditious resolution of negative karma.

54
A Purification by Fire
Burning emotion away

In this practice, entitled "Releasing in Fire," we will be extracting emotion from memory so we can allow a correction of *wrong perception* and a settlement of *unresolved memory*. The only thing that obstructs clear seeing more than non-intuitive thought is emotion, for emotion—negative or positive—has a wildness about it that can be scarily blinding and all but impossible to control.

In the practice of observation, observing stops when thinking begins simply because thinking and observing cannot occur at the same time. Yet the instant we catch ourselves thinking, we can fairly easily pull ourselves back into observation. This is not so with emotion.

If we fall out of our observation into emotion—especially powerful emotion—backpedaling into the cool detachment of observation is usually far less of an option than riding our emotion on out into its drained and exhausted dissipation. Because emotion is such an adversary of observation, the intent of this exercise will be to burn emotion out of memory.

Although this practice of "Releasing in Fire" will consist of writing our burdensome memories down on paper and burning that paper up, it must be made clear here we are not trying to erase our past. That which we have learned from the life we have lived thus far is important. We want to keep that. What we do not need to keep, because it confuses what we have learned, is emotion. Although it is true that emotion certainly has much to teach us, the primary substance of that teaching is that emotion is confusing.

Releasing in Fire

• In the top right corner of the next available page in your journal, write the date and time of this practice you are now beginning. In the top left corner, write "A Fire Purification."

• As you did in following the instructions outlined in Chapter 52, entitled "Observing," get comfortable in *sukhasana,* pull two-thirds within while focusing your *trataka* gaze upon some physical point, then successively adjust awareness to the consciousness of "I am not what I am aware of," "I am," and "I am the watcher."

• Once you have yourself established as the watcher, choose a memory of a negative emotional experience you had with another person. Then, write down—not in your journal but on a separate piece of paper—a description of that experience (see figure 10).

Figure 10: *The first stage of "Releasing in Fire"*

Figure 11: *The second stage of "Releasing in Fire"*

- After you have performed this exercise in recall, write a letter to the person with whom you had this experience (also on a separate sheet of paper). In this letter, fully and freely express all of the negative emotion you felt during that experience. Don't hold back. Be explicit. When you are finished, burn both your experience description and your letter. (See figure 11.) No need to make a ceremony of this. All you are doing is burning trash.

A note: In this exercise, we are focusing on memories of experiences you have had with other people since it is generally interpersonal relationships that stimulate the strongest emotions.

- Once you have performed this exercise with one negative, personal memory, do it again with other similar memories.

A note: Because the past only exists in memory, changing that memory changes the past it holds — as far as our subconscious is concerned, which is all that matters as far as we are concerned. If we choose to change the past by releasing emotion from the memory of that past, that memory then exists in the subconscious as experiential knowledge gained, minus the confusion of its emotion.

Remember, emotion must be released for its effects to be realized. Realizing emotional effect is important because this effect *is* the knowledge emotion has to offer. But it's a knowledge that can only come to light when emotion is observed in detachment.

- After you have completed your "releasing in fire," relax in *shavasana* and allow your intuition to respond to all that has just occurred.

- When you feel the time is right, sit up and open your journal. Under your title, "A Fire Purification," write down your reflections upon your experience of relieving memory of its emotion. As you reflect, consider the following two truths generally accepted by most mystics:

1. Other people are never the problem. If a person gets on your nerves for no apparent reason, it should be helpful to realize (though hard to face) this person represents something about yourself you have not yet understood through experience.

A negative reaction is very telling, for it indicates a rattling of our sense of security. We, whoever we think we are, want things to stay the way they are—for the sake of our security. Thus, when we are challenged with something we do not understand, we react negatively in defense of what we currently perceive to be our anchor of stability. Example: A teenager—highly influenced by peer pressure, his current "anchor of stability"—reacts in disgust to the lifestyle of his parents. Yet disgust turns to respect and understanding as this teenager grows up into the responsibilities of adulthood and has kids of his own who are disgusted with *his* lifestyle.

2. The subconscious is never the problem. It is our programming of the subconscious that makes this marvelously efficient computer-like part of us appear to be either our worst enemy or our best friend. To think the subconscious is the enemy is to program the subconscious with that wrong perception.

55
The Superconscious State
The mystical level of mind

Once we have become subconsciously adjusted to a sense of an "I" rooted in *being*, rather than an "I" driven by the impulses of the five senses or lured on by the ramification of thought and the novelty of the conscious state of mind, we have successfully positioned awareness on the threshold of superconsciousness.

Before we seriously focus deeply within, we experience superconsciousness in a general way—usually as something like a no-problem zone of inner space in which everything just seems to be okay. Because this nonspecific enjoyment of alrightness feels quite "natural" to us, we are left to assume that we are at least temporarily functioning in an "unnatural" state of mind when life does *not* seem to be "okay."

If we accept "natural" to mean *inherent* and "unnatural" to mean *acquired*, we will be inclined to perceive our superconscious state of mind to be *inherent*, and therefore the same for all of us, while we understand our subconscious and conscious states of mind to be *acquired*, and therefore different for each of us (since each of us acquires differently according to our individual experience).

Obviously, just living in a physical body demands an externalization of awareness out of "inherent" superconsciousness into "acquired" conscious and subconscious states of mind.

When we roll out of bed in the morning to brush our teeth and shower, each one of us must necessarily leave our inherent superconsciousness to live by thousands of little personally acquired memories. Although certainly we might manage to do all of this with a subconscious sense of superconsciousness, which would be wonderful, our waking life is still primarily an acquired existence formed consciously and subconsciously.

From this we can see, while we are awake in the physical realm doing physical things, the superconscious is at best only available to us as a secondary influence working through our subconscious to feed the background of our daily life with bliss, confidence, calm, compassion, inspiration and the like.

Tapping into superconsciousness in this way is wonderful to be sure. But to thoroughly experience this richest part of us, we must fully withdraw from our conscious and subconscious states of mind, enter the spiritual realm, and be there completely. Under normal physical circumstances, this cannot be accomplished easily. During periods of time set aside for the practice of a yoga that includes deep meditation, however, it can be.

During such withdrawal, we strive to become immersed in those magnificent qualities of *being—bliss, love, stillness, balance, peace, power, rapture, joy* and *awareness*. Just holding the "I" centered in any of these qualities invites Samadhi, intensifies an internal correction of *wrong perception* and *unresolved memory,* and programs our subconscious to flood our external life with an unfettered superconscious support that can and will sustain us even during our most trying times.

If we can then come out of this withdrawal to remain two-thirds within during the waking hours of our life, our subconscious will assist rather than block a more continual superconscious influence upon our physical life. This two-thirds-within positioning of awareness is easily attainable. In fact, it is so attainable we can be there and not know it.

Take, for instance, an elderly lady, washing dishes, humming a song and looking out her kitchen window at two robins nibbling sesame seeds off a bird feeder. As that lady rests in the bliss of *now*, enjoying the warmth of soapy dish water, the touch of slippery plates, the tap-tap pecking of the birds, and the sweet delight of humming her song—all at once—is she not a perfect example of the conscious, subconscious and superconscious states of mind working together harmoniously as one?

Moving like this in life is not difficult and does not demand we have a completely resolved subconscious. Even with a huge backlog of karmic "issues," we can work with ourselves to live and move easily, receiving superconsciousness like a welcome guest when it comes, awaiting it patiently when it doesn't.

Dealing with life in this manner, ever so lightly leaning upon and occasionally withdrawing completely into our internal nature, we invite our superconscious to more and more consistently move forward through our subconscious into our conscious states of mind until, finally, we are feeling at least a little bit of superconscious all the time.

When we have lost our sense of superconsciousness, we can get it back by simply becoming aware of that loss. Just that. With this simple adjustment of awareness—just recognizing and acknowledging we have temporarily lost our sense of inner bliss during a frenzy of mental or emotional distraction—we gift ourselves the only moment the *now* needs to help us gain back our option to feel and follow the rhythm and rhyme of our own intuitive mind back in and through inner realms to our superconscious home base.

56
Innersearching
Exploring being

In this practice, entitled "Innersearching," we will deepen our experience of *being* by exploring its qualities of *bliss, love, stillness, balance, peace, power, rapture, joy* and *awareness*. Through this inner investigation we will discover there are worlds within worlds within *being*, for *being* is superconsciousness, which can be experienced a little or a lot, deeply or not.

Innersearching

• In the top right corner of the next available page in your journal, write the date and time of this practice you are now beginning. Then, list the following qualities of *being*: *bliss, love, stillness, balance, peace, power, rapture, joy, awareness*. Under this list, write "Being Explored."

• As in the practices of Chapter 52, entitled "Observing," and Chapter 54, entitled "Releasing in Fire," get comfortable in *sukhasana* to become deeply centered in *watcher awareness*, first by holding awareness two-thirds within while focusing an open-eyed gaze of *trataka* upon a physical point, then by successively adjusting to the consciousness of "I am not what I am aware of," "I am," and finally, "I am the watcher."

- Once you have become comfortable in watcher awareness, look at the list of the qualities of *being* you have just recorded in your journal. As you focus your eyes upon the first word in that list, *bliss*, allow your intuition to guide your awareness into an actual bliss experience. As soon as you catch this bliss experience, even just a little bit, shift your eyes to the next word, *love*, and allow your intuition to do the same thing again—guide your awareness into the first glimmering of a deep love experience. After you have touched into this love, move your eyes and awareness in the same way on through all the other qualities listed —*stillness, balance, peace, power, rapture, joy*—until you are finally looking at the last word, *awareness*, and asking intuition to guide your awareness into an experience of *awareness aware of itself*.

A note: Awareness can move like lightning or sit still as stone. In yoga, we seek skill in moving as well as stilling awareness. A skillful moving leads to a skillful stilling.

Also, for those of you with little faith, we say, "please do not underestimate intuition." She needs no training to maneuver you within. Her guidance is unshakably flawless right now. Do yourself a favor. Let yourself be sure intuition will do her job if you let her.

- When you have guided your awareness to move quickly through your list once, go back and do it again—more slowly. Repeat this slowing cycle of deepening inner experiences for at least fifteen minutes.

A note: There is a key here: *Slower brings deeper, and deeper brings slower.* As you will discover for yourself, there will be little need for a purposeful internalizing of this exercise, for your slowing will quite naturally encourage a deepening and your deepening will quite naturally encourage a slowing.

- After about fifteen minutes of exploring *being*, remain in *sukhasana* to call up a memory of a negative emotional experience. As you observe that negative memory, intuit its vibration as contrasted with the vibration of the qualities of *being* you have just explored.

A Note: As you perform this last exercise, notice how *being* sits cool and emotion runs warm to hot. Notice also how the cool of *being* yields a natural sense of safe detachment from the pull of *outer* life just as the heat of emotion stirs up a blindness to the pull of *inner* life.

• When you feel the time is right, record in writing—under your title, "Being Explored"—your reflections upon exploring *being*.

57
Hidden Hybrids
Subconscious amalgams

The *wrong perception* and *unresolved memory* we hold in our subconscious are endowed with a strong magnetism that pulls toward them the correction they lack and need. Since this correction must occur through the events of our conscious, subconscious and superconscious existence, it could rightly be said we spend a good portion of our physical, mental and spiritual life dealing with our past if we are holding a considerable backlog of negative karma.

Because cognized memories no longer need or demand our attention, they lose their magnetism and leave us alone. As liabilities of ignorance that have become assets of wisdom, these understood and demagnetized memories drop back into our storage of experiential knowledge gained to become karma resolved. In that storage, they await our reference when it is sagacity born of experience we need.

This processing of memories the subconscious does is wonderfully logical and, because it is logical, easy to understand. There is, however, one curious portion of the subconscious that is not so easy to sort out because it does not perform in what might be considered a logical manner. Here is how that part of the subconscious works.

When two similar experiences get recorded into memory at different times, the impressions they make in the subconscious mix and mingle to form a very different third impression. This third impression is more than a simple mix of its two parent memories. It is a unique anomaly created by the subconscious itself. One baffling aspect of this anomaly is it often does not obviously resemble either of the two memories that spawned it.

Because these hybrid subconscious impressions are difficult to understand and for that reason tend to remain a mystery for long periods of time, they become increasingly magnetic as they strive to pull toward them life situations that would bring them out into resolution.

If these hybrids are positive, the situations they attract will also be positive, and being positive will be happily understood and enjoyed. If these hybrids are negative, however, the situations they attract will also be negative, and being negative will not be happily understood, nor will they be enjoyed. Not being understood or enjoyed, they will often be suppressed into repressions. To a great extent, it is this latter negative, mysterious and mostly repressed portion of our subconscious that gives rise to our more perplexing psychological behavior.

Here is an example of how one of these negative hybrids might get formed:

A young lady—we'll call her Jane—gets a little drunk at a party and kisses her best friend's husband, John. Because nobody sees the kiss, Jane thinks to herself, "No big deal. Forget it." A month later, John and Jane unexpectedly run in to each other in a grocery store where they talk for a long time in a somewhat flirtatious manner. Although Jane feels badly about this conversation afterwards, she manages to think again to herself, "No big deal. Forget it." And indeed, she apparently *does* forget both these experiences.

Yet, every time Jane sees her best friend, Sally—John's wife—she feels awkward and acts in a manner that appears to be unfriendly. Sally wonders what's wrong and assumes she has done something to offend Jane.

As the years roll by, Sally and Jane drift apart until, finally, Sally—in an awkward attempt to rekindle her friendship with Jane—invites Jane to a party celebrating the 25th anniversary of her marriage to John. When Jane receives this invitation, her stomach turns, her face flushes red and she feels like she's going to faint. For the first time, she takes an honest look at a most uncomfortable sense of guilt she has been carrying for so long and sees how that guilt stems from those two experiences she had with John years before.

Having now finally isolated her guilt, and having traced it to its two source experiences, she sees how it was caused. Looking squarely at that cause, she asks herself some tough questions: "Is there anything I need to do now? Do I need to talk with John or confess to Sally? Would I steal a kiss from or secretly flirt with another woman's husband now?"

As she contemplates these questions and finally decides her answer to all of them is "no," she allows herself to take a candid look at what she was actually thinking and feeling at the time of those two events. Much to her surprise, she gains a great sense of release and relief, not because she is able to analyze why she did what she did, but because, in frankly facing herself the way she was twenty years before, she can see now by comparison how she has grown since then. And in that seeing, her two past improprieties start looking like sequential chapters of a book that can now finally be closed and filed away in the library of wisdom gained, as she again becomes best friends with Sally.

Just understanding how the subconscious works, especially in its creation of these hybrids, is enough to inspire us to live a good life that will not hound us later with unfinished business of an oppressing, embarrassing or confusing nature. In a life lived thusly, our "voice of conscience" is easily heard and enthusiastically obeyed.

Also, when we understand how these subconscious hybrids are made, we can arrange our lives so that positive rather than negative combinations get created.

For instance, if we meditate for an hour every day at six in the morning for a full year, we will be absolutely delighted when we come to realize we have gained an indomitable faith in spirit no words from a book could ever instill—all because a year's worth of experiences that were both similar and positive got melded in our subconscious to produce one mammoth amalgamation of spiritual inspiration.

By contrast, if we do not understand or respect how the subconscious mixes similar memories and we live a careless life that treats the subconscious like a garbage can for a trash past that cannot really be thrown away, we experience suffering.

In suffering, we anguish between the screaming haunt of a bewildering mesh of negative subconscious impressions and the superconscious voice of our conscience incessantly reminding us that we ourselves have created the agony we are now experiencing.

When those negative subconscious hybrids begin to get demagnetized through understanding, the ego gets dismantled enough to allow awareness the freedom it needs to move from an externalized identification with anguish toward an internalized enjoyment of bliss as it reforms itself little by little into a sense of identity that more accurately reflects its essential Self.

58
Seeing
Anatomizing memory hybrids

In this practice, entitled "Seeing," we will be facing memory hybrids to understand their structure. This kind of seeing can be most effectively accomplished when awareness is poised lightly on the edge of waking consciousness, such as when we are going to sleep, waking up or deeply relaxing. During such times, a release of fear and desire allows a more willing observation of what might ordinarily be avoided.

Calling forth negative subconscious hybrids to be understood—whether we are receptive to them or not—does not usually require a lot of purposeful inducement, since all of these misconstrued impressions are already seeking their own resolution and release, regardless of our assistance or resistance. Thus, our mode of operation here in this practice of "Seeing" will center around *relaxing, allowing* and *observing*—*relaxing* the body, *allowing* a surfacing of subconscious secrets, and *observing* those secrets revealed.

Seeing

• In the top right corner of the next available page in your journal, write the date and time of this practice you are now beginning. In the top left corner, write "The Strands of my Binds."

• In preparation for this practice of "Seeing," follow your own intuition to perform any preliminary sequencing you feel will set you up to remain vitally awake yet deeply relaxed in a near-sleep state.

A note: Only you can be a true judge of how you should prepare for a session of intentionally elongating the "twilight zone" that ordinarily only occurs unintentionally just before and after sleep. Generally, any exercise that is physically invigorating followed by any combination of breath and body controls that are physically relaxing should work well in this preparation.

- When you are ready to begin "Seeing," lie back in *shavasana*. Relax as if you were going to sleep. (Morning—when you are not tired—is generally the best time to perform this exercise.) As you relax, maintain a gentle focus on your breath until images begin to emerge. Then, focus on those images.

    The first images to emerge will most likely represent simply a routine subconscious processing of your most recent memories. Let those images come and go. After about fifteen minutes or so, you should arrive at your *seat of consciousness*. This is that "ground zero" place within you that you naturally fall back to when you are not consumed in inner or outer activity. Once you have found your seat of consciousness—which may or may not be blissful—hold on to it as you wait and watch for deeper subconscious imagery to arise.

A note: If we are "pure," our seat of consciousness will be in *being*. If we are "impure," our seat of consciousness will suffer the beclouding confusion of our *wrong perception* and *unresolved memory*.

When we are experiencing *being*, we feel blissfully content. When we are not experiencing *being*, we feel uncomfortably discontent. Although this latter discontent registers in our nervous system as a fidgetiness that makes us want to do anything but sit still, it represents our intuition's initial unraveling of *wrong perceptions* and *unresolved memories*. In our fidgetiness, we experience this healthy inner work of intuition as a welling up of erroneous thought and negative emotion stemming from sources we find difficult to pinpoint.

Since purity is the essence of our spiritual nature, we are only going to feel impure if our spiritual nature gets covered up, which is exactly what happens when we are harboring a subconscious backlog of *wrong perception* and *unresolved memory* that gets all mixed up within itself to form a wall separating our inner and outer life.

If our seat of consciousness is perched on the outer side of that wall, sitting in that seat will not initially be a pleasant experience. Yet sit there we must in this practice of "Seeing" designed to help us dissolve the psychological distress that keeps our seat from being where it belongs in our essential, blissful and spiritual nature.

- As imagery begins to appear, remain the watcher. Try to avoid becoming consumed in a reaction to what you are watching. Instead, wait until what you are watching settles into bliss.

A note: In the case of negative imagery, it is common for the pictures emerging to trigger mental replays of the memories they represent. These "replays" often consist of alternative versions of what really occurred during the past being remembered—different imaginings of what we feel coulda-woulda-shoulda happened but didn't.

In this practice of "Seeing," our challenge will be to *not* get drawn into this mental replay, but instead watch it from a distance.

When positive images of a similar nature reveal to our detached awareness how they got merged to become positive character traits, we will be inspired to move on into a deepening life of selfless joy. When negative images of a similar nature reveal how they got merged to become negative character traits, we'll relish an understanding we are finally able to assemble from difficult experience. As a consequence of this latter, tougher, rougher revelation of wisdom, at least some of the psychological discontent muddling the bliss of our seat of consciousness will simply fade away like a headache that finally just disappears.

What this all comes down to in this practice of "Seeing" is waiting—waiting in detachment for misunderstanding to die back into understanding. This metamorphosis of ignorance into wisdom right before the very eyes of our "Seeing" will occur of its own accord if it is allowed, which it will be if we let it be from within our detached waiting.

- When you feel the time is right, sit up and open your journal. Under your title, "The Strands of my Binds," record your reflections having now practiced "Seeing." As you reflect, ask yourself, "How do I feel now as I relax back into my ground seat of consciousness? Better than before? The same? Worse?"

A note: Our subconscious is full of these memory conglomerates we are calling "hybrids" here. Some of these hybrids are "good" and some of them are "bad." The ones that are "bad" become "good" by simply being understood as we see how they came to be.

As we continually work to shift our base sense of identity, which generally occurs as we shift our "seat of consciousness," our correction of *wrong perception* and *unresolved memory* happens more quickly and easily, simply because we are so expeditiously moving who we think we *are* away from who we thought we *were* when we created the negative karma that must now be resolved.

59
Sleep
A release of waking consciousness

A lot of our internal confusion—especially the unique bewilderment generated by the subconscious itself as it forms mysterious hybrids of negative memories—gets automatically resolved during sleep. Sleep time is a good time for this kind of work because, during those hours, our life in the physical realm is quiet and our waking consciousness is not active.

During sleep, when our ever-so-beguiling conscious state of mind is not so busy luring us out with its novelty into the creation of new karma, our subconscious can more efficiently work with the superconscious to bring about a resolution of old karma. Some of our dreams are surface reflections of this deep nocturnal mending the subconscious and the superconscious achieve together. But renovating a negative past is not the only feat these two vast states of mind can jointly accomplish while our waking consciousness lies dormant. They can also provide us with valuable guidance for a positive future. This guidance can turn up in dreams.

From a mystical point of view, there are *mending dreams*, and there are *message dreams*. While *mending dreams* are predominantly subconscious and deal with the resolution of a primarily negative past, *message dreams* flower out of the superconscious to inspire in us the creation of a positive future. It is helpful to remember *message dreams*. It is not helpful to remember *mending dreams*.

During *mending dreams*, negative events get generated on the astral plane as part of a subconscious clearing process. If we isolate, remember and ponder these largely unpleasant astral experiences while we are awake, we bring them forward into our physical life where they—like anything we perceive in our conscious state of mind—get impressed into the subconscious. Due to their magnetism, these new, negative subconscious impressions attract events on the physical plane that generate a whole new set of negative karmas that might not have existed if we had not remembered those *mending dreams* in the first place. Because we do not want this to happen, we can appreciate why it is not advisable—whether we are practicing yoga or not—to remember or analyze *mending dreams*.

Message dreams, however, are quite different. Aside from *feeling* meaningful as they occur and are remembered, these nocturnal reveries prove themselves to *be* meaningful as their wisdom gets applied in life. *Message dreams* can be prophetic (revealing guiding glimpses into the future), symbolic (presenting esoteric knowledge through symbols) or visionary (igniting ecstatic spiritual experience).

As we work with dreams in our yoga practice, our first aim is to distinguish *message dreams* from *mending dreams*. Once we have this distinction established, our objectives are to understand the *message dreams*, and leave the *mending dreams* alone.

Mending dreams are often of a nonsensical and uncomfortable sort that we generally don't *want* to remember. Fortunately, these kinds of dreams do not tend to stay with us (unless we try to remember them) after we awaken from sleep. *Message dreams*, however, will always occur against a backdrop of good feeling, even if their message is of a somber or ominous nature. Also, *message dreams* will always bear a sense of significance that will inspire us to revive them. Unlike most *mending dreams*, these *message dreams* are usually vivid, understandable and easily remembered.

It is only in the physical brain of the physical body that we dream, for it is only the physical body and brain that require the downtime of sleep. Dreams form a portion of the minimal activity that occurs within the physical brain during sleep. *Mending dreams* mark the physical brain's registration of subconscious cleansing. *Messaging dreams* mark the physical brain's registration of superconscious instruction.

Although the *pranic*, emotional, mental and soul bodies mentioned in the *Vedas do not* sleep, they *do* function differently while the physical body *does* sleep. During sleep, the *pranic* body *(pranamaya kosha)* receives its primary revitalization, the emotional body *(manomaya kosha)* enjoys a freedom to move separately from the physical body, and the mental body *(vijnanamaya kosha)* takes advantage of a less hampered access to superconsciousness.

While it is true, in accordance with *Vedic* thought, that four of our five bodies exist only to facilitate the development of our one essential soul body—*anandamaya kosha,* "the body of bliss"—it is also true it is only through the experiences this innermost "soul body" has as it functions through the other four bodies that the "soul" can develop at all. Thus, it could be said, our soul needs bodies to live *in* as much as those bodies need a soul to live *for*.

Although *Vedic* thought asserts that any physical act we commit signifies a coordinated effort exerted by all of our five bodies in all three realms of existence, it is undoubtedly the physical body living in the physical realm that must endure the fullest brunt of *karmic consequence*, for it is in the physical realm, with all of its inherent limitations, that the law of karma can have its most complete and obvious effect.

Example: Although a man might think of robbing a bank a hundred times, it is only when he actually does that deed on the physical plane that he creates a karma requiring perhaps a significant portion of a physical lifetime to resolve.

As we go to sleep, our awareness—which is non-physical and never sleeps—jumps from the physical plane to the pranic, emotional, mental and spiritual planes to function there within the constraints of karma we ourselves have created primarily in our waking consciousness. There, in accordance with the nature of that karma, we either suffer in bondage or revel in freedom.

Yet, even though the function of our awareness during sleep is strongly influenced by karma, there is one thing we can do to set ourselves up for a meditative sleep. We can gloam.

60
Gloaming
Dwelling on the threshold of sleep

In this practice, entitled "Gloaming," we'll be learning and applying a yoga-meditation technique that was originally conceived as a preparation for deep sleep, but can also be performed as a meditation.

To gloam is to catch, hold and lengthen the state of transitional consciousness that lingers on the threshold of sleep. As a practice, "gloaming" can be easy, or elusive. It can be easy if we allow it to happen—the way it occurs naturally as we are going to sleep or waking up. It can be elusive if we attempt to force it, as in trying to make it obey too many preset rules. The aim of this "Gloaming" exercise is to enhance an experience we are already having *unintentionally* by making it a yoga we perform *intentionally*. By "intentionally," we mean *with intent*.

What can be encouraging here is knowing that even a meager attempt to practice gloaming can have a significant effect, for the very *intent* of any deliberate attempt to dwell in the thin but pure sliver of consciousness that has released waking but has not yet embraced sleeping aims awareness straight for Samadhi.

"Gloaming" is most effective when it is performed right before sleep because *the last place we focus our awareness on the physical plane in waking consciousness before we go to sleep sets the trajectory for the flow of our awareness during sleep.*

In getting good at "gloaming" before sleep, we open ourselves up to the grand possibility of extending our yoga into the nighttime hours, and from there into the 24 hours of a full day where yoga can then begin to abide within us as a state of *being* rather than a practice of *becoming*. That said, let's gloam.

Gloaming

- In the top right corner of the next available page in your journal, write the date and time of this practice you are now beginning. In the top left corner, write "My Twilight."

- Now, as in your preparation for the practice described in Chapter 58, entitled "Seeing," ready yourself for an alert but relaxed *shavasana* by following your own intuition to establish any preliminary sequencing you feel will prepare you to remain vitally awake yet deeply relaxed in a near-sleep state.

- As you become comfortable in *shavasana*, establish an *ujjayi* breath control that is evenly measured—like nine-counts-hold-one on the inhalation, and nine-counts-hold-one on the exhalation. Try to keep all of your focus on this breath control until you catch that uniquely calm bliss that precedes sleep. Once you have located this blissful calm, strive to consciously hold it in stillness. As you feel yourself sinking into sleep, pull yourself back—return to your *ujjayi* breath control if necessary.

A note: In the practice of any breath control, making the exhalation shorter than the inhalation invigorates and vitalizes, while the opposite—making the exhalation longer—calms and sedates. If you should decide to put this principle to work as you strive to keep from falling asleep during "Gloaming," you might apply a "9/7" count—breathing in nine counts and out seven—to your *ujjayi* breath control.

Although the practice of "Gloaming" is similar to the practice of "Seeing" (in Chapter 58), it differs in its focus. In "Gloaming," we are focusing upon the calm bliss that stands as a backdrop to that which we observe in the practice of "Seeing." In "Seeing," we are sitting in our seat of consciousness whether that seat is blissful or not. In "Gloaming," we are focusing upon finding and holding the bliss of *being*. In short, "Gloaming" is deeper than "Seeing."

- When you feel the time is right, sit up and open your journal. Under your title, "My Twilight," record your reflections having intentionally worked to hold awareness aware of bliss on the threshold of sleep.

A note: If gloaming is successfully practiced before sleep, its conclusion should be remembered upon awakening. This conscious recall will indicate you did not just drift off to sleep as you normally might, but instead intentionally left your gloaming to consciously enter sleep.

61
Externalization
Absorption in outer life

Just being aware in a conscious state of mind diminishes our subconscious sense of superconsciousness to a certain extent. Becoming immersed in a conscious state of mind, however, can obliterate that deeper sensitivity almost completely.

It is the superconscious functioning through the subconscious that keeps the subconscious working as smoothly as it does. And it is the superconscious functioning through the subconscious that *keeps us sane in a conscious state of mind.*

As pessimistic as we might allow ourselves to become about specific situations or life in general, there is and always will be within us an intuitive knowing that insanity—defined by the *New Oxford American Dictionary* as "a state of being seriously mentally ill"—could very well prevail if we were not forever living in the perpetual blessings of an always-present but not-always-apparent superconscious influence.

When our more direct conscious access to superconsciousness gets cut off significantly, life gets complicated. We create problems and ask questions that could not even exist if we were in a more internalized state of mind.

When superconsciousness is perceived directly, answers precede questions and solutions precede problems. When superconsciousness is perceived through the subconscious, questions flow into answers and problems flow into solutions. In a conscious state of mind, burdened by a heavy subconscious, questions can seem to have no answers and problems can seem to have no solutions.

Questions unanswered and problems unsolved yield action that results in karma unresolved. Experiencing a backup of this unresolved karma eventually drives us within ourselves to discover that simply internalizing awareness is a spiritual panacea that solves all problems and answers all questions by putting us in a place where solutions and answers will not let problems and questions exist.

In this understanding it becomes apparent how *externalization* can be such an obstacle to a yogi's success in yoking awareness back to it's source in Self.

Although it is true that in the instant we become aware we are externalized we are no longer externalized (because simply *being aware* of where we are in consciousness is a profoundly internalized state of mind), holding that awareness long enough to become substantially internalized is a challenge worth respecting with a plan of action for constructively dealing with fear and desire.

If we ask the wisdom of our own experience to explain "externalization," that wisdom might reply, "Awareness drawn out by desire and held out by fear is awareness externalized." If we ask that same wisdom to explain "internalization," it might reply, "Awareness drawn in by desire devoid of fear is awareness internalized."

In more closely observing externalization as an obstacle to yoga, we can see such outward entanglement is really only and always a consequence of some combination of *wrong perception* and *unresolved memory*. These latter two conundrums joined together in any form or fashion create a wall between our inner and outer existence that must eventually be faced and dissolved either slowly in life or a little more quickly through yoga or some such practice.

As we set about facing and dissolving this wall we have created, we change. With our resolution of subconscious confusions increasing and our blind submersion in conscious states of mind decreasing, how could we not change? If at any point in time we perceive ourselves to be who we are because of the way we think, feel and live, it should make sense that changing the way we think, feel and live must necessarily change who we think we are.

In its purest state, this "we" we keep referring to in this book is awareness. Yet "we" do not generally reside for long periods of time in a state of being aware we are awareness, simply because awareness generally keeps itself busy becoming what it is aware of. This *being aware* through *becoming* is the only way awareness knows how to be aware. Even as the watcher, awareness is more aware of watching than pure *being*, which is awareness aware only of itself.

If we allow ourselves to become habitually externalized, we forfeit our intuitive sense that we are not what we are aware of. This habitually nurtured disconnection from source leaves us precariously exposed to fear and desire. In this state of externalized vulnerability, fear drives us—whoever we think we are—into a corner where desire desperately strives to defend and protect us, even as it also works to make and keep us happy.

When we are born into physical life, a certain amount of this externalization of awareness must necessarily occur just so the physical body we live in can be taken care of appropriately. In our desire for the body's well-being and our fear of its pain and death, however, we generally immerse ourselves in physical consciousness more than is necessary. There, deep in the hold of physicality, we succumb to the lure of the conscious state of mind and become the unwitting custodians of *wrong perception* and *unresolved memory*.

When an excess of negative karma has us trapped in externalized living, our seat of consciousness gets cemented in place. This is understandable since, under a strong influence of fear and desire, the degree of security we feel as we sit in this seat does not come from where that seat is as much as it comes from the length of time we are able to keep that seat where it is. In other words, when we are externalized, having a seat of consciousness that stays put means more to us than having a seat of consciousness that is well placed.

If we are living two-thirds within, however, we will feel no need for a security derived from any part of our external life and will therefore be more inclined to happily allow our seat of consciousness the freedom it requires to eventually move in and up.

When we live externally and are therefore intentionally locking our seat of consciousness in one place for the sake of security, and we fortify that place with protection, we form an ego. Although the kernel of this ego is awareness, which is plenty wise, that ego itself is a creature of ignorance literally born to go astray. It is this ego, holding itself cemented in a conscious state of mind for the sake of security, that *is* the "I" creating negative karma in need of resolution.

The eradication of the ego back into its kernel of awareness occurs in sync with the resolution of negative karma. One brings on the other. But neither will happen expeditiously without the pull of a refined desire freed of fear. Once this high-level desire sets its pull into play and fear no longer holds sway, great progress can be made quickly in the conquest of karma on a quest for Self.

62
Defying Discontent
Intensifying inner life

In this practice, entitled "Defying Discontent," we will move awareness from the consciousness of *pursuing* a desire to the consciousness of *having fulfilled* a desire. This is a powerful practice that quickens yoga as it expedites the transmutation of desire.

Defying Discontent

• In the top right corner of the next available page in your journal, write the date and time of this practice you are now beginning. In the top left corner, write "My Fulfillment."

• Lead yourself through *hatha yoga* postures you sense will balance your physical body so you can sit comfortably for at least a half hour.

• After you have completed your chosen *hatha yoga*, get comfortable in *sukhasana* and adjust the centeredness of your breathing with either *surya bedha pranayama* or *chandra bedha pranayama*. Then perform *anuloma viloma pranayama*.

• Remaining in *sukhasana*, perform *ujjayi* breath control and ease your way back into the bliss of *being*. As fantasies stemming from urges begin to arise, pick one of those fantasies and identify its source desire. If that desire does not seem worthy of pursuit, modify it until it does. Once you have a desire that feels acceptable, visualize its attainment. Follow this procedure with as many fantasies as you like.

Example: As you are sitting with the intention of *being* in bliss, you suddenly find yourself immersed in a mental argument that is a reconstruction of a remembered conversation during which you were humiliated. Now, in your vindictive re-do of that conversation, you are the one doing the humiliating. As you catch yourself in this revenge fantasy, you are somewhat embarrassed. Yet you realize all you ever really wanted was respect. Once it becomes apparent to you that respect was your real aim, you sense an acceptable version of a desire to *receive* respect should include a desire to *give* respect as well. Now inspired to both give and receive respect, you visualize yourself respecting and respected.

A note: "Fantasies stemming from desires" constitute a specific category of visualization. Unlike random impressions that surface during everyday subconscious processing, or pictures projected to us from other people, or even thought images reminding us of "things we have to do," these "fantasies stemming from desires" usually consist of visual story lines we mold with imagination. In reality, these reveries are thought beginnings of and mental rehearsals for the physically manifested fulfillment of the desires they represent.

When we intentionally visualize ourselves in the fulfillment of a healthy desire, we are accomplishing two things. 1. We are constructively harnessing and focusing our tendency and ability to imagine. This releases the considerable powers of our subconscious to begin a process of physically manifesting what we are visualizing. 2. We are projecting our awareness to an imagined future in which we see ourselves having attained our desire's fulfillment.

As you will most readily discover, the primary challenge of this exercise will be to *not* unwittingly submit to gut-level fantasies as they appear before you in the forms they take and the stories they make. Because fantasies of this nature—examples: sexual, violent or vengeful fantasies—are driven by desires rooted in the primal urges of the instinctive nature, they can be especially difficult to resist. Yet such resistance will be well worth cultivating for the purity it will provide and the wisdom it will assure.

• As you remain in *sukhasana* for a half hour or so, you might upgrade one, two, three, four or more fantasies into positive visualizations of contented fulfillment. When you are ready, reflect upon your experience of using imagination to foresee the attainment of worthy desire and write as you are inspired to write under your title: "My Fulfillment."

63
Internalization
Absorption in inner life

Repressions are difficult to understand for at least two reasons. 1. They are buried deep in the subconscious. 2. They are almost always comprised of those mind-made, memory amalgamations we have been referring to as "subconscious hybrids."

Acknowledging that repressions manifest in life, often unexpectedly, as powerful urges and negative emotions, we can all sense how our own repressions have taken root in the background of our nature, and from there have occasionally stepped forward to assist in forming what might be referred to as the "dark side" of the person we are generally perceived to be. If this dark side manifests rarely, it can seem *out* of character as compared with the "character" we are usually perceived to be. If it manifests enough to look like it embodies a substantial portion of our known personality, it can appear to be scarily *in* character.

If we want to do something about this "dark side," we must honestly recognize and fearlessly face the repressions forming its core. An important principle to keep in mind as we approach this task is that such honest self-facing can only occur if we are willing to concede that our shortcomings are not someone else's fault but are instead creations of our own making for which we must personally take responsibility.

Once we have deemed ourselves accountable for what we have done, we can begin to see ourselves as others see us. This more detached and objective perspective engenders an ability to observe—without reaction—the surfacing of repressions. Not reacting in this context means not re-acting—as in not adding another action to the series of actions that created the repressions we are witnessing in the first place.

None of this self-facing is easy. And it would be wrong to imply it is. But striving to remain detached by living two thirds within can help tremendously—and in a surprising way. Once we have caught this idea of holding awareness a little more *in* then *out*, we come to realize that facing a repression in the non-reaction of detachment actually *is* the understanding of that repression. This is an important discovery.

When we are looking at life from two thirds within, it becomes apparent that understanding is a simple seeing that cannot occur if our *desire* to understand is making what we are *trying* to understand too up-close and personal.

When we are living in an externalized state of consciousness, we usually understand in hindsight rather than with foresight. This is especially true when we are dealing with desires that keep us externalized.

After having created a negative karma, lived for some time under the weight of that karma and learned a few important lessons of life through the resolution of that karma, we can look back and think to ourselves, "That could have been done another way." Example: Fame. It looks good on other people. So we spend the better part of a lifetime going after it. Then, when that life comes near to its finish and we have achieved some degree of that precious fame, and the adoring public knows far more about us than we want them to—and a few more things that really aren't true—and we cannot even go to a store without wearing a disguise, we look back and think to ourselves, "That could have been done another way."

In yoga, we try to understand what we desire *before* we go after it—or *instead* of going after it. This is not difficult. A little bit of waiting in detachment before acting upon a desire is all it takes. Our restraint of impulsiveness in this detached waiting holds desire in abeyance long enough for some objective scrutiny to occur. In scrutiny, intuition finds the only opportunity it needs to reveal a flash of knowing that could circumvent the creation of an unnecessary and negative karma.

This same use of reflective pause can be applied in unraveling repression. First, we step back in detachment. Then, as repressions begin to surface, we observe them as if they belonged to someone else.

If we need inspiration to approach an unraveling of our subconscious confusion in this way, it can be helpful to remember that a repression stems from a fear or desire that has not been allowed enough expression in (mental or physical) experience to be understood.

Seeking understanding, these fears and desires keep trying to surface in our experience by rising up as strong urges and intense emotions. Urges and feelings of this nature can be puzzling because they so often erupt suddenly with little or no provocation. A person with repressed anger, for instance, might be an absolutely wonderful person to be around—except when he or she occasionally flies into frightening fits of sudden rage for no discernible reason.

If we are harboring a lot of repression as we begin to meditate, we will discover through our own experience just how distracting repression can be. This discovery can be frustrating if we don't realize or cannot acknowledge that these repressions must be understood through detached observation before deep meditation can occur. When we have caught the idea that understanding repression is a positive and necessary part of an introspective yoga, and that a detached observation of repression *is* the understanding of that repression, we can drop our frustration to willingly do what must be done in what can then become a gratifyingly successful practice of a deeper yoga.

From this understanding of repression and the power of detachment, we can see why, in the eight steps of Patanjali's *ashtanga* yoga, *pratyahara*—the *practice* and *state* of detachment—is placed at step five, right before *dharana* (concentration), *dhyana* (meditation) and *Samadhi* (mystic oneness).

The *practice* of *pratyahara*—as in *trying* to observe anything from a detached point of view—actually stirs up repression. This is as it should be. With regard to repression, the difference between *pratyahara* and meditation is that in *pratyahara* repression is expected and awaited while in meditation it is considered a distraction.

Understanding that *pratyahara* is a necessary prerequisite to deep meditation, many responsible yoga and meditation instructors will warn their students that only when a *practice* of *pratyahara* (a condition of seeking detachment) has become a *state* of *pratyahara* (a condition of having successfully achieved detachment indicating repressions have been or are being understood) can meditation culminating in Samadhi be a reasonable expectation.

64
Cooling
Withdrawing from hot and cold

In this practice, entitled "Cooling," we will be withdrawing awareness from the over-caring *hot* of emotion and the uncaring *cold* of thought into the *cool* of loving detachment through a practice of *pratyahara* that focuses upon using the mind to calm the body and release emotion into the gaze of watcher awareness.

Pratyahara can be performed as a meditation or as a preparation for meditation. Here we'll make it a meditation so we can isolate and appreciate how powerfully internalizing this fifth step of *ashtanga yoga* can be when it is performed by itself.

This specific practice of *pratyahara* was developed with an understanding that certain chronic physical tensions represent repressions—repressions that can be released up into the light of watcher awareness when their associated physical tensions are relaxed. As this rising up of repressions occurs in this practice of "Cooling," our primary ambition should be to maintain watcher awareness.

Now that we know what "Cooling" is, let's be cool.

Cooling

- In the top right corner of the next available page in your journal, write the date and time of this practice you are now beginning. In the top left corner, write "My Cool."

- Lead yourself through *hatha yoga* postures you sense will be most helpful in balancing your physical body so you can relax.

- When you have attained what you feel is a suitably relaxed state of mind and body, get comfortable in *sukhasana*, and put this book—opened to show the list below—in a place you can easily see from your seated meditation posture.

Left foot, right foot
Left ankle, right ankle
Left calf, right calf
Left knee, right knee
Left thigh, right thigh
Left hip, right hip
Abdomen, chest
Lower back, upper back
Left hand, right hand
Left wrist, right wrist
Left forearm, right forearm
Left elbow, right elbow
Left upper arm, right upper arm
Left shoulder, right shoulder
Neck
Skull

- When you are ready, read the above list several times—enough to catch its pattern and memorize its sequence. Then close your eyes and move awareness quickly and agilely through each of the 30 body points named. Repeat this 30-step movement of awareness several times.

- After about ten minutes of this preliminary awareness-training, lie back in *shavasana* to begin again the sequential movement of your awareness through the list. But now, move your awareness as follows:

    As you focus upon the first body point, assert the mental command: "Left foot, relax." As you make this command, *feel* that your left foot has become so heavy it is sinking into the ground. Once you have caught this feeling of heaviness sinking, move your awareness to the next body point to assert the mental command, "Right foot, relax," and feel that foot heavily sinking into the ground. Continuing on, follow this procedure with each of the rest of the 30 above-listed body points, in the order they are listed.

    One relax-and-release pass of awareness through all 30 body points, followed by a short space of time spent enjoying the poised calm this exercise instills, constitutes one cycle of "Cooling." Each cycle of "Cooling" should take about five minutes to complete so that one session of this practice would last about a half hour and include five or six "Cooling" cycles.

A note: The greatest benefit of this practice will come from the *quantity* of cycles repeated, rather than the *quality* of your performance. Therefore, please don't feel pressured to execute this practice perfectly. Just know that any effort you make in performing this *pratyahara* will serve your purpose well enough since most of the internalizing of awareness this practice induces occurs subconsciously and superconsciously rather than consciously. Thus, your conscious focus here should simply be to remain detached as you keep awareness moving along from one body point to the next. Even your relaxation command does not have to be made in any particular way. It just has to be dispatched.

This permission you give yourself to be easy-going during this practice will be especially supportive when your subconscious begins to invade your focus with repressions disguised as distractions. Even if the length of your concentration span is long and you are able to sustain two or three cycles of "Cooling" without being significantly distracted, there will come a time during a session of this practice lasting a half hour or more when just staying with the basic program of moving awareness in detachment will be about all you can manage.

Because your externalized concentration has probably been conditioned to function hand in hand with an involuntary and unnecessary tensing of the physical body, the physical relaxation of this "Cooling" practice will quite likely bring about not only a release of repressions but also a general dispersing of focus until a new more internalized concentration, devoid of physical tension, has been developed through purposeful effort.

It is during this purposeful development of relaxed and internalized concentration during this practice of "Cooling" that repressions can most easily move unobstructed into the limelight of your awareness. As this new more mystical version of concentration gets cultivated in conjunction with complete physical relaxation, your *practice* of *pratyahara* will gradually become a *state* of *pratyahara* in which watcher awareness is able to observe released repressions from a distance that allows those repressions to be viewed not as distractions but as curious objects inviting investigation.

- When you feel the time is right, sit up, open your journal. Under your title, "My Cool," record your reflections having worked with the mind to relax the body into internalized observation. As you reflect, please consider the following:

   In everyday life, we often seek relaxation by switching the focus of our awareness from something we feel is stressful to something we feel is not stressful. Although this purposeful moving of awareness is an excellent skill to develop, it could not really be referred to as a practice of genuine relaxation.

   If, for instance, we are trying to induce a release of job-related worries by reading the newspaper, watching TV or surfing the Internet, what sort of calm are we going to find when we discover—from the newspaper, TV or Internet—the stock market has plummeted, unemployment is on the rise or another war is imminent? Even if we are successful in shifting our awareness from the stress of work to the non-stress of a genuinely pleasurable experience—like a sunset walk on the beach, for instance—how long will it take for that job-stress of ours to find its way through the back door of our consciousness even into our enjoyment of the incontestable beauty of a setting sun?

   When we shift the focus of our awareness from one external point to another external point, we are moving awareness *sideways* in consciousness—not *inward*. Yet, when we focus our awareness upon simply relaxing the physical body—through a practice like "Cooling"— we allow our awareness to fall in toward the mind's core through a temporarily weakened veil of subconscious tension. Although the calm we experience from physical relaxation may not last long, it can—while it *does* last—radiate a wave of beneficial effects through all levels of our mind and body, even as it allows the surfacing of repressions.

A note: As we perceive the events of the life we live from within the watcher awareness of what could be referred to as a genuine *state* of *pratyahara*, we not only enjoy those events from a distance rather than suffer them in close proximity, we also alter our memory of them with the insight of intuition rather than the blindness of emotion.

65
Vibration
The oscillation of consciousness

From a mystical point of view, life force—as well as that which life force manifests and animates—consists of a vibrating energy that is conscious. Since vibration is oscillation and oscillation is movement, neither this vibrating and conscious life force nor the mind substance it manifests and animates is ever really still. Even a rock—because it consists of a conscious life force vibrating at a certain rate—is a mass of living energy in perpetual motion.

Yet the vibration of a rock is different from the vibration of a tree. Actually, the vibration of one rock is different from the vibration of another rock and the vibration of one tree is different from the vibration of another tree, for every physical, astral and spiritual entity has its own distinctive energy that oscillates at its own unique level of intensity. A more intense vibration oscillates more rapidly and is considered more refined than a less intense vibration. In this sense, the intensity of an energy vibration indicates the level of its elegance.

In bringing this down to earth, so to speak, we would say the physical and lower astral realms, which are made up of *odic* force, vibrate at a low level of intensity; the higher astral realm, which is made up of *actinodic* force, vibrates at a medium level of intensity; and the spiritual realm, which is made up of *actinic* force, vibrates at a high level of intensity.

Odic force is the primal energy of the physical realm. This *odic* force stimulates attraction and repulsion between people, between things and between people and things as it functions through a masculine (aggressive) and feminine (passive) movement of energy. To the extent that we are aware in the physical body, we are experiencing the grip of *odic* force, for the physical body is *odic*.

When we are living in physical consciousness and feeling the influence of *odic* force strongly, we form likes and dislikes, establish friends and enemies, and register fear and desire powerfully, because *odic* force moves between polar opposites. Within a positive flow of *odic* force, we are inclined to form congenial relationships with business associates, friends, lovers, family members and marriage partners. Conversely, when *odic* force is flowing negatively, we are more likely to develop interpersonal relationships that are disagreeable or adversarial.

Actinic force is the spiritual energy of the rarefied superconscious substratum of manifestation that completely transcends the domain of *odic* force and the duality *odic* force vivifies. Within the influence of this *actinic* force, which is more innately attuned to what we might refer to conceptually as "absolute reality," any awareness of polarity is dominated by a sense of the oneness that forms the basis of all manifest existence. Such oneness-awareness, when aroused, initiates an effortless unraveling of those complications in life that get created within the dualistic realm of *odic* force. When we are aware in a flow of *actinic* force, we are blissful, fearless and desireless, for in that state we are as we are: beings cognizant of divine essence.

Actinodic force is a blend of *odic* and *actinic* force that begins to occur when our subconscious has become significantly relieved of its confusion. When this *actinodic* force becomes strong, it acts as a conduit for conveying the superconsciousness of our inner life out into the externalized consciousness of our outer life.

Resolving karma makes us a more spiritual person because it engenders within us an ever-growing, ever-flowing *actinodic* force. *Actinodic* force is not something we need to create intentionally. It creates itself in the absence of unresolved karma.

As our perspective on life becomes more internalized and less selfish (selfishness being an externalized state of mind), we become cool to the warm magnetism of the *odic* domain. Although from within the realm of *odic* force, "cool" might be read as a cold lack of love, it is perceived from an *actinic* point of view to be a clear expression of the very essence of love: *a living sense of the impersonal oneness of all.*

Being aware in an *actinodic* force yields an ability to quickly distinguish between impulses based in the intuition of spirit and impulses based in the fear and desire of instinct. This sorting of impulses occurs through a sensing of vibrations that run hot, warm, cold or cool.

Impulses arising from our instinctive nature express themselves through feelings that are hot, warm or cold. Behind these feelings are emotions stimulating thoughts plotting personal benefit. Impulses arising from our spiritual nature are cool. These inclinations inspire a direct revelation of an impersonal wisdom.

When awareness is held in one vibration (as in concentration), it becomes that vibration and intensifies it through focus. Because an intensification of a vibration through focus is also an intensification of consciousness, and consciousness intensified is also consciousness rising and internalizing, *focus* is the emphasis of the last three steps of Pantajali's *ashtanga* yoga.

When awareness is flowing through a conscious state of mind and is being lured out by novelty, it does not tend to remain focused. Non-focus keeps awareness externalized. When awareness gets focused and through that focus becomes internalized as it flows from *odic* into *actinodic* into *actinic* force, it leaves behind the conscious mind as it soars deeply into superconsciousness.

66

Sensing

Reading vibration

In this practice, entitled "Sensing," we will work to intentionally enhance our psychic sensitivity by focusing awareness upon the feelings that register in our nervous system as we move the focus of our eyes across a collection of external objects. The development of this sensitivity will help us to live in the action of *doing* while pulling on the latent potential of *being*.

For this practice, you will need three pieces of colored paper propped up vertically. Any three colors will do if they are significantly different. Three shades of blue, for instance, would *not* be ideal. Red, yellow and blue would work well. You will also need three portrait pictures of people (photographs or art renderings)—also propped up. Two of these pictures should be of people you know well—like friends or family members. The third should be of a person you know only vaguely—like a movie actor or a political figure.

In our preparation for this practice of "Sensing," we will be adding to our collection of yoga tools an ancient breath control called *bhramari pranayama*.

To perform this breath control, we inhale slowly and deeply through the nose as in *ujjayi pranayama*. Then, without pausing on a suspended in-breath, we exhale slowly while producing a long and continuous humming sound.

Bhramari pranayama is a blissful breath control that assists in the toning and balancing of the pituitary, a pea-sized endocrine gland that hangs suspended in a small blood-filled cavity off the bottom of the hypothalamus at the base of the brain in the center of the skull.

The humming of *bhramari pranayama* helps tone and balance the pituitary gland by vibrating the blood in which that gland is positioned. It is this harmonizing of the pituitary during *bhramari pranayama* that reveals the bliss for which this discipline is famous, and provides us with the ideal preparation for our practice of "Sensing."

Sensing

• Position your three sheets of colored paper in front of you to the left, and your three portrait pictures in front of you to the right. These six images should be placed far enough away that you can see them all without having to turn your head from side to side.

• In the top right corner of the next available page in your journal, write the date and time of this practice you are now beginning. In the top left corner, write "What My Sense Says."

• Lead yourself through *hatha yoga* postures you feel will balance your physical body so you can sit comfortably for at least a half hour.

• After you have completed your chosen *hatha yoga*, get comfortable in *sukhasana* and adjust the centeredness of your breathing with either *surya bedha pranayama* or *chandra bedha pranayama*. Then perform *anuloma viloma pranayama*.

• Remaining in *sukhasana*, perform *bhramari pranayama* until you feel a blissful stillness. Then, without moving your head, let your eyes repeatedly pass from left to right and right to left across the six images placed before you. As you go, successively slow down the movement of your eyes so you can more and more closely observe the inner shifting of vibration that occurs in sync with the passing of your physical gaze from one image to the next.

A note: It is your awareness of the shifting of vibration occurring in coordination with the movement of your eyes that will deepen your perception of vibration. Once you have caught the feeling of one vibration in its contrast with another and the others, you will be able to more successfully seek its source.

During this exercise, it is best to let your perception remain at a feeling level. This is to say, let your perception grow without thought, knowing thought should and will come later.

• When you feel the time is right, open your journal. Under your title, "What My Sense Says," record your intuitive perception of each of the six images you have been observing. Now is the time to think back over your experience and put that thinking into words. As you reflect upon each of the colors you have chosen, ask yourself, "If this color was a person, what would he or she look like?" As you reflect upon each of the people that you have chosen, ask yourself, "If this person was a color, what would that color be?"

A note: Getting good at sensing vibration is invaluable in dealing tactfully with life's challenges—especially in facing new experience with foresight so that later hindsight is less necessary and the creation of karmas due to blundering is less frequent. Learning to sense vibration is also a pivotal accomplishment in the practice of yoga.

67
Nada
Sound: the first manifestation of life

Nada means "sound." In our yoking with essence, a deep understanding of sound is fundamentally important, for—according to the *Vedas*—life first manifested out of Self as sound. This same perception of life first manifesting as sound is reflected in the *Bible,* which says, "In the beginning was the Word, and the Word was with God, and the Word was God." Whether or not we are serious about stepping awareness back into its un-manifest source, this primal stirring of *nada*—this first word that "*was* God"—is worth investigation.

Nada yoga—another offspring of *raja yoga*—is an ancient metaphysical science and practice based not only in an understanding that life first manifested as sound but also that each manifest thing consists of a unique vibration that can be distinguished as a sound. Each tree, for instance, has its own distinctive sound, as does each rock—and as do we, each one of us.

In *nada yoga,* sound is classified into four categories: 1. *Vaikhari,* also referred to as "ahatha," is audible sound. 2. *Madhyama,* also called "anahatha," is "unstruck" sound. In this context, "unstruck" simply means "not audible." 3. *Pashyanta* is subconscious sound comprised of noise emanating from unresolved karma. 4. *Paranada* is the original "sound of sounds," or "soundless sound," as it is sometimes called.

Although this last-mentioned but first-occurring *paranada* is called the "soundless sound" because its high vibration is nearly indiscernible, it issues forth the *Aum* from which all other sounds come and within which all other sounds are contained. *Nada yogis* extol *Aum* as the *nada-nadi shakti*, which means "life force as sound." In his *raja yoga sutras*, Patanjali refers to *Aum* as "the sound that expresses the divine absolute."

For practical purposes, it is helpful to think of the practice of *nada yoga* as the art of listening. We can begin our exercise of this art by focusing upon certain carefully chosen audible or "struck" sounds that soothe and calm rather than excite and agitate.

Contemplative music can serve us well as a first point of focus in our beginning *nada yoga* practice, but this music should be instrumental and not vocal. Because the human voice tends to personalize and therefore externalize awareness, listening to music that includes vocal sound is not generally considered helpful in the practice of *nada yoga* where our goal is to internalize awareness into the impersonal realm of spirit.

As our mind settles down while we are listening to the unobtrusive sound of contemplative music, we find the "struck sounds" we are listening to have a sum-total vibration we can first feel, then hear as "unstruck sound." In this careful listening we also discover that unstruck sound reveals itself by itself simply because we allow it to through our enjoyment of it.

From this understanding, we can extract three useful hints for achieving success in the practice of *nada yoga* when music is our focus: 1. Choose nonvocal music that is delightful yet calming. 2. Let enjoyment lead. 3. Remain content.

Some *nada yoga* traditions emphasize the principle that the subtle source of the "unstruck sound"—translated as "anahata" in Sanskrit—is located within the *anahata chakra* of the soul body (corresponding to the center of the chest of the physical body). Not surprisingly, those who follow these traditions are encouraged to focus awareness on the *anahatha chakra* during their sound meditations.

In *nada yoga* traditions advocated by teachers who emphasize that each person emanates a one-and-only sound, students will often be encouraged to seek out, identify and focus upon the one sound that is the unique *nada* signature of their teacher. The intention of this practice is to approach a merging with the ultimate *paranada* through a merging with a specific *nada* that is highly refined.

In India, just as the physical or nonphysical *darshan,* or "sight of the divine," is highly revered, so is the inaudible *nada nadi*, or "sound of the divine," held in lofty esteem. Thus it is that yogis and yoginis born in or influenced by Indian culture often seek out a Sat Guru's *whispered* initiation and blessing into a higher practice of yoga.

68

Eeeing

Listening to an inner sound

In this practice, entitled "Eeeing," we will be listening with our inner ear to our inner *eee*. There are certain *nada yogis* in India whose one and only yoga practice is listening to this intense inner sound.

The *eee* is a tone that anyone can hear, even though—because it is heard with an inner ear—it can be overshadowed by the noise of external life. If you cannot easily hear this *eee*, cup your hands over your ears. What do you hear when external sounds are ignored? The roar of the *Aum* and the shrill of the *eee*: the two grand sounds of internality.

Although this *eee* is ever-present because it is a superconscious sound, it varies in its intensity. Each intensity of *eee*—indicated by a difference in pitch and volume—represents a specific level of superconsciousness. A more intense *eee*, higher-pitched and louder, issues forth from a deeper and higher level of consciousness than a less intense *eee*, lower-pitched and softer.

Through our own experimentation, we can easily discover how simply holding an awareness of the highest *eee* we can hear will naturally intensify that *eee* even further in and up. Certain *nada yogis* perceive focusing upon the *eee* as a direct path to Nirvikalpa Samadhi.

A sophistication of this form of *nada yoga* is to gaze upon a picture of a saint or a sage while listening to the inner eee. In this more refined form of inner listening, there unfolds a subtle consciousness in which different intensities of the inner *eee* are heard simultaneously.

As we hold awareness in this greater sensitivity, we learn that one of these *eee's* we are hearing is ours and another is of the saint or sage in the picture we are observing. We also discover, just by focusing on both these eee's at once, we can begin to hear and feel these *eee's* merging, as does our consciousness merge with that of the holy person pictured before us.

What can be disconcerting and therefore misleading in this practice is that an *eee* of a higher vibration than ours can sound and feel uncomfortable at first. This is only because we have not yet adjusted to its greater intensity. What can be consoling and therefore assuring in this practice is knowing that becoming adjusted to a higher *eee* than we are used to hearing requires only listening to that *eee* long enough for this adjustment to occur. Not surprisingly, this happens most efficiently if we have a confidence born of faith and a tenacity born of will.

The intention of this particular practice of "Eeeing" is to simply become accustomed to perceiving and holding on to the sound of our own highest *eee*.

Eeeing

• In the top right corner of the next available page in your journal, write the date and time of this practice you are now beginning. In the top left corner, write "My Eee."

• Lead yourself through those *hatha yoga* postures you sense will allow your physical nervous system to resonate with the bliss of *being*.

• After you have completed your chosen *hatha yoga*, get comfortable in *sukhasana* and adjust the centeredness of your breathing with either *surya bedha pranayama* or *chandra bedha pranayama*. Then perform *anuloma viloma pranayama*.

• Having balanced body and breath, lie back in *shavasana,* close your eyes and listen to outer sounds—the chirping of birds, the barking of dogs, the whoosh of passing cars—whatever hits the tympanum of your physical ear. Hear as many of these external sounds as you can.

• After about five minutes, shift your listening within. (In this effort, you might find earplugs helpful.) Once you have caught the sound of the inner *eee*, listen inside it for different renderings of its pitch. As you come to hear these different pitches, focus on the highest one (it should also be the loudest). Spend at least fifteen minutes doing this.

• When you feel the time is right, sit up and open your journal. Under your title, "My Eee," record your reflections upon listening to *eee*.

A note: Like the high *eee*, the low *Aum* can be heard internally. Generally speaking, however, touching into the psychic sound of this background *Aum* is usually a later development in the practice of *nada yoga*.

69
Mantra Japa
The repetition of empowered sound

Japa just means "repetition." According to this simple definition, any action that repeats is "doing *japa*." Likewise, any person who performs a repeating action is "doing *japa*." In yoga, *japa* is regarded as a form of focus in which a repeated action is used to keep awareness from wandering and to achieve an aim intimated in the unique energy of the action being repeated. In this yogic context, the "action" of *japa* is usually the repetition of a *mantra*.

Although *mantra* is a Sanskrit word that literally means "instrument of reflection," it might be more clearly defined as "an empowered sound." To be more specific, we could say a *mantra* is a sound used as a word to express a specific power, that specific power being that word's "meaning." When a person "does *japa*" upon a mantra, he is performing *mantra japa*. When a person does *mantra japa* upon a mantra that expresses a positive, spiritual energy, he is performing one of the mightiest mystical practices known to humankind.

Since life is consciousness, consciousness vibrates and vibration is a repeating action (of oscillation), it could be said that life itself *lives* in the *japa* of its consciousness. This means, when we perform *mantra japa*, we are doing something we—as living, conscious beings—already know how to do and can therefore do easily and well.

In India, the motherland of yoga, *mantra japa* is more popular than meditation—not because meditation is innately difficult, obscure or less effective, but because meditation can seem distant when we are not *already* in higher consciousness. Since most of us with yogic aspirations are not always *already* in higher consciousness, we generally find—especially when we are more acutely feeling the tugs and pulls of lower consciousness—*mantra japa* and its tangible method can seem more inviting, accessible and beneficial than meditation.

When we are doing *japa* on a mantra, we can "read" the unique energy of that mantra by feeling its vibration as we repeat it. This reading by feeling is an important ability to develop as we begin our repetition of a certain mantra because it can assist us in understanding where the mantra we are repeating is taking us.

Because some mantras express negative energies, or are meant to establish connections with certain inner-plane entities we might not be interested in getting to know, the mantras we choose to use should be at least fundamentally understood before we repeat them extensively. If we have not yet developed the faculty of "reading by feeling," and we are not being tutored by a qualified teacher, reading a book definition of a mantra we have chosen to repeat can help. In a best-case scenario, a written meaning of a mantra can tune us right into that mantra's more authentic energy meaning.

While a positively charged mantra is being repeated for its specific purpose, it can also work for us like a general panacea to defuse ego-based character flaws like pride, arrogance, jealousy, fear and confusion. It should be noted, however, a purification like this can really only occur when the *ignoring* of *ignorance* gets replaced with the *observing* of *observance*. Intimated here is an important truth: Before we can be relieved of impurities that exist only because we cannot or will not see them for what they are, we must be ready and able to look at them. Then, we must be able to face them without reacting emotionally so our intuition can dissolve them into knowledge gained. Although this is generally not something easily accomplished, it can occur less painfully in the vibrational cocoon of good *mantra japa* where there is always an abundance of power and protection, as well as an assured connection to the bliss of *being*.

Yet still, there is a stage of trial we must go through in our practice of a positive *mantra japa*—a period of time during which the intensity of our discipline arouses karmas we either succeed or fail in seeing and facing in detachment. What can catch us by surprise is that these karmas might not arise *during* the practice of *mantra japa*, but rather *around* it in the newly intensified life we come to live as a consequence of practicing this discipline of *mantra japa*.

While we are living through this kind of adjustment, we might be quite satisfied with our practice of *mantra japa*—perhaps ecstatically so. Yet our everyday experiences are feeling unreasonably sped up—often caught up in a whirlwind of difficulty filled with stressful circumstances coming at us too abruptly to be handled with ease.

Although this "whirlwind of difficulty" is but an accelerated resolution of negative karma, what it feels like is an onslaught of inconvenient experiences that cannot be foreseen and therefore cannot be avoided. Examples: Your credit card gets stolen. A truck backs into your (properly) parked car. Your dog has "an accident" on your white living room rug just as you are leaving for work.

If experiences like these are causing us suffering, and we are finding it difficult to correlate this suffering with our enjoyed *mantra japa*, it should be fortifying to understand that the very practice galvanizing this negative intensity will also dissolve it, *if that practice is maintained*. Herein lies *mantra japa's* greatest test—and that test's implied question: Can we, when faced with negative intensity, sustain our practice of *mantra japa* long enough for intuition to resolve the negative karmas aroused?

In and through all of this, we must appreciate that failures in life are steps forward in life, for it is in the survival of failure that *will* is motivated, *ego* is humbled and *success* is eventually deserved and therefore achieved. The older we become, the more we realize this principle in experience, and the more we know experience does not lie.

At this point, it must be reiterated that mystical disciplines—like those of yoga—simply hasten natural processes. Yet even as we assert that life itself will eventually force us through the barriers we have created in ignorance, we must also concede that life must necessarily drive us into some variety of intentional mystical effort (like yoga) to get us past a certain point in penetrating those barriers. We feel this later drive as a genuine need for purity, clarity, love and illumination.

A word of warning: If we have chosen to perform a positive *mantra japa* in response to a wholesome feeling of spiritual need, it is good to understand the mantra we have chosen to use might have a greater intensity of energy than we are prepared to handle effectively *at the time we have decided to perform japa on that particular mantra*.

In yoga, as in life, more energy than we can handle effectively at any given point in time is almost never a good thing. Thus, it is generally advisable to at least initiate the performance of *japa* upon powerful mantras with the blessings and advice of a qualified teacher.

The over-stimulation of negative karma through an over-intensification of life due to *japa* performed on a mantra two powerful (for us right now) can spur mental and emotional disturbances that are at least uncomfortable. Ironically, these disturbances can manifest as those very psychological imbalances—like anxiety, panic and depression—that we should rightly expect the balancing of yoga would correct.

If our *mantra japa* is churning up negative psychological conditions and we are not benefiting from the consoling assistance of a qualified teacher, we can work ourselves into thinking we have summoned up some sort of demon and should stop our *mantra japa* altogether.

Stopping a positive *mantra japa* is almost never necessary. Generally, when we feel the practice of a certain *mantra japa* starting to reach an intensity we cannot adjust to within a relatively short period of time, all we ever really need to do is back off to a more peaceful mantra, a mantra designed to calm rather than agitate negative karma into resolution. One such mantra is *Aum*. Although *Aum* is plenty powerful, its power is the power of peace.

During periods of psychic intensity, we can also gain some degree of inner relief from contemplating two well-accepted mystical principles: 1. As challenging as any life circumstance might seem to be, we can never really be confronted with more difficulty than we can handle. 2. If our intentions are positive, we will always be fortified with the beneficial assistance of unseen, inner-plane beings. And if we request this assistance, directly through prayer or indirectly through a sincerity of spirit, that assistance will be greatly accentuated.

70

Empowering
Doing mantra japa

In this practice, entitled "Empowering," we will be performing *japa* on seven *bija mantras*. Although these seven "seed sounds" are powerful, they will never be so powerful they cannot be put into practice comfortably if the focus of our practice is to simply *be* the energies these mantras invoke. The seven high energies these seven mantras express are the seven powers of the seven chakras that form the core of our spiritual body. Since no explanation can surpass experience, let us now move on into our own experience of "Empowering."

Empowering

- In the top right corner of the next available page in your journal, write the date and time of this practice you are now beginning. In the top left corner, write "My Japa."

- Lead yourself through *hatha yoga* postures you feel will allow your physical nervous system to resonate with the bliss of *being*.

- After you have completed your chosen *hatha yoga*, get comfortable in *sukhasana* and adjust the centeredness of your breathing with either *surya bedha pranayama* or *chandra bedha pranayama*. Then perform *anuloma viloma pranayama*.

- Having balanced body and breath, perform *bhramari pranayama* (the "humming breath") until you feel a blissful stillness.

- Sit up in *shavasana* and place this book so you can see the mantras listed below. Then, occasionally referring to this list, spend about one minute chanting each of the listed mantras aloud. As you repeat, feel the location and visualize the color of the chakra each mantra represents.

Lam - first chakra, base of the spine, red
Vam - second chakra, sacral region, orange
Ram - third chakra, solar plexus, yellow
Yam - forth chakra, heart region, green
Ham - fifth chakra, throat, blue
Sham - sixth chakra, third eye, purple
Aum - seventh chakra, crown, white

• Once you have performed this (approximately) seven-minute exercise aloud, do it again with whispered repetitions. Then do it a third time with mental repetitions.

A note: It is during the mental portion of this exercise that we can most easily feel ourselves slipping into a full enjoyment of the blissful energy the mantra we are repeating reveals. This most agreeable merging is the "becoming" leading into the *being* that we are seeking in this practice.

Of the many approaches to *being* we have experimented with on the path of this book, this access through mantra repetition is one of the most powerful, for it offers a method that forms a base and frame for holding awareness still through the winds of distraction.

• When you have finished the three-phase internalizing of your mantra repetition, spend another fifteen minutes or so repeating the mantras successively. One round of this exercise would consist of going through all seven mantras in sequence, pronouncing each mantra once as you sense its location, feel its vibration and visualize its color. As with the previous exercise, perform this successive mantra repetition in three phases: aloud, in a whisper and mentally.

A note: The ease with which you move from one mantra to the next in this successive-repetition exercise will be determined by how deftly you can sense, feel and visualize. Because this demands concentration, especially in the beginning, it should be reassuring to understand that while nothing is gained by performing this exercise hurriedly, any performance of it—done well or not—will be a significant achievement.

• When you feel the time is right, sit up and reflect upon your experience of working with these seven *bija mantras*. Then open your journal and clarify these reflections by recording them under your title, "My Japa." As you write, please keep in mind the following six well-accepted mystical principles associated with mantra repetition:

1. Although all mantras are powerful, the degree of each mantra's power is relevant to the unique energy it expresses.

2. Although each mantra's power is as unique as the energy it expresses, each mantra's energy is but a manifestation of the one primal energy that always feels the same when it is experienced in *being*.

3. The highest achievement in any *mantra japa* is to arrive at and remain within the one primal energy that forms the core of each mantra's unique energy. Becoming centered in this core power during *mantra japa* allows the unique purpose of the repeated mantra to realize its fullest potential, unobstructed and as intended.

4. If awareness is allowed to wander during *mantra japa*, that to which it wanders becomes the recipient of the japa's power. If, for instance, awareness wanders into anger during the repetition of a positive mantra, that anger will become accentuated. This means "problems" sometimes said to arise from the repetition of mantras conceived to yield benevolent effects often come as much from a lack of concentration as from the intensity of the mantras themselves.

5. When subconscious disturbances arise to distract us during *mantra japa*, it should be our determination to remain centered in the energy of the mantra we are repeating. In this center is *being,* in *being* is detachment, and in detachment is the stability of our greatest security.

6. The sustained repetition of positive mantras can depolarize and transmute our creative powers, resolve our subconscious turmoil and withdraw the vital forces of our body into the spine—there to be drawn up into the heady energies of superconsciousness.

71
Affirmation
A repeated declaration of an aspiration

Having investigated *japa* with *mantras*, we will now explore *japa* with *affirmations*. An affirmation is a declaration of a physical, mental or spiritual goal—worded as an attainment of that goal—repeated, preferably aloud, with the intent of commanding the subconscious to make that goal a reality.

There is a primary difference between *mantra japa* and *affirmation*. *Mantra japa* works from the inside out. *Affirmation* works from the outside in. In *mantra japa* we are using the repetition of certain sounds to achieve chosen goals through the invocation of inner powers. With *affirmation* we are using the repetition of carefully worded statements to achieve goals, external or internal, through the control of thought. "I have all I need" or "this body is strong and healthy" are affirmations designed to achieve external goals. "I am" is an affirmation aimed at the achievement of an internal goal.

A nicely conceived affirmation should consist of a short, simple and positive statement worded in the present tense to inspire a visualization catalyzing a feeling of being in the attainment of the condition the affirmation describes. The mystical principle here? To affirm, visualize and feel the attainment of a desire guarantees that attainment, and quickens its coming.

Because an affirmation functions like a command to the subconscious—a mind born to obey in a literal way—that affirmation should be constructed as if each word of it will be perceived separately and at face value *now*. In an affirmation like "I will not eat meat," for instance, the subconscious registers the word "meat" and does its best to bring us meat. It also registers the word "will" as an instruction telling us that nothing need be done *now* since fulfillment *will* occur in the future. If becoming a vegetarian is the aspiration behind the affirmation: "I will not eat meat," a better wording would read in a positive present tense and not even mention meat. Example: "I love eating delicious and healthy fruits and vegetables."

Affirmations can also be used to confront and eventually overpower old and negative subconscious programming. A new and positive subconscious program introduced by a well-intended and carefully-worded affirmation, backed by a freshly transmuted desire, will always be of a higher and more powerful vibration than an older, negative programming established haphazardly through poor thinking habits. Because it is higher and has more power, the newer programming will always win out if the repetition of its affirmation is sustained for a significant period of time.

When a negative subconscious impression is forced to face a positive subconscious impression during the repetition of a positive affirmation, the two impressions will war. If we affirm, for instance, "I can do what I decide to do," we are likely to find the subconscious coughing up memories of past experiences in which we failed to do what we decided to do and thus suffered feelings of personal inadequacy. Perhaps those memories have coalesced within our subconscious to form the conviction: "I *can't* do what I decide to do." If we expect this kind of subconscious warring during our repetition of affirmation, we will not be surprised or deterred when it occurs, even though such warring might require us to live through relatively difficult periods of adjustment.

If we can manage to persevere in the repetition of an ambitious affirmation, we will discover that the more we can endure difficulty in the dignity of non-reaction, the less such difficulty will bother us—and the less such difficulty bothers us, the sooner it won't bother us at all. Acquiring skill in dealing with difficulty through perseverance in non-reaction contributes to the cultivation of indomitable will, genuine detachment and noble character.

Usually, by the time we have learned about affirmations and figured out how to create and use positive affirmations effectively, we will have come to understand enough about desire and its fulfillment to realize, for the attainment of any kind of sustained contentment in life, desire must be whittled down to need and need must be minimized. This basic insight into the nature of desire and need usually occurs to us about the same time we learn from experience that the fulfillment of a desire exceeding our need will generally create at least a negative karma of self-indulgence. As these several intuitive flashes hook themselves together into an epiphany, they form a net sum total revelation about affirmation that might get expressed as a guideline for affirmation-making something like this: "Create and practice affirmations with forethought in accordance with genuine need. Yet, let the need of one be the need of all. And let that all be served."

From within an unselfish framework of thought like this, we can enthusiastically create and wholeheartedly embrace the practice of an affirmation like "I have ten million dollars now," as we visualize having, using and sharing money wisely in the joy of selfless service.

As soon as we start consciously creating and performing positive affirmations framed in the present tense, it becomes embarrassingly apparent how we have unconsciously created and used negative affirmations in the past. Example: Complaining. When we repeatedly complain, we are unknowingly affirming and thereby incessantly commanding the subconscious to manifest what we are complaining about. If we say again and again, for instance, "Jane drives me crazy," will it not be only a matter of time before Jane does just that? Or if we repeat, "This job is awful," how could that job ever be wonderful?

Repeated profanity is another example of a supremely negative affirmation. Every time we say, "god damn it," for instance, we are calling upon God to damn what we are referring to in our moment of emotional upset. And when we repeat this negative affirmation, we do indeed damn, for in the truest sense, cussing is cursing. This warrants a word to the wise: Repeated cursing is a negative affirmation that will transform us into a giver of curses and the recipient of that karma.

As we gain a healthy respect for the power of affirmation, we come to realize we would be well advised to acknowledge and eliminate our unconscious repetition of negative affirmations before we go too far into a conscious creation and repetition of positive affirmations. If we apply this wisdom in experience, the building of force we stimulate through our positive affirming won't be frustratingly undone by the dissipation of force we allow through our negative affirming.

For maximum effect, affirmations should be visualized as they are repeated. This visualizing will key in feeling. Feelings are stronger than pictures and pictures are stronger than words. Feelings conjure up a mental enactment of that which is being affirmed and visualized. That mental enactment will eventually become physical, if the saying, seeing (visualization) and feeling of the affirmation are sustained. Of these three—saying, seeing and feeling—feeling is primary. Rhythm in the repetition of an affirmation enhances feeling.

Consistency in the practice of affirmation (as in any activity) is a broad-range form of rhythm. When we practice positive affirmation at the same time and place every day, we can be sure—because of this day-to-day rhythm—a reasonable manifestation of our affirmation's intended result will soon occur.

72
Shaping Fate
Creating and performing an affirmation

In this practice, entitled "Shaping Fate," we will be creating and performing affirmations aimed at achieving worthy and unselfish ends.

In preparing to create these affirmations, we will modify the desires we intend to affirm into minimal needs, then establish those needs as motives and goals.

In creating these affirmations, we will compose terse, potent and positive statements to be spoken in the present tense as if the goals they express have already been achieved.

In practicing these affirmations, we will strive to see and feel what we are saying as if we are experiencing what we are saying, seeing and feeling right now.

Shaping Fate

- In the top right corner of the next available page in your journal, write the date and time of this practice you are now beginning. In the top left corner, write "My Affirmations."

- Lead yourself through *hatha yoga* postures you feel will allow the nervous system of your physical body to resonate with the bliss of *being*.

- After you have completed your chosen *hatha yoga*, get comfortable in *sukhasana* and adjust the centeredness of your breathing with either *surya bedha pranayama* or *chandra bedha pranayama*. Then perform *anuloma viloma pranayama*.

• Having balanced body and breath, perform *bhramari pranayama* (the "humming" breath) until you feel a blissful stillness.

• Sit in *sukhasana* with your journal in your lap, pen in hand. In preparation for composing three need-based affirmations, write down—under your title, "My Affirmations"—three desires you feel are or could be made worthy and selfless.

• Then read those written desires aloud as motives. (Remember, a motive will always be worded like the desire it expresses.)

If these desires sound worthy and selfless when they are voiced as motives, your intuition will leave you with a feeling of contentment. If they do not sound worthy, you'll feel a discontent.

If you sense one or more of those desires needs to be made worthy if it is not, or worthier if it is, stay with your discontent until it motivates within you the creation of what you feel is an appropriately worthy desire. Once you have crystallized this desire, whittle it down to an unselfish need. Then, in your journal, cross out your old desire and write in your new need.

When all three of your desires sound good voiced as motives addressing worthy goals trimmed down to selfless needs, compose your affirmations. As you write these affirmations, economize your words. Keep in mind: The fewer words you use, the greater will be their effect. Make sure to write your affirmations in the present tense, as if they are manifesting now.

Example: If you word an unselfish need, "I want to control my anger," and this wording feels good as a statement of motive, which in turn helps you clarify your goal as "anger control," you might be led to compose an affirmation like "I am cool, calm and collected" or "I am calm"—or just "I am."

• Once you have written your affirmations, give them a test run, one by one. As you repeat your first affirmation for about five minutes, work to see and feel what it would be like to dwell in the fulfillment of that affirmation. Then, in the five minutes following your *action* of affirming, let your *reaction* to that action teach you something.

When your reaction resolves itself into understanding, try to word that understanding in your journal. Follow this procedure with each of your three affirmations.

A note: Because we might ordinarily resist dealing with our reactions when an adjustment of seemingly reliable beliefs and attitudes might be required, the primary challenge of this practice could well be in *facing reactions fearlessly* and *learning from reactions humbly*.

• After journaling your reactions, write down a new title: "Reflections On Affirming." Under this title, record your reflections on conceiving and composing, then saying, seeing and feeling your three affirmations. Please include in your reflections upon how you feel the repetition of affirmations compares with the repetition of mantras.

73
Determination
Will: a tool and a fuel

In life as in yoga, *will* is both a *tool* and a *fuel*. As a *tool*, it is a narrowing of focus we use to initiate and maintain an action. As a *fuel*, it is a power we deliberately exert toward the accomplishment of an action. The power of *will* is determined by the intensity of the *desire* it follows, for *will* only exists to activate and fulfill *desire*. Although the strength of *will* as a *fuel* is automatically established by the desire it follows, the strength of will as a *tool* can be intentionally cultivated. In life as in yoga, the purposeful cultivation of *will* as a *tool* is most beneficial.

If we approach yoga having developed will as an efficient tool, we can expect to move within quickly and easily, *if we want to*. This *wanting* is crucial, for all the will in the world can't pass up desire, the leader of will. Yet, because desire is a beast that is never satisfied until it consumes itself, and one desire fulfilled with no need of will morphs into another desire unfulfilled in need of will, the story of evolving desire is also the story of evolving will.

If our first thrust into the practice of yoga has been disciplined by a will cultivated enough to catalyze within us an intuitive sense that our perpetually unsatisfied desire is not our enemy but is instead our friend and guide, we find ourselves willing ourselves to humbly accept that we must allow *who we think we are* to slowly become *who we really are* through a sequential fulfillment of desires. Understanding and acknowledging that we cannot sidestep this path of evolving desire, we strive only to expedite our progress on that path by continually honing our use of will as a tool.

A will well developed assures our attainment of the ultimate end of yoga, *even if that end is not our current desire*, for as surely as one desire grows into another by the action of our will, so shall our last desire finally find peace in desirelessness when our will be done.

Once desire transmutes into an intense yearning for spiritual unfoldment, we begin to identify ourselves as *actinic* beings. Moving in sync with this transformation of identity, our will becomes *actinic*.

An *actinic* will is quite different from an *odic* will. While an *odic* will, working in compliance with the whims of our lower instinctive nature, occasionally fights even the manifestation of intuition, an *actinic* will always works to support and reveal intuition.

In meditation, an *actinic* will moves toward the Self like a heat seeking missile moves toward infrared radiation. Undistractedly attuned through intuition to its ultimate power source, this self-propelled, *actinic* will neither falters nor fails as it self-adjusts its way toward the fulfillment of its divinely ordained destiny.

It is also with this intuitively influenced, *actinic* will that we make our one-hour-a-day *practice* of yoga a 24-a-day *attainment* of yoga. In this more expansive use of an *actinic* will, every action we perform—from brushing our teeth to paying our bills—becomes an opportunity to live in the *now* by focusing our will upon the task at hand. This constant development of will as a tool builds a great worldly confidence, as well as a profound spiritual faith.

A precaution: Just as any skill must be maintained and improved through use, so must an *actinic* will be cultivated through application. If not cultivated, this *actinic* will can slowly become *odic*.

It is through the continual use of an *odic* will that we become overly involved with and attached to the external world and through that enmeshed attachment begin to perceive that external world as the only reality.

74
Juxtaposing
Comparing willing and willful

In this practice, entitled "Juxtaposing," we will contemplate our own life experience to determine the difference between an *actinic* will of willingness and an *odic* will of willfulness.

When we scrutinize our lives for the play of an *actinic* will, we are looking for a drive that works in agreement with intuition and moves easily with the flow of life. We'll know we've located this easy motivation when we are feeling like "nothing is happening," even while so much is getting done. Once we have consciously identified when we are experiencing this effortless efficiency, we will know by contrast when we are not.

When we are not experiencing an *actinic* flow of effortlessness, our will is *willful*. When our will is willful, we are working from within an *I'm-going-to-have-my-way-no-matter-what* consciousness that functions in obedience to an instinctive sense of *self* as opposed to a superconscious sense of *Self*.

Juxtaposing

- In the top right corner of the next available page in your journal, write the date and time of this practice you are now beginning. In the top left corner, write "My Two Wills."

- Lead yourself through *hatha yoga* postures you feel will allow the nervous system of your physical body to resonate with the bliss of *being*.

- After you have completed your chosen *hatha yoga*, get comfortable in *sukhasana* and adjust the centeredness of your breathing with either *surya bedha pranayama* or *chandra bedha pranayama*. Then perform *anuloma viloma pranayama*.

- Having balanced body and breath, perform *bhramari pranayama* (the "humming" breath) until you feel a blissful stillness.

- When you are ready, lie back in *shavasana,* relax into detachment and think back through the last three days of your life. First, let your intuition guide you to blissful memories of experiences when you felt "nothing was happening." Then, by contrast, allow yourself to become aware of experiences when that feeling did *not* exist. As you become aware of these two kinds of memories, one by one, recall the specific impetus you were responding to as you initiated action by will.

A Note: How you direct yourself to act during any given experience will be in accordance with whom you perceive yourself to be at that moment. If you are at work, thinking of yourself not as awareness but as a sales representative who will only get promoted if he "performs," and you are working under pressure to finish a certain project, you could easily find yourself generating and suffering aggressive thought and heavy emotion. Such ego-oriented externalization makes intuition all but impossible to perceive as the thrust of your misdirected determination drives you to willfully manhandle the tasks at hand.

    If, however, you are at work simply doing your job as you would do any job that needed doing, and you are so involved in what you are doing you have no consciousness of passing time, your identity *is a nonentity.* In your egoless oneness with your work, your will is flowing easily with necessity in work that seems to perform itself. And as you function in this effortless efficiency, you're a nobody—who might just get promoted for "performing."

- When you feel the time is right, sit up and open your journal. Under your title, "My Two Wills," draw a vertical line down the center of the page to create two columns. Entitle the first column "Willingness" and the second column "Willfulness." Then, as you reflect upon your last three days, record three memories of willingness experiences under "Willingness" and three memories of willfulness experiences under "Willfulness." Once this is done, record your reflections upon your experience of willingness and willfulness.

A Note: As we have discovered often on the path of yoga outlined in this book, pure awareness functioning through simple observation is a powerful tool for understanding. As this practice of "Juxtaposing" will likely show, nothing can motivate us toward *willingness* more than simply seeing our own *willfulness* for what it is.

75
Sex
The great connector, baby maker

The sexual urge is the driving force of the instinctive nature and the primal impetus for the perpetuation of life on earth. We all have a good sense of the existence of this force. Because it is hard-wired into the brain and nervous system of our physical bodies, each and every one of us has felt it strongly.

When we perceive this sexual urge as a simple surge of force that must be expressed rather than suppressed, yet we sense that such expression should be beneficial rather than harmful, we are well prepared to live life with a wise and healthy control our instinctive nature. As an adult, seeing the sex force in this way, having long felt its sway, is not so much to ask. When we are young, however, and experiencing this primal stirring of libido as a new and exciting fascination, we are not likely to perceive it as anything but an irresistible impulse to do precisely what it is compelling us to do.

Since young adults are surrounded by grown-ups who were once teenagers, opportunities for youth to express their sexual feelings impulsively are generally restrained. Such sexual restraint usually comes at home and in school through disciplines of body and mind imposed by elders. These disciplines typically keep the body active with physical exercise and the mind busy with memorization and thought application. As comprehensive and praiseworthy as these disciplines are, however, they do not usually include a substantial amount of deep sex education.

At some point during our tenuous teenage years, some senior member of our family—usually one of our parents—might give us the "sex talk," that generally awkward discourse on what can happen when boys and girls rub their bodies together.

Depending on the cognition of the adult doing the talking, what gets said can be helpful or not. Yet even when helpful, it is not likely to clarify an understanding of the more internal consequences of sexual intercourse. This would be no fault of the talker whose words might well be admirably insightful. It's more a matter of the fact that an in-depth understanding of the sex act is an obscure bit of occult knowledge not well known.

When a man releases sperm into the vagina of a woman during coitus, a connecting tube between that man and woman gets formed on the astral plane. This tube, created of very real astral matter that can be seen with psychic sight, forms the beginning of a bond that will become stronger with each act of sexual intercourse that man and woman perform together. Through this tube there flows a continual exchange of mental, emotional and spiritual energy. Not surprisingly, a man and woman in this kind of unifying sexual relationship will often think, feel and express the same thoughts and emotions at the same time. Over time, two such people can actually begin to look alike.

Please notice there has been no mention of love in this description of the astral tube that gets created during sexual union. Most undeniably, this tube is a consequence of sexual intercourse only.

Since the highest purpose of sex is to express love and create a child, the highest function of an astral tube created by the sex act is to provide a conduit through which an exchange of love can develop a parental relationship that will fortify a long-term maturation of children. For this reason, that tube is sturdily built—and immediately so. An astral tube created by only one act of intercourse will last twelve years.

If two virgins in love begin a sexual relationship, and neither has sex with another person or other people, their energy exchange through their connecting astral tube will be contained. Being contained, it will nurture and develop them both.

If, however, a man or a woman has loveless sex indiscriminately, his or her primal life force will flow through as many tubes as there were sexual partners. Since there was never any love in this flow, the energy being exchanged is more likely to manifest as thoughts and feelings that confuse, fragment and dissipate rather than nurture, coalesce and develop. For a person who has created many such connections, life can be motivated by thoughts and feelings that seem to be his or hers but are quite literally not. An extreme development of this kind of confused over-sharing can engender the creation of a psychological instability — not to mention an abundance of negative karma.

In yoga, as in most any mystical practice, the sexual fluid is generally regarded as a physical form of sacred life force meant to be contained — either in one body or in two bodies joined as one in love. If this fluid is *not* contained, the mind and body become sluggish due to a wasting away of that fluid's life-giving potency. If this fluid *is* contained, the reverse occurs. Both mind and body grow as powerful receptacles of a flourishing life force.

This accumulating life force will naturally flow in and up if it is not allowed to flow out and down. Such inwardly ascending energy empowers the practice of yoga as it glows the mind and body and facilitates the resolution of negative karma.

76

Unrepressing

Eliminating buried confusion

In this practice, entitled "Unrepressing," we will revisit the *Releasing in Fire* practice described in Chapter 54 to focus upon exposing and relinquishing the emotion of sexual repression. As in our previous *Releasing in Fire* practice, our intention here will not be to erase or analyze our past, but rather to de-emotionalize it so that intuition might see it more clearly and, in that clearer seeing, let it be reconciled as experiential knowledge gained. Be prepared! This practice will seem like a confessional as you write down and burn up embarrassing sexual memories.

Unrepressing

- In the top right corner of the next available page in your journal, write the date and time of this practice you are now beginning. In the top left corner, write "An Aftermath."

- Lead yourself through *hatha yoga* postures you feel will allow the nervous system of your physical body to resonate with the bliss of *being*.

- After you have completed your chosen *hatha yoga*, get comfortable in *sukhasana* and adjust the centeredness of your breathing with either *surya bedha pranayama* or *chandra bedha pranayama*. Then perform *anuloma viloma pranayama*.

- Having balanced body and breath, perform *bhramari pranayama* (the "humming" breath) until you feel a blissful stillness.

- When you are ready, either think back through your life from your present to as far into your past as you can remember, or think forward from your earliest memory to your present, as you look for embarrassing or "bad" sexual memories. These memories can include things you did or things done to you, comments you made or comments made to you, conversations you had—even mental fantasies you privately nurtured.
  As these memories surface, write them down on a separate sheet of paper. Try to fully and freely express all you recall. Don't hold back. Be explicit. When you are finished, burn that sheet of paper.

A note: An inclination toward secrecy in handling an embarrassing past can catalyze the suppression of a memory into repression—an impression tucked away so many times no one, not even you, can easily find it. Since such closeted memories also retain unfulfilled desires and unfaced fears, they are like little power packs of escalating force all too ready to explode. Pulling these memories out of their closet, writing them down on paper and burning that paper up relieves them of their pent-up emotion so their essential power can be understood and thereby released into constructive usage.

- When you feel the time is right, sit up, open your journal and ask yourself how and what you feel in the aftermath of this practice of "Unrepressing." Then, under your title, "An Aftermath," describe that feeling. Please also describe why and how an exercise like this might benefit the practice of yoga and meditation.

A note: Nothing frees awareness to move—both happily in life and deeply in yoga—like the release of repression. During any preparation for deep meditation, some manner of dealing with repression positively and courageously is not an option; it is a must—for repression and deep meditation cannot coexist.

77
Concentration
Focusing

In the yoking of yoga, meditation is the goal of concentration. Because concentration consists of nothing more or less than repeatedly hauling awareness back from distraction to a given point of focus, it is forever a work in progress that never gets what it is after until it morphs into meditation where *doing* becomes *being* and distraction holds no sway.

What is referred to as a "bad meditation" is usually just concentration. What is referred to as a "good meditation" is usually just meditation—especially since meditation cannot be, in its contented balance of opposites, either "good" or "bad." To this we might add that any attempt to concentrate will always be "good" in the sense of being positive, because concentration pursued will always yield meditation.

So, the up-front concentration of any meditation is where all the work of that meditation is. And the work to be done is in the grind of persistently dealing with distraction. In maintaining perseverance through distraction, faith helps, of course—faith in the truth that, as surely as a river will flow toward a sea, so will concentration move toward meditation to eventually yield a full merger of doer, doing and done in a bliss so all-consuming it loses its separation from Self.

Because concentration is an action of *doing* and meditation is a state of *being*, making a statement like, "Today, we are going to meditate," would not be entirely accurate. A more precise wording of a statement like that might read: "Today, we are going to try to remain focused long enough to find a little peace, which will become a lot of peace if we can stay with it."

Patanjali might simply have said, "Today, *samyama*." In Sanskrit, *samyama* literally means, "holding together, tying up or binding." In Patanjali's use of this term, what is being bound into a one unbroken sequence named *samyama* is *dharana* (concentration), *dhyana* (meditation) and *Samadhi* (absorption).

If we take up the practice of *samyama* in yoga and we are living a disciplined life—either by choice or necessity—the rigor of the concentration portion of that *samyama* will not be so difficult to survive on into meditation. Having developed a habit of focus by living in discipline, we will be more inclined to approach the chore of concentration routinely and without being surprised or annoyed by its challenge.

When we are *not* living a disciplined life, we often assume our concentration will or should be easy, and balk when it's not. This frame of mind leaves us less inclined to approach concentration with the stamina required to see it on through into meditation, and sustain meditation on through into Samadhi.

Besides a general lack of discipline, there are a number of other conditions that can complicate our efforts to concentrate. These include promiscuous sex, chronic physical pain, poor health and diet, unresolved subconscious issues (especially repressions), an inflated sense of self, too much thought or emotion, not enough devotion, insufficient or erroneous training, a lack of faith, too many external concerns and more.

As should be expected, meditation itself can eliminate *all* of these conditions. The catch here, of course, is that, to get into meditation, we must necessarily pass through the concentration that dredges these conditions up. So, wise is the yogi who strives to alter or eliminate as many of these "obstacles" to meditation as he can *before* he does a lot of *samyama*.

Here, we may take heart in the fact that *all* of these obstacles do not have to be completely eliminated before we even try to concentrate. We only need to nullify enough of them to get through concentration into meditation just a little bit. As we will then readily see, even a small amount of genuine meditation works wonders in eliminating obstacles even as it flowers a fresh faith in the potential of yoga.

In the interest of making all of this a little more practical, we now offer here below seven specific hints for surviving concentration into meditation:

1. As Patanjali advises in his *ashtanga yoga sutras*, make the focal point of your *samyama* something you find interesting.

2. Preface each *samyama* session with some yogic sequencing. Using the eight steps of Pantanjali's *ashtanga yoga* as a loose model, you might start your preliminary sequencing with some worship and prayer, then move into a series of your favorite *hatha yoga*, *pranayama* and *mantra japa* practices before settling down into *samyama*.

3. Begin your concentration with your eyes open in *trataka*, even if the object of your *samyama* is internal. Remember, the eyes are a physical version of awareness and can therefore be used to help steady an internal focus. A common practice is to keep the eyes open during concentration, then close them as meditation dawns.

4. Because slumping brings sleeping, sit up straight (during a sitting meditation) to allow a natural and unobstructed rise of power (a natural consequence of your *samyama)* from the base of your spine up into your head. Until concentration has become a well-learned skill, *sukhasana* is usually a better position for meditation than *shavasana*.

5. Make a plan for dealing with distraction. Some suggestions: A. Ignore it. B. Make a mental (or physical) note to deal with it latter. C. Designate it as the new focus of your *samyama*.

6. Give up the idea that thoughts come in and go out of your mind like visitors come in and go out of your home. Instead, hold on to the idea that you are a traveling point of awareness moving *through* thoughts like the physical body moves *through* physical events.

7. Because awareness and breath are intimately related, use breath control to help move, stop and focus awareness.

78
Stepping In
Following a path to meditation

In this practice, entitled "Stepping In," we will internalize our awareness through a series of deepening states of consciousness. In this pragmatic approach to concentration, we will accommodate the natural tendency of awareness to move by *requiring* it to move along a step-by-step path.

One distinctively new feature of this practice will be its directional orientation of the physical body. This physical alignment of the body is important because the positioning of our head during sleep or *shavasana* meditation and the direction we face during *sukhasana* meditation has a strong effect on the flow of our internal energies.

Scientists tell us, just as the planet we live on rotates upon an axis with a positive pole to the north and a negative pole to the south, so do our bodies balance upon a similar axis with a positive pole at our head and a negative pole at our feet. Because like poles repel to produce a negative effect and unlike poles attract to produce a positive effect, our sleep and meditations are most supported by a positive flow of energy when the directional positioning of our head during sleep or *shavasana* meditation and the direction we face during *sukhasana* meditation is to the *south* (*against* rather than *with* the earth's polarity).

Scientists also tell us our planet revolves from west to east, which means the sun's magnetic force field effects earth from the east side. With regard to an east-west flow of force, this means our sleep and meditations are most supported by a positive energy when the directional positioning of our head during sleep or *shavasana* meditation and the direction we face during *sukhasana* meditation is to the *east* (*against* rather than *with* the incoming effect of the sun's force field).

Bottom line: For an optimal sleep or *shavasana* meditation, position your head to the *south* or *east*. For an optimal *sukhasana* meditation face either *south* or *east*. Since it is generally accepted that a southern focus favors mystical pursuits and an eastern focus favors mental pursuits, yogis could well be expected to choose (though not exclusively) a southern focus.

Stepping In

• In the top right corner of the next available page in your journal, write the date and time of this practice you are now beginning. In the top left corner, write "My Path Within."

• Lead yourself through *hatha yoga* postures you sense will allow your physical nervous system to resonate with the bliss of *being*.

• Once you have become comfortable in *sukhasana*, facing either south or east, proceed through the following five steps, spending two to five minutes with each exercise:

1. Establish ujjayi breath control—nine counts in, hold one; nine counts out, hold one.

2. Feel the natural warmth of the physical body. At first, this warmth can be most easily identified in the main torso.

3. Feel the primal life force flowing through the nervous system of the physical body. This feeling should surface as a tingling sensation felt throughout the entire body, but most obviously in the hands and feet.

4. Trace this primal life force that you feel flowing through your nervous system back to its origin in the spine. Enjoy this spinal energy, which should feel more like a still presence than a moving flow.

5. Pull the focus of your awareness from the feeling of the energy of the spine back into awareness aware of itself. Awareness aware of itself can be triggered by the simple thought: "Before I am aware of any thing, I am just aware."

The usual tendency is to make the attainment of this pure state of consciousness more complicated than it actually is. You will know you have caught an awareness of being aware when you feel a certain distinctive heady energy.

A note: Usually, after having held awareness aware of being aware for three to five minutes, you would proceed on into a *samyama* of your choice. Since the purpose of this practice of "Stepping In" is to simply learn and experience a method for getting through concentration into meditation, all you are going to do next in this exercise is externalize awareness back out into your "normal" waking consciousness.

• To return to "waking consciousness," practice the above five steps in reverse, moving backward from step five to step one. When this reversal of your internalization has been completed, lie back in *shavasana* to enjoy the blissful aftermath of your methodical control of awareness.

• When you feel the time is right, sit up and open your journal. Under your title, "My Path Within," record how you feel about following a structured path through concentration.

79
Meditation
Intuiting

We know we have moved from concentration into meditation when we find ourselves musing on our focal point. In this musing, our budding absorption has overpowered distraction and awakened observation.

When we are observing something, we are not preoccupied. In this full presence of focus, we are seeing what we are observing as it is, and in this seeing are moving toward it through a becoming of it. This movement toward the merging of becoming occurs simply because we have gained interest and lost distraction.

As observation blooms into full meditation, we experience an intensity of energy that flutters the heart with bliss and floods the head with power. The distinction of this particular intensity is that it always feels the same, regardless of what we are meditating upon. Because of the stable nature of this unique intensity, a state of genuine meditation stands solid like a fort offering us—should we choose to accept it—a guaranteed protection from distraction in the sublime insulation of authentic detachment.

In this most genuine detachment of meditation, we are not forever unaware of distraction. We simply see distraction, when we see it, as a distantly unobtrusive curiosity. And the more we become absorbed into a oneness with the object of our meditation, the less even that distant curiosity seems to exist.

What we are feeling in the intensity of meditation is both the high vibration of the spiritual world and *our lack of adjustment to that vibration*. As soon as we become adjusted to one level of this new meditative intensity, that intensity deepens to another level, which requires another adjustment. In this way, we flow in and in simply by continually adjusting to one new level of meditative intensity after another.

Although it may seem, as we follow an internalization of energy during meditation, we are relinquishing our hold on our meditation's original point of focus, what we are actually doing is penetrating into the core of that focal point. This leads to a deepening of the "I."

During our first efforts to concentrate, we make a clear distinction between subject and object. We perceive ourselves to be an "I" locked in a physical body trying to focus upon a point either inside or outside that physical body. As this "I" moves from concentration into meditation and leaves body-consciousness to merge with the object of its focus for the sake of understanding that object, two wonderful things occur. 1. A oneness is won. 2. An "I" is lost. If we do a lot of this loosing of the "I" in the oneness of controlled becoming, that "I" will have to eventually stop seeing itself stuck in any one place and start seeing itself free as the wind, forever moving and merging, moving and merging. Once awareness gets freed to move like this, it has no anchor to restrain its ascension into Self Realization.

In the inner worlds, souls of similar development exist together in the same place. High-minded souls live with other high-minded souls on one level while low-minded souls live with other low-minded souls on another level.

In the physical world, it is different. In that realm of earth, air, fire and water, embodied souls at different levels of development get thrown in together. Losers mix with winners. Saints walk with sinners. This mixing of mismatches—which actually stimulates learning and evolution—forces clashes of vibration that eventually make meditation look like an attractive oasis of inner relief.

When we are in a deep state of meditation, we have left the physical realm to explore its origins at the source of manifestation. In this exploration, we gain solace as we merge with energies both harmonious and sublime. In this merging, questions become answers and ignorance becomes wisdom like concentration becomes meditation and meditation becomes illumination. And as we come out of meditation to perceive life from inside out, we see the physical world for what it is, and what it is not. And we see that nothing is right or wrong or out of place.

80

Flowering

A meditation

In this practice, entitled "Flowering," we will be working with a meditation that focuses upon using memory and thought to stimulate intuition. For this meditation, all you will need is a flower. Any flower will do, but one you find interesting will do best.

Flowering

- In the top right corner of the next available page in your journal, write the date and time of this practice you are now beginning. In the top left corner, write "My Flower Meditation."

- Lead yourself through *hatha yoga* postures you feel will allow the nervous system of your physical body to resonate with the bliss of *being*.

- When you are ready, get comfortable in *sukhasana,* facing either south or east, place your flower on the ground three feet in front of you. Then follow the five steps below (summarized from pages 206 and 207):

1. Establish *ujjayi* breath control — nine counts in, hold one; nine counts out, hold one. 2. Feel the natural warmth of the physical body. 3. Feel the primal life force flowing through the nervous system of the physical body. 4. Feel the energy of the spine. 5. Pull your awareness from the feeling of spinal energy back into awareness aware of itself.

- Once you have arrived at awareness aware of itself, open your eyes and perform the Flower Meditation in the following manner:

    Look at the flower and observe its obvious physical qualities: color, size, smell etc. When you come to the end of these observations, recall what you have been taught (by people, from books or otherwise) about flowers like the one you are observing. If you have been taught a lot, this could take some time.

    Finally, when you have come to the end of what you have learned and you find an emptiness allowing an openness to intuition, crystallize into thoughts and then into words the intuitive flashes you feel coming through this new openness. When put into words and repeated mentally, these intuitive thoughts might read something like this: "This flower is an entity with an identity." "This flower inspires poetry rather than prose." "The petals of this flower explode effulgence."

- When your flower meditation culminates and feels like it wants to end, lie back in *shavasana,* close your eyes and withdraw into *being.*

- When you feel the time is right, sit up and open your journal. Under "My Flower Meditation," record your reflections having used a flower as a focal point for internalizing awareness.

A note: The method conveyed in this *practice* could be applied in a meditation upon any point of focus — an everyday problem or a philosophical question, for instance. By drawing forth out of yourself all you see and all you have learned, you make yourself empty and available for the rising up within you of what you did not know you knew.

Also keep in mind, after you have finished a meditation like this, your subconscious will continue to work with your superconscious to keep bringing you insights. As these insights come, they will feel like gifts for which you will want to give thanks. Yet who can there be to receive this thanks but your Self?

81
Samadhi
Awareness absorbed

Samadhi is often described with indistinct title phrases—like "the ultimate attainment of yoga" or "union with the divine." There is a valid rationale behind this nebulousness. *Samadhi* really is a phenomenon that is not definable.

As skillfully as *Samadhi* evades practical definition, teachers wanting to position it as a yogic goal will define it anyway. Trying not to be overly abstruse, they might call it "an absorption in oneness." Although the words "absorption" and "oneness" leave us with hints of where we are going in this quest for an indescribable, they are not distinct enough to provide us with much concrete guidance, especially since "absorption" and "oneness" name experiences we are all already having all the time.

When we become absorbed in a book or a movie, are we not experiencing a oneness? Even when we "forget ourselves" in an argument, are we not experiencing a oneness (with anger)? Obviously, none of these adventures in oneness is the Samadhi we seek. But each of these events is an experience of absorption in which doer, doing and done are temporarily one.

In trying to understand an everyday sort of oneness as it relates to the oneness we are supposed to be pursuing in our yoga practice, it is important to recognize the significant difference that exists between a oneness we induce by will and a oneness we are seduced into by the will of others or the conditions of circumstance. By the same logic that would assess a willed oneness to be a consequence of well-focused concentration, an un-willed oneness would have to be evaluated as a result of something akin to hypnosis.

When we allow ourselves to live life in reaction—forever becoming blindly absorbed into situations manipulated by other people—are we not submitting ourselves to a sort of hypnosis in which we give up a voluntary control of our existence and thereby open ourselves to suggestions and directions coming to us from outside?

In yoga, it is important to master a control of awareness. This awareness control allows us to consciously choose that with which we become one. Without this awareness control, we will not have the necessary freedom, agility and skill to intentionally maneuver our way through the mind to its edge on "the brink of the Absolute."

During the concentration stage of *samyama*, we are intentionally holding awareness aware of a chosen focal point. During the meditation stage of *samyama*, our concentration becomes a distraction-free enjoyment of our chosen focal point. In the Samadhi stage of *samyama*, our meditation becomes an enjoyment of enjoyment in which our chosen focal point becomes irrelevant as we blend with the bliss we feel. This latter merging with bliss eventually yields the one-and-only non-experience of *That* which emanates all—even existence and consciousness.

In the aftermath of this ultimate non-experience of Source, we realize we have just emerged from Samadhi. Having emerged from Samadhi, we do not feel like we have attained anything. The Self is no more explainable than it was before. We haven't gained any new knowledge about manifest existence. All we know is that life is different. Life now feels less permanent—like it could vanish at any moment, yet somehow doesn't. And it seems to coexist with something not so noticeable before, yet now unmistakably obvious. Rock-solid real yet having no form, this "something" seems to contain life and permeate it at the same time. As we carry an awareness of this unalterable permanence around with us through our daily experience, we find fear and desire have lost much of their capacity to mesmerize us.

What we have just described is an *ultimate* Samadhi. Because the term "Samadhi" is used to name both a rarefied but explainable superconscious experience in the world of manifestation as well as an unexplainable non-experience at the source of manifestation, there are said to be two Samadhis. The superconscious *experience* on the "brink of the Absolute" is called Savikalpa Samadhi. The indefinable *non-experience* of the absolute at the source of manifestation is called Nirvikalpa Samadhi. In yoga we seek to patiently nurture an *experience* of Savikalpa Samadhi so the *non-experience* of Nirvikalpa Samadhi can arrive in its own timing.

Although Savikalpa Samadhi is a simple experience, it is not an easy experience to have. Born to explode out of simplicity into complexity, awareness has trouble staying home inside itself unless a desire to stay home has been cultivated, which can only occur when all other desires have played themselves out.

The same desire that takes awareness away from Self brings awareness back to Self. Truly, if we were viewing our life as a trail of progressive experience, we would have to say desire is the trailblazer. Even at trail's end, the necessary determination to hold a focus on focus long enough for that focus to implode upon itself is contingent upon a desire—a desire for Nirvikalpa Samadhi.

Thus it is that the ultimate attainment of Nirvikalpa Samadhi requires the ultimate transmutation of desire. Right up to the end, it holds true that we *will not* get what we *do not* want and we *will* get what we *do* want. Plenty of people have become very good at meditation yet have not discovered the ultimate Samadhi only because they have not yet arrived at a final wanting.

Although the phrase, "Self Realization," is often understood and used as an alternate label for Nirvikalpa Samadhi, it more specifically refers to the experience of realizing, in the aftermath of a genuine Nirvikalpa Samadhi, that an ultimate non-experience of merging with Self has just come to pass.

After the non-experience of Self in Nirvikalpa Samadhi, we enjoy an easier access to superconsciousness. The spiritualizing of our life that naturally occurs through this more effortless enjoyment of our deepest nature assures that karma will be more readily resolved as it is created so that a clear subconscious can allow a more continual guidance of intuition. In the illuminated living that evolves from this state of uncluttered consciousness, we fear no past and want no future for we have all we need in the *now*.

82
Being aware
Holding awareness aware of itself

In this practice, entitled "Being aware," we will work to lengthen the simple yet challenging experience of sitting on "the brink of the Absolute" in *being*. This practice, which is a *samyama* focused upon focus but anchored in bliss, is a discipline aimed directly at the attainment of a Savikalpa Samadhi on the threshold of a Nirvikalpa Samadhi.

Being Aware

- In the top right corner of the next available page in your journal, write the date and time of this practice you are now beginning. In the top left corner, write "My Awareness."

- Lead yourself through *hatha yoga* postures you feel will allow your physical nervous system to resonate with the bliss of *being*.

- Once you have become comfortable in *sukhasana*, facing either south or east, proceed through the following five steps:

1. Establish *ujjayi* breath control—nine counts in, hold one; nine counts out, hold one. 2. Feel the natural warmth of the physical body. 3. Feel the primal life force flowing through the nervous system of the physical body. 4. Feel the energy of the spine. 5. Pull your awareness from the feeling of spinal energy back into awareness aware of itself.

- Sit for at least one half hour focusing upon holding awareness aware of itself as you enjoy the bliss of *being*.

A note: Being aware of being aware *is being*—*being*, approached through awareness. Although awareness—as it is generally perceived—has no feeling, *being* certainly does. The feeling of *being* is the feeling of *bliss*.

In this practice of "Being Aware," we are striving to hold awareness aware of itself as we are also striving to catch and hold the bliss of *being*. These two aspects of this one practice are important to delineate because—in this practice—it is an awareness of being aware *in conjunction with* the feeling of *being's bliss* that will keep us from intellectualizing our effort.

To be aware of being aware, we must think a thought first. In this thought—however we construct it—we must form an *idea* of awareness and from within that idea sense ourselves to *be* awareness. Yet as soon as we begin to become one with awareness, *which occurs through feeling*, we find we must let go of any sort of awareness-idea. In this relinquishment of thought, we begin to experience a genuinely blissful absorption of awareness into itself.

When even the bliss of awareness aware of itself becomes simply an intensity of energy we can only sustain in a perfect stillness, we intuitively know we have got what we must simply hold to eventually discover the ultimate yoking of yoga.

• When you feel the time is right, open your journal. Under your title, "My Awareness," record your reflections after having held awareness aware of itself long enough to feel the bliss of *being* long enough to sense within that bliss the beginnings of awareness merging into a oneness with its Self.

83
The Yogas of Spine and Mind
Unnecessary pursuits

Of all the yogas that flowered out of *raja yoga*, the two that didn't really have to were *kundalini yoga* and *jnana yoga*. Although this is a bold statement to make, it's one that would make sense to those who have discovered the flourish of *jnana*, "wisdom," and the rise of *kundalini*, the "serpent power," are natural consequences of *raja yoga* well performed and do not need to be sought as separate goals of freestanding yoga practices.

As isolated methods, *kundalini yoga* and *jnana yoga* can look attractive if they are viewed as shortcuts to enlightenment. Unfortunately for those holding this view, the unrelentingly balanced law of *you-get-what-you-pay-for* tells us that any means cut short will naturally yield an end proportionally less fulfilled because the end of any pursuit is a grand-total tally of its means.

The term *kundalini* has been around so long no one really knows when it was coined. Frequently referred to as a "serpent power" and often depicted as a snake, this *kundalini* is thought to be a powerful, primal energy either sleeping in dormancy or rising in manifestation. Although this potent energy is often considered ominous, most yoga adepts agree it is really just a concentrated form of the one pure life force flowing in and through all things.

Common sense tells us that understanding the intensified force stimulated in the practice of *kundalini* or any yoga should precede its intentional arousal.

One well-accepted school of mystical thought asserts that the *kundalini* quite naturally awakens, ascends and successively activates the first three chakras of memory, reason and will as we grow up from a child into an adult and learn to live in the world. Later, according to this same thinking, the *kundalini* can be coaxed into rising on up into the four higher chakras of cognition, love, divine sight and Samadhi if there is an cultivated interest in sophisticating life through the pursuit of some artistic, religious, spiritual or mystical study and practice.

As we translate concepts of *kundalini* into experience, we learn that, as the *kundalini* ascends, time must be allowed at each level along the way for the physical, pranic, emotional, mental and spiritual bodies to adjust to the intensity of the higher and deeper spheres of consciousness being awakened, and that rushing this adjustment through extreme practices can complicate what should be a fluid, easy and natural process. Fortunately, the very experience of this complication usually provides those doing the rushing with plenty of incentive to slow down and let the upward ascent of this powerful force occur on its own.

A note of caution: There is a teaching in the ancient traditions of yoga that warns of a rare circumstance in which the *kundalini* can rise up through the feminine *ida nadi* or masculine *pingala nadi* rather than through the central *sushumna nadi*—the principle psychic nerve current of the soul body that coexists with the spine in the physical body. According to this teaching, this off-center rise of power, which can cause certain temporary sensory, motor, mental or emotional disorders, is more a consequence of impurity (negative karma) than an intensified practice of yoga rushing the dissolution of this impurity.

The most common practice of *kundalini yoga* consists of nurturing the feeling of power released during and after the performance of certain *hatha yoga* postures in conjunction with specifically designated breathing exercises—especially a breath control called the "breath of fire." The "breath of fire" is a fast, light and shallow "sniffing breath" in which the inhalation and exhalation are of equal length and force.

The main difference between *kundalini yoga* and *raja yoga* is, in the former, the rise of serpent power is pursued directly and intentionally while, in the latter, it is allowed to occur indirectly as a natural consequence of other *(raja yoga)* practices.

The "wisdom" of *jnana yoga* is not nearly as ominous as the "snake" of *kundalini yoga*, at least with regard to causing sensory, motor, mental or emotional disorders.

Jnana yoga is perceived as a philosopher's path. On this philosopher's path, the philosophy followed is Advaita Vedanta—a set of principles put forward in the first century CE by a man named Adi Sankara.

According to Advaita Vedanta, God as Brahman is the only reality; the world of time, form and space is completely illusory; suffering is a consequence of ignorance; liberation is the eradication of ignorance in knowledge; and knowledge is understanding the true nature of God and the world.

An accomplished *raja yogi* would take no issue with any of this philosophy, for he would see it as a simple statement of fact—a worded version of the perspective on life that awaited him as he emerged from his first Nirvikalpa Samadhi. In fact, an accomplished *raja yogi* could rightly be referred to as a *jnani yogi* with respect for what he came to know about life having penetrated its source.

Yet, *jnana yoga,* as it is generally perceived, is a path for thinkers, a path upon which wisdom is perceived to be a consequence of smart thought founded on the precepts of Advaita Vedanta. What is lacking in *jnana yoga*, as it is generally understood, is a path of attainment based on the idea knowledge is something more than intellectual perception.

The path of *raja yoga* should begin with a firm intellectual grasp of where that path will end—in the direct realization of the truths asserted in Advaita Vedanta. With this stable start, the *raja yogi* can attain the goals of *jnana yoga* as well as those of *kundalini yoga* in a safe *raja yoga* context.

84
Settling In to Learn
Leaning on the spine

In this practice, entitled "Settling In to Learn," we will pull *kundalini yoga* and *jnana yoga* back into *raja yoga* to focus awareness upon the power of the spine.

Although feeling *being* while dealing with the swirl of everyday life can often seem difficult if not impossible, leaning on the power of the spine is always easy. Try it now. All you have to do is sit up straight, wiggle your spine back and forth a little—just enough to remind yourself where the spine is and how the power flowing through it feels—then become centered in its force. It's that simple, and it's that easy. When you remain centered in this spinal force long enough to feel it coursing up into your head—which takes perhaps three to five seconds—you'll know, in the real *jnana* of your own superconsciousness, the blissful energy you feel is a vital life force you share with all creation.

Although this leaning on spinal power is an easy move to make, it can be a surprisingly difficult move to *remember* to make when a conscious acknowledgment of that power could yield its greatest benefit. *Developing a habit* of "leaning on the spine" when you least need its power can help make that leaning automatic when you need that power the most, for a predominately distinctive characteristic of habits—and an advantageous one if those habits are "good"—is they do not require a conscious summoning.

Those who do not lean on their own spines generally lean on other people. In yoga this leaning *out* instead of *in* is a tendency to avoid, for yoga is a celebration of independence in which we repeatedly show ourselves we need nothing we do not already have.

In this practice, we will be leaning on our spine to settle in to learn what we didn't know we knew.

Settling In to Learn

- In the top right corner of the next available page in your journal, write the date and time of this practice you are now beginning. In the top left corner, write "My Jnana."

- Lead yourself through *hatha yoga* postures you feel will allow your physical nervous system to resonate with the bliss of *being*.

- Once you have completed your hatha yoga, sit in *sukhasana* facing either south or east, become centered in the power of your spine and feel that spinal power flowing up into your head. Every time you become distracted, pull your awareness back into your spine to again feel that power moving up into your head.

A note: This should be a pleasant and easy experience—one that does not require an extensive preparation. Once you discover how truly easy it is to "lean on your own spine," and you have performed enough of this leaning for it to become at least a little bit of a habit, you will find you have found a most powerful way to keep yoga with you all day.

- After about twenty minutes, lie back in *shavasana,* ask yourself the question, "What do I need to know right now?" Then await your answer with alert attentiveness.

- When you feel the entirety of your answer has composed itself under the watchful eye of your awareness, sit up and open your journal. Under your title, "My Jnana," write a letter to yourself telling yourself what you need to know from within yourself *now*.

85
Powers
Liabilities going in, assets coming out

Traditional *Raja yoga* adepts will generally insist that, in the practice of yoga, seeking Nirvikalpa Samadhi should precede or even supersede the development of occult powers. These qualified practitioners prioritize the ultimate attainment of yoga in this way because they know realizing the Self in Nirvikalpa Samadhi requires a lot of focus and a lot of transmuted desire. And they know the thrust of the quest to realize the Self will dissipate if too much focus and desire is channeled into other pursuits, like the development of occult powers.

There is another reason why occult development is best pursued after Nirvikalpa Samadhi, if at all. Before we have come to know our Self, our interest in occultism is selfish. It has to be. The *self* of *selfish* is still who we think we are. Once we have lost *self* in *Self*, we are *selfless*. To be selfless is to be impersonal—no person, no self. When we have no personal and selfish desire to develop occult powers, we don't. Yet, after we perceive our *self* as *Self* in Nirvikalpa Samadhi, those powers *can* get developed within us in response to need, as need is perceived from an impersonal and selfless point of view.

Where there is a person and a self, there is vulnerability. Where there is vulnerability, there is fear. Where there is fear, there is a desire to self-protect. Where there is a self to protect, there is a propensity to act blindly and by such action create negative karma.

Where there is no person and no self, there is no vulnerability. Where there is no vulnerability, there is no fear. Where there is no fear, there is no desire to self-protect. Where there is no self to protect, there is a propensity to act wisely in the moment in accordance with a selfless need, and by such action create minimal karma.

After Nirvikalpa Samadhi, our interaction with our superconsciousness has greater breadth than it did before. During the Savikalpa Samadhi preceding Nirvikalpa Samadhi, we are experiencing superconsciousness peripherally as we hold awareness aware of itself with an intention of canceling that awareness out and back into its Self.

Reentering manifest life after Nirvikalpa Samadhi, our focus is not narrowing in. It's opening out. Having fulfilled our intent to realize Self, we are now simply present in the moment with no place to be other than where we are. In this full presence, we revel in a sense of freedom. In this freedom, we see the all of manifestation from the top down and from the inside out, as if we were entering that all for the first time.

From within this ultimately open mind, we see no questions that cannot be either eliminated as irrelevant or answered from a variety of perspectives. And we see no problems that are not surrounded by an abundant assortment of possible solutions. Yet we ask no questions and pose no problems. With no self to serve, yet strategically positioned to be of service, we are just there. Just being there, we attract the attention of beings like us. As these kindred souls gather around, we feel their presence as a blessing. Feeling blessed, we bless. Blessing and being blessed, we serve.

86
Impersonalizing
Seeing the impersonal in the personal

In this practice, entitled "Impersonalizing," we will be performing a *samyama* focused upon a person. Our aim will be to see within that person that which is impersonal.

As our yoga deepens, our life becomes more and more impersonal. This dismantling of our person through the practice of yoga occurs quite naturally as our shifting sense of "I" internalizes from selfish to selfless points of view.

If we can accept that our personal life is mainly selfish and our impersonal life is mainly selfless, we can see that to be impersonal is *not* to be uncaring. All around us, we can see that spiritual qualities like compassion—defined in the *New Oxford American Dictionary*, as "sympathetic concern for the sufferings and misfortunes of others"—are impersonal *because they function with no personal preference*.

With this understanding of impersonal selflessness, it becomes apparent how and why we can be a most agreeably enjoyable person to be around when our impersonal and selfless qualities are allowed to shine. Therefore, with due respect for the importance of impersonal selflessness, the intent of this practice, entitled "Impersonalizing," will be to recognize the impersonal in others so we might more deeply appreciate and nurture that same impersonality where we find it in ourselves.

In preparation for this exercise in *samyama*, you will need a picture (a photograph or an art rendering) of a person you know and like *personally*. A living person active in your life now would be preferable. This picture should be fortified so it can be propped up vertically.

Impersonalizing

• In the top right corner of the next available page in your journal, write the date and time of this practice you are now beginning. In the top left corner, write "Good Memories."

• Lead yourself through *hatha yoga* postures you sense will allow your physical nervous system to resonate with the bliss of *being*.

• Once you have performed the *hatha yoga* of your choice, get comfortable in *sukhasana* facing either south or east, place the picture of the person you have chosen about three feet in front of you, propped up vertically. Then perform the following five steps:

1. Establish *ujjayi* breath control — nine counts in, hold one; nine counts out, hold one. 2. Feel the natural warmth of the physical body. 3. Feel the primal life force flowing through the nervous system of the physical body. 4. Feel the energy of the spine. 5. Pull your awareness from the feeling of spinal energy back into awareness aware of itself.

• Using the picture before you as a focal point, keep your eyes open as you reflect upon the nature of the person you are observing. As you let your mind wander into the best of the past you shared with this person, choose five pleasant memories to describe in your journal under: "Good Memories." As you write, include an explanation of how the person you are meditating upon helped to make those memories "good."

Example: As you gaze upon a photo of your dad, you find yourself recalling a wonderful experience that occurred when you were five years old. Your dad was showing you how to skip rocks on a still lake.

Your journal: "My dad was teaching me something new: how to skip rocks. And it was wonderful. He was just letting me learn as if I were playing and could do no wrong. In his fun love, learning was easy and the excitement of skipping a rock two, three, four and five times was oh so thrilling. As I record this memory now, I can see what I could not see then: That whole event was a gift from my dad—an experience just for me born of his deep affection. Now, every time I'm standing by a still lake, I want to skip a rock."

A note: A challenge of this exercise will be avoiding a recall of negative experiences revealing the selfish, personal side of the person you are meditating upon. A discovery of this exercise will be seeing that good memories often reveal impersonal unselfishness.

- Once you have your five "good" memories described in your journal, write down a new title: "Seeking the Imperson." Then lie back in *shavasana* to complete your *samyama* by enjoying the bliss of *being*.

- When you feel the time is right, sit up and open your journal. Under your title, "Seeking the Imperson," describe what you learned about the "person" you focused upon as you summoned forth good memories of him or her. Did those good memories reveal an impersonal unselfishness? Did you see the "Imperson" in the "person?"

An example description of an unselfish *imperson*: "My dad was often a gentle, kind and humble man who showed his deep love and compassion through unobtrusive deeds that often went unnoticed and unappreciated." Perhaps dad was also occasionally grumpy, moody and sullen. But that would be dad as a "person"—not an "imperson." In this exercise, we are looking for the "imperson."

A note: As you record your reflections, keep in mind that everyone has a selfless and impersonal side. And every effort you make to perceive that selfless side of others will help you perceive that side of you.

87
The Shining Ones
The higher beings of inner realms

At this juncture of our journey, we must acknowledge the influence of unseen beings as they affect both our life and our yoga. For those who are not clairvoyant and/or clairaudient, the very existence of these beings must necessarily be conjectural and therefore accepted on faith, rejected in doubt or questioned with an open mind. Even for those blessed with extrasensory perception, much of what will be said here about these beings will be speculative. Yet where it is speculative, it will be constructed upon occult convictions widely accepted across a variety of mystical traditions.

We will begin by asserting that none of us is ever alone, even while we are experiencing what we perceive to be physical solitude during waking consciousness. This means, wherever we go, whatever we do, we move and act under the helpful or harmful influence of unseen beings living in unseen worlds. This is experiential fact for those who have directly or indirectly perceived the existence of inner-plane entities, and speculative theory for those who have not.

Christians refer to these veiled beings as "angels" and "demons." Hindus and Buddhists call them "devas" and "asuras." An *asura* is a "demon." A *deva*—literally, a "shining one"—is an "angel." If we are living lives more selfless than selfish, we enjoy the blessings of the shining ones. Yet, even if we are living selfish lives, and in those lives are enduring the haunt of *asuras* to one extent or another, we are never without the benevolent assistance of a special breed of inner plane beings called "guardian devas."

At birth, according to a widely accepted mystical conviction, each of us comes under the care of one or more of these "guardian devas." Although these specialized helpers do not live in physical bodies while they are assisting us from within, they have lived on Earth and will again. They have chosen to work with us and we have accepted them because they are so like us they could "live in our skin." Yet because they live within and can therefore better comprehend what we cannot see might come to be, they are in a most favorable position to fulfill their destiny of keeping us alive. This is their first and primary job—to keep us alive. Their secondary job is to keep us happy in a life unburdened by the consequences of poor decision-making. While these guardian devas stay with us throughout our lives, other inner-plane beings come and go to work with us in accordance with what we are thinking and doing.

For sensitives, as mystics are sometimes called, it is not a matter of speculation that, if we are pondering compassionate thoughts and performing benevolent deeds, we will attract the positive influence of higher inner-plane beings *for as long as we are functioning at a high and positive level of consciousness*. Conversely, if we are thinking selfish thoughts and gratifying those thoughts with selfish action, we will attract the influence of astral entities who would be thinking similar thoughts and performing similar deeds if they were alive in a physical body. Since the motive of these lower entities is selfish—like ours if we are aware at a low level of thought and emotion—their influence will never be in our best interest. It will always be in theirs. For their own pleasure and benefit, they will not hesitate to motivate us toward action that would yield, even at best, no possible good for us.

According to popular mystical thinking, all inner plane entities—*devas* and *asuras*, angels and demons—are only different from us because they aren't currently living in physical bodies. And it's only because they are not physically alive right now that they are so intent upon developing a relationship with us. What they want from us is a vicarious fulfillment of their desires on the physical plane.

Yes, *devas* and angels have desires—desires of quality. While the *asuras* and demons desire to take selfishly, the *devas* and angels desire to give selflessly.

After a desire has taken form and shape as a thought on the astral plane, it must "come to life" as an action on the physical plane to achieve its fulfillment. By the law of cause and effect, this action bringing satisfaction must be followed by a reaction creating a karma in need of resolution. When the reaction to an action is understood and its karma is resolved, the desire that manifested that action can be transmuted into a higher desire to thereby affect a higher quality of life.

If we can accept through our own experience this understanding of the nature and function of desire, we can more deeply appreciate why disembodied entities on the astral plane are so dead set upon getting into physical life through us or any way they can just to sweat out the satisfaction of their desires.

As we come to understand how the guardian devas and higher astral entities we work with will benefit as much from vicariously fulfilling and transmuting even their most refined desires through us as we will benefit by moving more safely and happily through the world with guidance we receive from them, we must also warily concede that the lower astral entities we allow to influence us will provide no such helpful guidance. All they will do—for all they *want* to do—is disrupt our lives for their own selfish enjoyment of their own selfish desires as they carelessly instigate the creation of negative karma for us in the process.

88

Praying

Conversing with the shining ones

In this practice, entitled "Praying," we will be conversing with people we cannot physically see.

As we address those of you who know from experience or accept on faith that beings in worlds beyond your physical sight *do exist*, *want to help* and *can hear you* when you talk to them, we forthrightly suggest this practice of "Praying" will yield obvious benefits.

As we address those of you who do not currently feel drawn toward conversing with the nonliving and therefore feel disinclined to perform this practice, we would ask you—in the spirit of experimentation—to please go ahead and perform this practice anyway, since all you stand to lose is a conviction the nonliving do not exist.

Praying

- In the top right corner of the next available page in your journal, write the date and time of this practice you are now beginning. In the top left corner, write "My Prayer Preparation."

- Lead yourself through *hatha yoga* postures you sense will allow your physical nervous system to resonate with the bliss of *being*.

- Sitting comfortably in *sukhasana* facing south or east, open you journal and—under your title: "My Prayer Preparation"—compose a list of needs you would like to address in prayer.

A note: You might find it helpful to refer back to that gathering of needs you accomplished during the practice described in Chapter 18, entitled "Needalizing." Since that "Needalizing" practice was one of your earlier exercises on the journey of this book, you might find your needs have changed since then—perhaps drastically.

- Choose one of the needs from your newly created list—perhaps the most urgent one. Write a prayer addressing that need. Make the "invisible" recipient of that prayer anyone you want—God, Buddha, Shiva, a departed relative, even "Whomever will listen."

A note: Unless you are extrasensorially perceptive, your chosen recipient will probably be a concept in your mind at first. Yet the very act of choosing a conceptual recipient—in and of itself, even before a prayer is formed—sends out a very real call to a very real astral entity. In response to nothing but your conception of a recipient, an appropriate astral entity—however he or she is addressed—will get set to respond to your prayer.

Prayer is not just a psychological exercise. It is a very real communication between two or among several very real beings. If you offer a low-level prayer like: "Please vanquish my enemies so I can succeed," a real inner plane entity will be right there to assist you in the fulfillment of that request. This is to say that whatever you request to be done *can* be done with assistance from inner plane beings, even should you have to make a karmicly costly deal with a demon to do it. Therefore, in prayer, beware of whom you ask and what you ask for.

Sometimes the answer to a prayer will come to you even as you are writing that prayer down on paper. If this should happen, from where does this response come? You? The entity to whom your prayer is addressed? You'll never know. Not really. If the answer you receive is helpful, who cares where it came from? If it is not helpful, again, how or why does it matter from whence it came?

In the aftermath of prayer, your own intuitive perception should be allowed to have the final say in the value-assessment of any responses you feel you are receiving. To put this even more strongly, nothing entering your mind—in response to prayer or not—should be allowed to bypass or oppose your own intuition.

To implement this principle in prayer, simply practice a little introspective discernment right after you pray. And have faith that intuition needs less than a fraction of a second to shout out its acceptance or rejection of the response you have summoned.

In your moment of introspection, you should sense this intuitive reaction as a simple "yes" or "no."

- When you are ready to pray, please do so in the following way: Offer your written prayer aloud or silently to your chosen recipient as if that recipient was physically present in front of you. Then try to intuitively feel an incoming prayer response. Once you have caught a sense of that response, put it into words. If those words feel favorable, write them down in your journal and offer your prayer again, this time intuitively awaiting an elaboration upon the first response you received. If and when this elaboration begins to show itself in a way that feels good when put into words, write it down in your journal as you did before. Should this praying and waiting evolve into a conversation, let that conversation be. This is prayer at its best. If a prayer-conversation like this should occur, summarize its gist in your journal when it is done.

A note: When a high-level prayer becomes conversational, that conversation is a three-way interchange. The three parties involved in this interchange are your conscious "I," your superconscious (intuitive) "I" and the "I" of the recipient to whom you *were* praying and with whom you are *now* conversing.

A prayer-conversation, which will usually occur too quickly for you to record while it is taking place, will usually form up as a philosophical discussion during which the three "I's" involved gradually merge as one as they become more and more agreed upon precisely how the wisdom they are discussing might best be brought down to earth and summarized in words. The merging of "I's" occurring during this inner conversation is the particular yoking of yoga that prayer can yield when it is pursued at its highest level.

- When you feel the time is right, sit up and open your journal. Write down a new title, "Reflections on Prayer." Then summarize in words your experience of "Praying."

89
Worship
Surrendering in communion with God

A religion is generally understood to be a belief in and worship of a personal God (or gods), a personal God generally perceived to be a self-aware entity that can be approached as one would approach a person. What this perception of religion implies religion is *not*, especially in Western theologies, is the belief and realization that we *are* God.

If we are passionate followers of a religion that either subtly or emphatically denies the existence of an intrinsic oneness of God and soul, and we are meditating to realize our Self, we can expect an arousal of a certain amount of mental conflict and confusion. Fortunately, this bewilderment can be easily resolved through some clear-minded sorting out of what we actually do and do not believe.

In its *general* application, yoga does not qualify as a religion—even though it was originally conceived in a religious (Hindu or Vedic) context. In some of its *specific* application, however, it does. For example, *bhakti yoga*, a system developed out of Patanjali's encouragement to worship *Ishvara* (in his fifth *niyama*, entitled *Ishvara Pranidhana*), might be classified as a religion because the worship of a personal God is central in its practice. *Bhakti yoga* means "union through devotion."

Also, yoga schools forming up around spiritual gurus whose teachings frame distinct beliefs can start looking like small religions if the gurus of those schools are receiving some degree of veneration or if those gurus advocate the worship of a personal God or Goddess.

While worship is generally considered a religious observance, it can—like prayer—be practiced apart from religion. In his fifth *niyama*, *Ishvara Pranidhana*, Patanjali not only encourages worship, he encourages worship of a personal God. *Pranidhana* means "surrender," and *Ishvara* means "personal God."

By including this *niyama* in a series of practices designed to eventually trigger the "non-experience" of Nirvikalpa Samadhi, Patanjali exposes a hint of his most comprehensive view of God. He is saying—though not overtly—we would be well advised to worship God externally if we intend to realize Him internally. This implied advice is based upon a mind-stretching perception that God is the unmanifest source of all existence, the primal life force flowing in and through all form, as well as the first and supreme Soul of souls—all at once.

A yoga practice based upon this broad, deep and sweeping perception would consist of worshiping God *outside*, merging with God *inside*, and realizing God as the essence of both *outside* and *inside*.

The *worship* portion of this approach allows us to give up *who we think we are* in preparation for realizing *who we really are*. The *merging* portion of this approach allows us to remain on the brink of the Absolute long enough to sink into and return from *That* to realize we have just merged with God as our Self.

In all of this, worship is of fundamental importance, for worship builds faith, and faith builds tenacity. By the firm resolve of tenacity, our external worship forges on to become an internal worship that will allow the death of an ego in a merging of awareness with Self.

In the feeling and expression of reverence and devotion that *is* worship, we find ourselves participating in a divine exchange of an "I" for an "I"—a *self* for the *Self*— couched in a feeling of a growing adoration for a God we perceive to be not unlike a very wise person who is just very good at giving and receiving love. A relieving surrender is what we experience on our side of this divine exchange. That to whom we are surrendering is not a figment of our imagination. He/She is absolutely real, but absolutely real in our experience—not in our concept.

Notice Patanjali's personal God is not specified (other then by the name of *Ishvara*, which only means "personal God"). By leaving it up to us to perceive this "personal God" any way we would like, Patanjali is intimating that any concept of God we come up with will work well enough to initiate our practice of that all-important worship that can lead to a very real merger of extoller and extolled.

90
Worshipping
Giving up, going in

In this practice, entitled "Worshipping," we will surrender. When we think and talk about giving up a wrong sense of "I," that's exactly what we are doing—thinking and talking. When we surrender in worship, we actually *are* giving up a wrong sense of "I."

From most any mystical or religious point of view, prayer is perceived as a *communication* that can exist either between man and God or between man and *devas* (or angels), while worship is perceived as a *communion* that can *only* occur between man and God. In a sophistication of this view, it is generally accepted that, although our perception and worship of God must necessarily change as we change, God will never have any problem accepting our perception and worship of Him in any way it comes.

A side note: Nothing in correctly presented yoga teachings should preclude your experimentation with those teachings to see if they work for you. We make this bold claim because the very idea of yoga rests on the principle that *value is relative to need* on a path of illumination each of us must walk alone. Thus, yoga teachings are tools—tools for us to use either freely and creatively or not at all. One of these tools—a powerful one—is worship.

In preparing for external worship, we ready our *self* to be surrendered as we muster all the faith we can find. If worship is new to us, we can gather faith from the positive changes we have witnessed worship producing in others. If worship is not new to us, we can gather faith from the positive changes we have experienced worship producing in ourselves. However we assemble it, faith is invaluable. The more we have of it the better our worship will be. The feeling of a faith in worship is a sense of an imminent transformation of heart and mind.

As we delve into external worship, we begin to sense how certain physical items are imbibed with *actinic* force through *devotional* use, just as certain physical items are imbibed with *odic* force through *practical* use. We can, for instance, sense we have enriched a rosary of beads with *actinic* force because we have used that rosary in devotional worship, just as we can sense we have individualized a shovel with *odic* force because we have used that shovel in physical work.

When we use a physical object as a symbolic representation of a personal God—however we perceive that personal God to exist—God reciprocates by using that same object as a conduit for a flooding out of His blessings. We know this because we can feel those blessings coming through that object now made sacred as a fulcrum for the exchange of energies both devotional and divine.

Now, with all this we know about worship, let's see if we can actually do some surrendering of *self* through external devotion.

Worshipping

• In the top right corner of the next available page in your journal, write the date and time of this practice you are now beginning. In the top left corner, write "My Surrender."

• Lead yourself through *hatha yoga* postures you sense will leave your physical body not requiring your attention.

• Choose an object for worship.

A note: If you are not accustomed to worship, you might feel more comfortable working with an object that has already been made sacred, such as an image in a shrine, temple or church. If you decide to use an object never worshipped, either hold it in your right hand if it is small or touch it with your right hand if it is large and chant *Aum* aloud for a few minutes before you begin your worship.

• As you prepare to worship, sit up straight—about three feet away from your point of focus, facing either south or east. If you are doing this in a public place, you might be limited by circumstance.

• As you begin your worship, keep your eyes open. Through the image you are worshipping, try to feel a connection extending from God to you and from you to God.

A note: It is important to keep in mind that you are not worshipping an object. The object you have chosen is a conduit. If you could see God, you wouldn't need a conduit.

• Once you have your inner connection well established, use *ujjayi* breath control to initiate a managed exchange of force between you and God. As you begin to feel this exchange occurring, give God your negative feelings of hurt and pain on your out-breath so you have a vacated space within to receive His blessings back on your in-breath. Eventually, after you have surrendered the bulk of your negative feelings and are nearly filled to the brim with the bliss of His blessings, give Him the "I" you thought you were when you were experiencing all those negative feelings you just gave up. Keep giving up this "I" in exchange for blessings until all you have to give are the blessings given to you.

A note: There is not much thought in this process. It is all feeling-based. And the feelings felt are primarily in the chest where we can sense the presence of the *anahata chakra,* our mystic heart within. It is from deep within this mystic heart that we surrender suffering. And it is deep into this mystic heart that we receive blessings.

Although we say we first surrender "negative feelings," then surrender the "I" we thought we were when we were experiencing those negative feelings, all we are really doing from start to finish is giving up what we feel in the chest. At first this feeling is psychic pain; later it's soulful bliss. Once we have arrived at offering bliss because we have no more pain to give, the bliss we give is a "thank you" for the inexhaustible flow of blessings we have received and are continuing to receive.

When we are giving back the bliss of our blessings, our breath is nearly still. In this near stillness, the blessings coming in meld with the blessings going out so the bliss of both, blended as one, is all there is.

- When you feel the time is right, sit up and open your journal. Under your title, "My Surrender," record your reflections on your experience of internal surrender through external worship.

91
Evil
An impermanent consequence of ignorance

Few would deny that physical life is challenging. In light of this common assessment, it is understandable why so many of us perceive being selfish as a fundamental necessity for survival in the physical world. It is even understandable why we might think we have to be selfish to be unselfish as in: "I have to make money before I can give money," or "I have to take care of myself before I can take care of others."

Although all of this thinking might well constitute what most of us would be reluctantly willing to call a pardonable point of view, it can still leave us feeling badly about the way we live our lives—as if something is just not as right as it could or should be. In an effort to get feeling "right" and thinking a little better about ourselves, many of us turn to mainstream religion, hoping that becoming involved with a socially acceptable form of worship will somehow correct any imbalances we have set into play through living what we perceive to be a necessarily selfish life. Because the discontent of our secret remorse *is* significantly assuaged as we step into the ranks of a religious congregation that is fortified from within itself by the common belief and mutual support of its members, we often understandably conclude our decision to commit to religion was a good one. And if we come to this conclusion, we often understandably allow ourselves to think our selfishness is now okay because we are now religious—and thinking this way is okay because so many others are thinking this way as well.

When a goodly number of embodied souls gather together to think the same way for any of many reasons—religious, business, political, social or otherwise—they form a daunting coalition of force, regardless of the integrity or validity of their reasons for gathering. From the inner worlds, this grand energy amalgamation looks like a one dynamic presence—a one very powerful person.

Both the *devas* and the *asuras* see working with a *being-made-of-many* as a *many-in-one* opportunity to exert a strong influence upon the physical plane. Therefore, just as these *devas* and *asuras* vie for the attention of individuals, so do they also vie for the attention of groups. When *devas* dominate the attention of religious groups, there is holy rejoicing. When *asuras* dominate that attention, there is holy war.

As we live our lives upon the battleground of earth, forever enduring its unrelenting clash of opposites, we cannot dodge dealing conceptually with what we see and experience—as much as we might like to. In an attempt to derive some sense out of what too often seems like nonsense, we find ourselves unavoidably grappling with concepts of good and evil.

If we turn to religion for an understanding of these two opposing forces, we might gain considerable solace from holding views that seem solid not so much because they make sense but because they are believed by many.

If we do *not* turn to religion as we try to understand these two forces, but instead take a more philosophical approach, we will still have to deal with religious issues, for concepts of good and evil are inextricably connected to perceptions of God, soul and life in general.

With regard to perceptions of God, soul, good, evil, life, death and such, views reflected in Eastern religions like Hinduism, Buddhism and Taoism are vastly different from views reflected in Western religions like Christianity, Judaism and Islam. This difference is highlighted by the fact that Buddhism and Taoism do not even qualify as religions in the strictest sense because their adherents do not believe in or worship a personal God.

Since yoga was born in the Hindu culture of India and meditation is performed to one extent or another in all Eastern approaches to spirituality, it could well seem logical that anyone practicing yoga and/or meditation would be looking at life from an Eastern religious or philosophical point of view. Actually, such is not always the case.

Now that yoga is internationally popular, there exists a phenomenon in which sincere aspirants who have grown up in a Western culture dominated by Western religious traditions are diving into a system of mystical introspection that is rooted in Eastern thought. Ironically, the conflict-to-resolution this scenario forces into play in the minds of sincere Western aspirants often produces stronger rather than weaker yogis and yoginis.

Although Easterners are advantaged because they do not have to significantly alter their philosophy and lifestyle to practice the deeper disciplines of yoga effectively, Westerners who succeed in reconciling Eastern mysticism with Western religious conviction, just to conceptually prepare themselves for the deeper experiences of yoga, often build a stronger philosophical foundation for their yoga practice than many Easterners have. This foundation these "Westerners" earn through hard effort is all the more fortified because they come to Eastern thought knowing what it is *not*.

From the perspective of Eastern mysticism, there is no intrinsic evil. All is good, for all is God, and God is intrinsically good. In this belief system, there is no acknowledgement of a Satan who personifies a force opposing God. Although from this perspective evil *is* perceived to exist, it is recognized as a temporary anomaly resulting from actions performed in an ignorance that will eventually become wisdom through the sufferance of karmic consequence.

From the perspective of Western religion, evil is deemed a living force directly opposing the will of God. Embodied as Satan and existing in man as one of his tendencies, this version of evil is perceived to be a permanent enemy of good and God.

From the perspective of Eastern mysticism, hell is perceived as a state of mind in which there is suffering due to the creation of negative karma. From this point of view, hell is not a physical place, nor is it eternal.

From the perspective of Western religion, hell is a physical place where bodies burn forever without being consumed, and there is eternal anguish. In this Western religious credo, there is a prominent belief there will come a Judgment Day when the physical body of each soul that ever lived on earth will be summoned back to life to stand before God to be judged and, in accordance with that judgment, be consigned to heaven or hell everlasting.

In yoga, our first and last guru is intuition. Dwelling in the balance of East and West, intuition takes its stand as the harbinger of life's only rigid rule: the wisdom of the moment. If we can allow ourselves to impartially contemplate the views of East and West in the purity of the *now*, intuition will unfailingly light a path of wisdom from where we are to where we next should be on our journey from *self* to *Self*.

92
Coming to Terms
Accepting or rejecting indoctrination

In this practice, entitled "Coming to Terms," we will be directly confronting what we have been taught, what we think about what we have been taught and what we now believe in contrast to or in sync with what we have been taught about hell, sin and evil.

Coming to Terms

- In the top right corner of the next available page in your journal, write the date and time of this practice you are now beginning. In the top left corner, write "Hell, Sin, Evil and I."

- Lead yourself through *hatha yoga* postures you feel will leave your physical body not requiring your attention.

- After you have completed your chosen *hatha yoga*, get comfortable in *sukhasana* and adjust the centeredness of your breathing with either *surya bedha pranayama* or *chandra bedha pranayama*. Then perform *anuloma viloma pranayama*.

- Having balanced body and breath, perform *bhramari pranayama* (the "humming" breath) until you feel a blissful stillness.

- Lie back in *shavasana*, your head positioned to the south or east and relax into *being*. Then think back over your life in a general way to isolate what you have been taught about hell, sin and evil.

A note: This particular remembering is investigative. If, for instance, you remember being indoctrinated with the idea you would go to hell if you committed a "mortal sin," you might try to recall if anyone described "hell" or defined a "mortal sin" for you. Or if you remember saying, "deliver us from evil" while repeating the Lord's Prayer every Sunday for years, you might try to recall if anyone ever clarified for you exactly what evil it was you were requesting deliverance from.

• After about a half hour of this targeted delving into the past, sit up and open your journal. From the memories you have found, write down—under your title: "Hell, Sin, Evil and I"—a core summary of what you have been taught about hell, sin and evil. Then, after asking yourself if what you have been taught is what you believe now, record in your journal how you currently perceive hell, sin and evil. In this record, please also include your reflections upon why it might be said, "our perception of hell, sin and evil has a fundamentally pivotal influence upon our deeper practice of yoga."

93
Sufferance
A catalyst for introspection

In the mystical perception of the East, to sin is to knowingly cause unnecessary harm. Although no one would deny that causing *some* harm is an inevitable reality of life, anyone can sense there is a way to live that does not cause *unnecessary* harm. This "way" is specified as the *Tao* in Taoism, and *dharma* in Hinduism and Buddhism.

The meaning of the word *dharma* conveys both a principle of life and a method of living that might be described as follows: "There is an inherent order within the all of manifest existence. Within that order there is an inherent way of living. When we are living in this inherent way, we are following dharma."

It is difficult to describe exactly how to go about following "an inherent way of living." If we say that living in accordance with dharma is moving *with* the flow of life rather than *against* it, we would also have to say that such living is not passive or aggressive exclusively, but rather passive or aggressive when necessary, neither when possible.

Following dharma could also be construed as living in a balance of *being* and *doing*. Yet such balanced living is all but impossible if we are overly selfish, for the way of selfishness, which is the opposite of selflessness, is *adharma*, which is the opposite of *dharma*.

We know we have caught the knack of following dharma when we feel ourselves being led by a sensitivity that pares desire down to need. In this sensitivity, we see ourselves moving as fluidly flexible entities fitting seamlessly into the flow of that one energy that forms the basis of all life. In the sense of wholeness this approach to life engenders, we do what we must, graciously accept what we need, give what we can, and cause the least amount of harm possible. As strange as it might seem to those hankering after a life of personal pleasure, this dharmic existence is delightfully enjoyable.

By contrast, when we are following adharma, we are selfishly chasing desire with fear snapping hot upon our heals. In this haunted pursuit, we care nothing for those who cannot help us or that which will not benefit us personally. We do what we want, we take what we can, we give as little as possible (unless giving will bring us profit), and we don't care who we hurt in the process.

Then there is *dharma/adharma*. In our first involvement with this particular touching of opposites, we are occasionally torn away from our indulgent selfishness into bouts of conscience during which we suffer the humiliation of facing the bottom side of the person we have allowed ourselves to become. As these dealings with our conscience become more frequent, our suffering intensifies enough to drive us up into a better quality of life.

This is all in accordance with the natural order of things in which nothing is out of place and all is as it should be, where an escalation of suffering leads to an end of suffering.

The sense that nothing is happening even amidst intense activity, or the sense that we are doing nothing even as we accomplish much, is also the feeling of following dharma. From within this feeling, we enjoy a way of living in the world without being of the world.

If we are inwardly receptive, our "voice of conscience" can lead us along this path of *dharma* in an easy way, for it is up through the ease of effortlessness that the base order of all existence can rise to the surface of our lives to provide us with a simple knowing of what to do *now* and how.

As we unfold in a life more and more saturated with dharmic living, we learn to see suffering as a catalyst for introspection. When we can appreciate suffering in this way, we can accept it as an integral component of living and thus allow it to engender within us a transcendence of suffering. In this transcendence, we are ripe for the "end of ends."

94
A Water Purification
Washing emotion away

As in the practice of "Releasing in Fire," the intent of the practice of "Releasing in Water" is to purge memories of emotion so those memories might more easily be understood and reconciled. Although "Releasing in Fire" and "Releasing in Water" share the same goal, they differ in practice.

While "Releasing-in-Fire" *directly* seeks out memories charged with emotion, "Releasing-in-water" allows those emotional memories to surface *indirectly* in the periphery of another yoga practice. Also, while the "fire method" focuses primarily on dealing with memories of experiences involving the negative emotions of difficult interpersonal relationships, the "water method" allows for the handling of any emotional memories coming into view. These practices work well with each other—either one coming first.

"Releasing in Water" should be performed by a flowing stream or river. If such a physical location is not available, this entire practice can be performed as a meditative visualization.

Releasing in Water

- Gather at least 50 flowers or petals in one basket and at least 50 leaves in another basket. Then, take these two baskets, along with your journal and pen, to a flowing stream or river. (If a stream or river is not accessible, this procedure can be visualized.)

- Take a seat or visualize yourself taking a seat by your chosen stream or river (facing south or east if possible). Open your journal and—in the top right corner of the next available page—write the date and time of this practice you are now beginning. In the top left corner, write "A Water Purification."

- Focusing on the flowing water (physical or visualized), let emotional memories rise of their own accord as you repeat *Aum* deeply so it resonates "aa" in the chest, "oo" in the throat and "mm" in the head. As each emotional memory surfaces: 1. Take a leaf from your leaf basket. 2. Mentally flood that leaf with the emotion of the memory that has just surfaced. 3. Place that leaf into the stream or river to be carried away by its current. 4. Thank the stream or river by giving it a flower or a flower petal (see figure 12).

A note: The emotion you are seeking to release does not have to be negative. It can also be positive. Example: Suddenly, as you are sitting by your chosen river, you find yourself remembering your grandmother's death, an experience that was difficult for you because of an emotion you were feeling—an emotion that was initially positive.

What you first felt for your grandmother was a positive emotion of *odic* attachment. Because positive and negative emotions are but flip sides of a one *odic force* forever bouncing back and forth between polar opposites, that first positive emotion you felt when your grandmother was alive *had* to give way to a negative emotion when she died.

Now, what you are seeking to give up from the memory of your grandmother and her death is the first positive emotion you felt for her. If this release is successfully accomplished, a letting go of the following negative emotion should occur naturally. In the vacuum of the absence of both these emotions, a higher impersonal but spiritual love born of understanding can move in to allow the memory of your grandmother's death to be viewed from the knowing distance of detachment.

• After about thirty minutes, or when you feel the time is right, open your journal. Under your title, "A Water Purification," record your reflections on working with water to release emotion. Include in your reflections how you feel this practice compares with "Releasing in Fire." As you reflect, please consider the following:

The subconscious does not rationalize. It records and categorizes according to a preset program. And it takes what is submitted to it quite literally. If it is receiving impressions that negative emotions are being put into leaves and washed downstream, for instance, it will dutifully record and file those impressions in the annals of memory as deeds done as actually as any deeds are ever done.

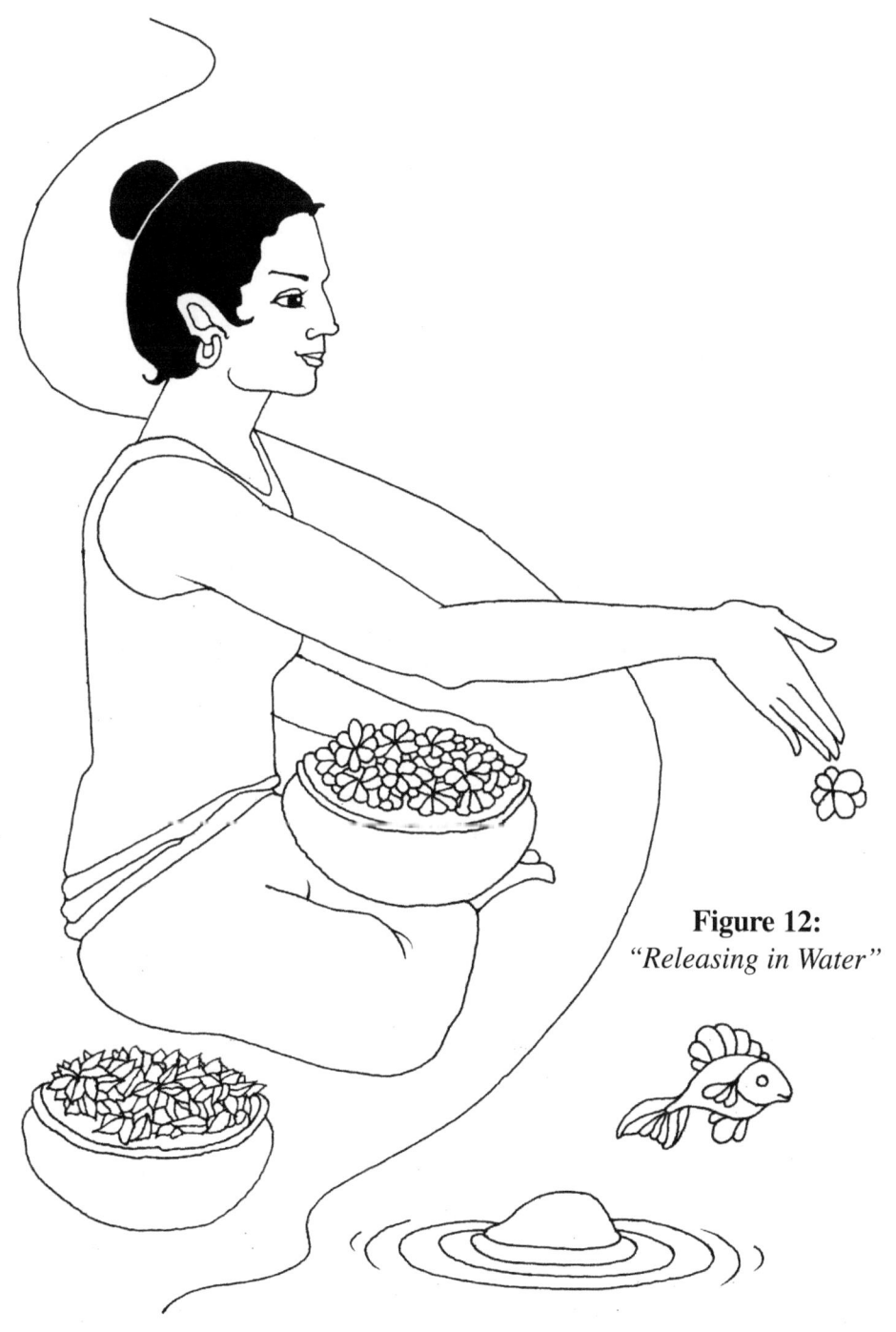

Figure 12:
"Releasing in Water"

PART FOUR
THE ABSOLUTE

95
Evolution
A journey through time

Because a capacity to penetrate the depths of consciousness ebbs and flows with the rise and fall of fears and desires, any sense of progress during the first months of a sustained yoga practice can be expected to occasionally waver. If we experience this wavering during our practice but do not let it stop us, we can expect to eventually receive feedback from our more genial colleagues and associates indicating our yoga is yielding positive results.

This feedback is important. It offers us an *external* support when we are not yet able to intuit an *internal* support. Comments from friends and relatives like, "you've really changed," "you've become so calm," "you're such an inspiration to be around," or "you look so healthy," offer us oblique but concrete indications we are making progress in the transmutation of desire, the transcendence of fear, the honing of cognition, the refinement of character and the development of physical vitality. Not surprisingly, this outside support inspires us to continue our practice with a sense that we are passing through some sort of transformation—a transformation making itself known to us through physical effects that can be recognized by others.

To continue on with a positive yoga practice that doesn't require external encouragement, we would be well advised to work toward supporting our yoga experience with good, solid philosophical thought. When we can maneuver ourselves into an intellectual stance that supports what our yoga is showing us through intuition, we will have positioned ourselves well for the enjoyment of a powerful inner life that will stand strong, independent and self-contained.

From a mystical point of view, thought's highest function is to process intuition in two ways: first, by validating it in the world of thought with solid logic; and second, by applying it in life through skillful decision-making. To fulfill this two-fold purpose, thought should make itself a flexible servant of intuition by remaining both open and intelligent.

As our nature changes in correlation with what we learn from intuition through a long-term practice of yoga, the concepts that form our philosophical outlook on life will also quite naturally have to change—perhaps many times.

With regard to soul evolution—an issue of central importance in any mystical pursuit—our first philosophical stance might be somewhat elaborate since, in the beginning of our yoga practice, we could be wanting lots of good reasons for doing what we are doing, and lots of good explanations for what experience has not yet taught us. Since yoga was originally conceived as an Eastern mystical practice, our first philosophical stance might get worded something like this:

The soul first manifests from the unmanifest as an entity with a sense of identity separate from its Self. As this soul entity experiences the all of manifest existence, one piece of that all at a time, it evolves through many lives in many bodies to create and resolve every possible karma until there is nothing left to learn from experience, and therefore nothing left to do but return to source in Self.

This philosophical perspective relates the practice of yoga to the needs of life. It allows us to appreciate how *hatha yoga* and *pranayama* can help us build a healthy and happy physical body so we can freely strive to cognize the deeper mysteries of life through a meditative process aimed at expediting a journey we are all already on—a journey of many lives that will eventually end in our ultimate merging with God as our Self. This kind of interlaced logic emerging out of a positive philosophical stance that accurately reflects the wisdom of intuition gives us lots of reasons for continuing our yoga practice *while we need those reasons for continuing*.

There comes a time, however, when our practice of yoga needs no reason to be a part of our life. At that point, its value is so intuitively obvious there is no need for logical support. When our yoga has become that, we will have either changed our philosophical perspective drastically or thrown it out altogether, for we will have found our way into a fortress of inner stability that has no need for wisdom supplied secondhand through thought.

Wisdom is a fact. Thought is a tool. Certainly, as a tool, thought is also a fact, but the content of thought is relative to its use and its need to be used. If there is no use for thought, it has no reason to be. A newborn baby girl, for instance, has little use for thought. As that girl grows up into a young lady, she will need thought, of course. But as a baby, she's just fine without it. For a baby, thought is a tool that lies dormant on a shelf.

As our *practice* of yoga matures into a *state* of yoga, we become childlike in our requirement of thought. Our sense of and faith in knowing what we need to know without overly thinking sustains us in a yoga that fulfills itself by itself.

96
Goal Digging
Assessing the quality of current desires

In this practice, entitled "Goal Digging," we will be assessing the degree of our *beingness*—the extent to which we have become comfortable in *being*—by digging up and looking at desires that keep us rooted in the world of *doing*.

If our yoga is based in *being* and is therefore more a *state of arrival* than a *method of arriving,* we will have less of a tendency to see life as a process of evolution, for in our simple *beingness*, we will not be feeling a need for *becoming* perfect. We'll just be enjoying the bliss of *being* that *is* perfect right *now*.

If, on the other hand, we are just *on our way* into our yoga practice, are not yet solid there and feeling the pangs of fear and desire strongly, our life will as yet be lacking the background *beingness* that gives a saint or a sage his or her aura of sublimity. Without this *beingness*, we'll feel a need for thought to keep churning up reasons why we do what we do, reasons derived from concepts of progress, evolution, growth and the like.

Because a lot of our lack of *beingness* exists as a result of unfulfilled desire, we will be working in this practice of "Goal Digging" to consciously dig up and revise some of our unsatisfied desires into a "wish list" that works *with* rather than *against* our yogic efforts.

Goal Digging

- In the top right corner of the next available page in your journal, write the date and time of this practice you are now beginning. In the top left corner, write the title, "My High Wish List."

- Lead yourself through *hatha yoga* postures you feel will leave your physical body quiet and balanced.

- After you have completed your chosen *hatha yoga*, get comfortable in *sukhasana* and adjust the centeredness of your breathing with either *surya bedha pranayama* or *chandra bedha pranayama*. Then perform *anuloma viloma pranayama*.

- Having balanced body and breath, perform *bhramari pranayama* (the "humming" breath) until you feel a blissful stillness.

- Lie back in *shavasana* with your head positioned to the south or east and tune into *being*.

- Once you have become comfortable in *being*, sit up facing south or east, open your journal and review the *needs list* you composed for Chapter 18 (*Needalizing*) and the *desires list* you composed for Chapter 20 (*Facing*). From those two lists, create a one new list—under your title: "My High Wish List"—comprised of those needs and desires you feel are acceptable now as you consider them next to a hunger for yoga's ultimate "end of ends." Then, rewrite these acceptable needs and desires as goals in a prioritized list that begins with Nirvikalpa Samadhi.

A note: Even if the first and highest goal of your life at this point is not this ultimate Samadhi—or even if you are not convinced Nirvikalpa Samadhi should be life's first and highest goal—we would suggest you perform this exercise anyway so your own experimentation might have an opportunity to reveal some useful insight.

- After your list is composed, lay back in *shavasana* and again touch into *being*. From within that still state, review your list.

• When you feel like it, sit up and open your journal. Under a new title, "The Degree of my Beingness," record your reflections regarding where you feel you stand on the path to Self through need and desire.

97
Involution

A non-journey in now-awareness

The mystical frame of reference we evolve into after several years of yoga practice might seem to contradict the philosophical stance we chose to maintain as that practice began. Though both our earlier philosophical understanding and our later mystical cognition might have been inspired by clear intuition, they could appear to be at variance, simply because they were each evoked at different times and from different points of view. From this we can see that intuition works with us in accordance with where we are in time, space and consciousness. In this mode of operation, it lets us know what we need to know *now*—no more and no less.

When we are deeply immersed in a world of people and things, for instance, intuition could be expected to inspire us to perceive God as immanent love. If, however, we are deeply involved in a world of introspection and meditation, intuition might more likely motivate us to perceive God as our own transcendent Self beyond time, form and space. Although logic could understandably deem these two seemingly opposing concepts of God irreconcilable, it would not dispute that each of these two could appear to be true from different points of view.

If we merge these two concepts, if we pull God-as-love together with God-as-Self, we set up a philosophical problem logic cannot solve. This failure of logic forces a deepening of yoga. A deepening of yoga brought about in this way offers an ideal use of thought—as a catalyst for shoving us toward that which cannot be touched upon by thinking.

When God is experienced as love and realized as Self, thought is forced to see love as the sense and feeling of a oneness that was never two—except in thought. As far as it can be put into words, this is the culmination of *raja* or *any* yoga.

What we come to at the end of what thought perceives to be "evolution" is what intuition cognizes to be "involution." *Involution* in this more mystical context means internalizing awareness out of thought, straight in toward Self and away from any notion we are an entity evolving from one state of progress to another and another.

Anyone who has awakened psychic vision enough to see auras will confirm that thoughts happen *outside the physical body* where they can be seen in living form and color. This means, when awareness is focused in thought, it is actually *more externalized* than when it is focused in the physical body.

In involution, we pull awareness deep into the source of the energy of the life of the physical body. In this depth that thought cannot pierce, awareness is simply aware of itself. When we find ourselves immersed in this ultimate focus of awareness, there is not even a notion of "self coming home to Self," or "*we* becoming one." There is only awareness dissolving into an inability to observe any second thing—even itself.

This does not mean all the previous effort we spent working with ourselves, motivated by concepts of evolution, was not worthwhile. All of that led us here to this turning point where evolution ends and involution wins its final dive within from self to Self.

98
Side Stepping

Accessing the in-tell of intelligence, now

In this practice, entitled "Side Stepping," we'll be stepping out of our preset methods of practice to follow our own intuitive guidance even with regard to our yoga's modus operandi.

This "stepping out" does not mean "spacing out," as in allowing awareness to be moved submissively from one distraction to another. Nothing about this approach will require forfeiting the very control that makes this practice a yoga. All we are doing here is listening in to intuition for instructions on *which* control to follow—listening in to the in-tell of our own intelligence for directions on *what* to do *when*.

In this effort, we are choosing to face yoga as we must face life. In life, especially during its more challenging moments, we do not always have the luxury of being able to follow a preset method for dealing with what comes.

If we get up in the morning, for instance, and rigidly fix our determination upon remaining the watcher all day long, we are setting ourselves up to become unnecessarily frustrated when life draws us into itself out of our watcher awareness. This seemingly unavoidable forfeit of our preset method for dealing with our day can be discouraging—to say the least.

In the flexibility this "Side Stepping" allows, we give ourselves an opportunity to apply all we have learned from yoga in accordance with the needs of the *now* rather than the rules of a preset method. In the self-reliance this *now* practice of yoga inspires, our faith in the guru who is the mystic in-tell of our own intelligence will empower us to trust what we didn't know we knew as we lead ourselves from we to one.

Sidestepping

- In the top right corner of the next available page in your journal, write the date and time of this practice you are now beginning. In the top left corner, write "Following My In-Tell."

- Lie back in *shavasana* with your head positioned to the east or south. Then hover still in waiting for your practice to begin. Have no plan. Take no stand. Let freedom be your flow. Let freedom be your steed to ride. Let freedom let you know. Then *do* what comes to you to *do* to *be* in *being* more—to build a faith in you to do what lets your spirit soar.

Example: As soon as we close our eyes and we are first feeling the absence of "something to do," *being* rises up to hold us in stillness. In this stillness, we feel confident the thing to *do* is to remain in this stillness. Yet as soon we make this decision, there comes a distraction. Suddenly, it's just there—distraction. And we are consumed by it. As soon as we become aware we are distracted, we sense the thing to *do* is regulate our breathing. "Ah yes, that works," we think to ourselves. And so we stay with this regulated breathing.

After about five minutes of this, our breath feels like it wants to pause and rest. So we let it. We let the breath suspend itself in stillness until it wants to move again. During this breath suspension, we experience a noticeable bliss. "Ah yes," we think to ourselves. "Bliss is good." So we stay with it. We stay with our bliss until—much to our dismay—we again become distracted. "Back to the breath," we think. And back to the breath we go until we are again feeling blissful. Soon enough, however, there she is again—distraction. This time, however, she is distant—too distant to consume us. So, we ignore her. In this sublime ignorance of distraction, our bliss holds us undistracted.

Now, as we sense ourselves becoming so accustomed to our bliss we can't even feel it building, we begin to fall into a sleep-like complacency. Yet, just as we are about to sink below waking consciousness, a powerful thrust of energy erupts within us to flood up from our body into our head. In response to this upward thrust, our skull tilts back a little. Our eyes roll in and up. The high eee shrills. And the inner Aum howls its wind sound.

As our heady energy intensifies, all we can do is work to hold awareness centered, even though the energy we are experiencing is too powerful to feel blissful. After about a minute of this, this energy begins to spread. And as it spreads, it begins to feel blissful again. Yet this bliss is different from the bliss we felt before. It has an electricity about it.

Just as we are starting to relish this new blissful energy, it stops feeling blissful as it again starts flooding up. Now this flooding-up is coming in groups of pulses interspersed by periods of stillness. During the pulses, there is a feeling of intensifying power. During the periods of stillness, there is a feeling of intensifying bliss. The pulses propel the energy *up*. The stillness's pull the energy *in*. This in-and-up rhythm of energy-movement continues until, finally, the pulsing stops and there is only stillness. After some time we are realizing we are coming back into consciousness, having been away.

- When you ready, sit up and open your journal. Under your title, "Following My In-Tell," record your reflections having worked with your guru of intuitive intelligence to penetrate within.

A note: Our intellect is not always intelligent. A truly *intelligent* thought will always be an *in-tell agent*—an *agent* of intuition's *in-tell*—while a thought produced by the *intellect* will too often *elect* to ignore that *in-tell*. An *intelligent* perception—even at its worst—is at least an agreement of intuition and logic. By contrast, an *intellectual* perception—even at its best—is but an excess of memory manipulated by learned and repeated patterns of thinking, perhaps sprinkled with a bit of intuition getting through any way it can.

99
The I's

The many false identities of the one and only Self

As we prepare to shift and simplify our focus from soul evolution to spiritual involution, we become aware of the ties we have forged with the mind of manifestation through a spiderlike hold we have fixed upon a multitude of "I's."

Just as any yoga based on a concept of soul *evolution* could be characterized as a path of transmuting desire, a path of transcending fear or a path of resolving karma, so could a yoga of *involution* be characterized as a non-path of side-stepping out of desire, fear and karma into a final withdrawal of awareness from all of its many subsidiary "I's." According to its use, each of these add-on "I's" is conscious, subconscious or superconscious.

A conscious "I" is an out-front personality we seek to intentionally establish in our conscious state of mind for the sake of functioning, as we would prefer, in a physical body on the physical plane. This external personality, a version of us we would most like other people to see, has many faces—one for family life, another for work, perhaps several for social events, and many more for the negotiation of a variety of everyday functions. If this conscious "I," with all of its many faces, is overly important to us and we are completely identified with it, we will be "self-conscious" to a fault, dangerously vulnerable to external influences and generally unaware of or unreceptive to internal guidance.

Through our yoga practice, this most external "I" changes quite a bit. By the time we have readied ourselves for a completely internalized yoga, we see this "I" as something separate—like a set of clothes we wear only when we are performing certain tasks.

A *subconscious "I"* consists of a largely secret disposition that forms itself by itself from the substance of unresolved karma, unfulfilled desire, misunderstood experience and unfaced fear. Because even we can only understand this version of ourselves in bits and pieces as it sporadically pops up and out of our subconscious into our conscious mind, we have little control over it. Because we lack this control, this private "I" is an identity we generally try to keep hidden—even from ourselves. Through yoga or any regime of practice that motivates us to "face ourselves," our *subconscious "I's"* gradually become exposed and polished away to nothing. Before this polishing gets done, however, the messes these "I's" have made constitute our greatest obstacles on a quest for the Realization of our truest "I."

A *superconscious "I"* is the deepest sense of self we can have in the world of time, form and space. This inner *"I"* is *that self* that's attuned to *the Self* through *being*. In this superconscious identity, we experience ourselves as the existence, consciousness and bliss of *Satchitananda*. When we are looking at the world of manifestation through this "I," we see that world from its core. Although this self is a most stable "I," it can seem obscure, for it stands in the background of our life behind those veils we ourselves have created through our overactive conscious individuality and our unresolved subconscious nature.

As our conscious and subconscious "I's" become soaked and thus purified in a working relationship with our superconscious "I," our three "I's" become one. In this oneness of "I's," evolution ends for involution to begin, as the *self* of "I" becomes the *Self* of all, again and again.

100
Deidentifying
Relinquishing false identities

In this practice, entitled "Deidentifying," we will be focusing upon relinquishing our identification with external "I's"—even those external "I's" that are functional and helpful.

As we concentrate our way into meditation, we strive to temporarily ignore as many of our external "I's" as we can. When the "I" we use at our job steps in to distract us with a question or a problem, we ask that "I" to wait, or we deal with it directly and immediately for a polite amount of time before respectfully requesting it to leave us alone for an hour or so. When the "I" we use at home tries to interrupt us with a reminder of a household chore that "just has to be done right now," again, we either put that "I" on hold or we expedite a handling of its consternation so we can get back to our temporary withdrawal from external responsibilities. Yet when we come out of our specified time of inner retreat to jump back into everyday life, we realize those "I's"—with all their questions and all their problems—have not gone away nor will they, so long as we stay externalized.

The deeper we delve into an introspective yoga, the more obvious it becomes that any *identification* we establish with an externalized "I"—even an "I" that is helpfully functional—inhibits our attainment of Savikalpa and Nirvikalpa Samadhi. This more accurate perception of the innate illusoriness of *identifying* with any "I" placed anywhere but in *awareness* or *Self* is simply our hard working intuition leading us along a path that looks less and less like a path the further we follow it.

Somewhere just before this path of *evolution* morphs into a non-path of *involution*, we see that suffering can only exist if there is a sufferer, just as a path can only exist if there is a path follower. In this seeing, the all of our yoga coalesces in the *now* to allow an ultimate merging of we into one—into the "I" of all.

In the following practice of "Deidentifying," we will prepare for involution by working in a practical way to back out of our many subsidiary "I's" right *now*.

Deidentifying

- In the top right corner of the next available page in your journal, write the date and time of this practice you are now beginning. In the top left corner, write "An Impersonal Plan."

- Let your own intuition guide your preparation for *samyama*. Make yourself ready for a period of deep introspection.

- When you feel the time is right, lie back in *shavasana* with your head positioned to the east or south and sink into *being*. After about five minutes, *choose* to observe "a personal problem." Once your chosen problem stands before you, clearly stated in *personal* terms, ask: "Who are the "I"s sharing the weight of this problem?"

A note: Say, for instance, your personal statement of the problem you have chosen to face is: "I barely have enough money to live."
    Obviously, the first "I" experiencing the weight of this problem will be the "I" centered in the physical body, for it is the physical body that will most immediately suffer if there is not enough money to pay for the basic necessities of physical life like food, shelter and clothes. When you are *identifying* with this "I," you might become understandably yet excessively concerned for your physical well-being.
    A second "I" experiencing the weight of this problem might be the "I" centered in that out-front character you would like others to think you are. When you are *identifying* with this "I," you might quite understandably feel an excessive inclination to cover up your destitution by appearing to be more financially stable than you are.
    A third "I" experiencing the weight of this problem might be an "I" centered in a largely secret disposition comprised of unresolved karma, unfulfilled desires, misunderstood experiences and unfaced fears. When you are *identifying* with this "I," you could—depending upon the specific structure of your subconscious—find yourself churning and bubbling with negative emotional feelings, like anger, resentment, envy and depression.

- Once you have isolated the external "I"s struggling with the burden of the problem you have chosen to solve," ask your intuition: "Which of these "I's" can help solve this problem?"

A note: With regard to our example problem stated personally as: "I barely have enough money to live," neither the "I" concerned only with out-front appearances nor the "I" preoccupied with unresolved karma can be of any assistance, for these "I's" themselves pose problems needing solutions. The "I" identifying with the physical body, however, *can* be helpful. It can set the physical parameters of its poverty dilemma. It can specify precisely how much money the body it is living in needs to feel secure in a given physical circumstance.

- Once you have isolated the most helpful external "I," take what it has to offer and release it as you pull back into awareness-aware-of-itself. When you have maintained awareness aware of itself long enough to feel the bliss of *being*, focus again upon your problem, this time from the "I" of watcher awareness. From within this high "I," restate your problem in *impersonal* terms. Then practice *samyama* on that impersonal problem statement.

A note: An *impersonal* but fact-filled rewording of our example poverty problem, which was *personally* worded: "I barely have enough money to live," might read something like this: "Within a single year, this body will need $100,000 so that $20,000 can be set aside for retirement and $80,000 can be provided for a modest life in a New York City apartment." Upon the foundation of an impersonal and factually rich problem statement like this, our superconscious intuition can build a practical plan for making a hundred thousand dollars a year.

    As you approach a *samyama* on your chosen problem, know the "I" you are is *awareness*—your superconscious self. Since awareness is the only "I" that can perform *samyama*, any preoccupation with any other "I" will make *samyama* impossible.

- When you feel the time is right, sit up and open your journal to write, under your title: "An Impersonal Plan," a summation of the strategy your *samyama* revealed for impersonally solving the "personal" problem you decided to face.

101
Transparency
The absence of personal presence

If we are going to pull back from the world of external responsibility to practice a rarefied yoga within, we must be reasonably sure everything will be okay while we're away—at least to the extent that awareness has the freedom it needs to become significantly internalized.

As we work toward preparing ourselves for internal retreat, we'll feel an intuitive inclination to move as transparently as possible in everyday life. In this context, moving transparently means living tactfully, as in flowing with the river of life, letting come what comes, letting go what goes. We'll know we've caught the spirit of this transparent living when we find ourselves easily settled in *being*, doing a lot with the feeling of doing nothing.

The underlying principles we are working with here are that change is the only constant in external life, that external life is subordinate to and dependant upon inner life, and that inner life—centered in *being*—is the stable origin of that externalized existence in which *being* is so dominated by *doing* life seems unstable.

When we are flowing with the river of life, the banks we are flowing between are opposites—*all* opposites, as in pleasure and pain, good and bad, right and wrong. If we can bring ourselves to go with the flow of this river as it surges between its banks, we'll find ourselves moving transparently along a *middle path,* evading the creation of avoidable karmas while expediting the resolution of unavoidable karmas.

To live transparently our conscious and subconscious "I's" must humbly offer up their sense of importance or prominence to the "I" of awareness. As a result of this surrender, our many outer "I's" are freed to flow in sync with the one and only inner "I."

Once our outer nature has become transparent, our inner nature becomes apparent. As our inner nature becomes apparent in outer life, patterns of living are in less need of external controls, for we are increasingly guided by an evolving energy that is forever moving in and up. In this in-and-up flow of force, we are not so inclined to pull back into thought and memory to pigeonhole what we are experiencing as kundalini rising, chakras opening or anything else. We are not so inclined because we don't care about naming or explaining what's happening. All we care about is following what's happening wherever it goes, especially when we perceive it is going *in and up*—all by itself.

As we strive to stay with this self-propelled involution of life force, we occasionally get pulled out into the way we were before. When this happens, we return to the practice of external yogas until we're back following again the inner energy that seems to move on its own.

And so we go on like this. Caring little for what got us where we are or whether we are better or worse for having done what we have done thus far, we enjoy a mystical freedom born of living in a faith and confidence only the nameless feeling we are feeling can give. And as we are made to soar within on the wings of this feeling, we reach an impenetrable peak that can only be sustained in stillness.

102

Gracefulizing

Learning from the past for the future, now

In this practice, entitled "Gracefulizing," we will study our past to locate patches of non-flow—congested spans of time when we were so unnecessarily involved with outer life we could not feel those ever-present inner *qualities of being* like *bliss, love, stillness, balance, peace, power, rapture, joy and awareness.*

Once we have located these memories of locked-up congestion, we will seek to mentally relive them *with* rather than *against* the flow of the river of life. In this mental modification of a negative past into a rehearsal for a positive future, we will prepare ourselves to live *now* without getting stuck on life's banks for lack of grace in dealing with people and circumstance.

Gracefulizing

- In the top right corner of the next available page in your journal, write the date and time of this practice you are now beginning. In the top left corner, write "My Sweet Grace."

- Guide yourself through a preparation for deep introspection.

- Lie back in *shavasana* with your head positioned to the east or south, tune into *being* and simply allow "difficult" memories to surface. As these memories arise, allow intuition to reveal ways the experiences those memories hold could have been lived more gracefully.

A note: In a practical sense, "grace" means "elegance." In a Western religious sense, a phrase commonly used to define grace is, "the favor of God." In an Eastern mystical sense, "grace" can mean "permission," *consent* given to begin certain activities; or "protection," *shielding* provided against trial and tribulation; or "revelation," an *unveiling* allowing an unobstructed experience of inner realms hitherto unknown; or "absolution," *exoneration* from past misdeeds; or "blessings," special *gifts of spiritual energy* bestowed in acknowledgement of good deeds done or inner unfoldment attained.

Taking pains to move through outer life with outer grace—as in living skillfully, transparently and respectfully—earns the blessings of inner grace in all of its various forms, for grace expressed externally springs forth from a humility that molds a most deserving recipient of an internal grace.

Humility—too little extolled in life—is a superconscious power yielding a unique ability to move transparently in the physical world.

The benefit of humility is not obscure because it is not obvious. It is obscure because it is ignored. It is because the benefit of humility is ignored that humiliation exists. Although humility finally appreciated through humiliation usually comes with some extra baggage (like anger, resentment and a diminished sense of healthy self esteem), it *is* humility nonetheless—humility acquired the hard way.

Humility gained in any way is an asset in spiritual life. Sooner or later, in some way, we all become humble. And within that humility, however and wherever we find it, we stand naked in a rain of grace.

- When you are ready, sit up and open your journal. Under your title, "My Sweet Grace," record your edited versions of those memories you have now remolded with your own sweet grace.

103
Simplicity
A condition of clarity

Life surrounding the yoga of involution is uncomplicated. In that life, there is a general settling back into a sense of the oneness pervading all things. As we gravitate toward this consciousness of oneness, thinking becomes unembellished enough for us to see life as intuition sees it: a repetition of variations on prototypal themes.

From this simple perspective, a body that is fat is simply one version of a body that could be thin, because there is only one prototypal body. Or the anger that impels one man to kill another is simply one version of an anger that might impel another man to honk his horn when he gets cut off in traffic, because there is only one prototypal anger. This perspective allows us to catch the crux of manifest life at its blueprint foundation where we can glean its patterns and interrelationships.

When manifest life starts looking like an entirety that could be experienced—one prototypal piece at a time—through a succession of physical lives, we will have entered the thought realm of speculation. If we go one step further to accept into belief the idea we are souls evolving by experiencing everything life has to offer through the process of reincarnation, we will have moved even more deeply into speculation.

Philosophies and religions are built upon speculation, speculation consisting of theories that are—like the patterns of life—variations on themes. Although it is true that even speculation must work within the bounds of a certain preset, prototypal blueprint, there is within that blueprint infinite potential for variation.

For instance, although both Hindus and Buddhists believe in

reincarnation, they do not agree on what reincarnation is. While most Hindus accept the speculation that we are souls evolving through reincarnation, Buddhists do not. Buddhists do not acknowledge that *souls* reincarnate. According to their most commonly accepted belief system, what moves forward from life to life is not a soul but a one continuum of experience propelled by the momentum of its own cause and effect.

In yoga—as it is practiced by Hindus, Buddhists or anyone else—speculation is valuable as long as it inspires us to keep practicing yoga. When the fact of our own experience provides us with all the inspiration we need to continue our inner search, we have little use for speculation. Once awareness is relieved of its need for speculation, it is freer to move more deeply into that which it has not yet experienced.

In the aftermath of a profound meditation transcending speculation, we see ourselves as a seamless part of a manifest existence that is what it is with no particular need for our interpretation or judgment of it. If, having arrived at this inner sight of a "seer," we get pulled out into an excitement of fear or desire, we intuitively know what to do: pull back within. And as we retreat within, we sense again—without a lot of laborious thought—how desire can evolve beyond its urge to surge, just as fear can ascend above its need to be.

104
Differentiating
Looking past life to death

In this practice, entitled "Differentiating," a simple yoga will help us distinguish between conceptual speculation and experiential fact as we ponder the ultimate source of both.

Differentiating

- In the top right corner of the next available page in your journal, write the date and time of this practice you are now beginning. In the top left corner, write "Who Survives?"

- Guide yourself through a preparation for deep introspection.

- When you are ready, sit in *sukhasana* facing east or south or lie in *shavasana* with your head positioned to the east or south as you perform *samyama* on the following set of two questions: "When death comes, who survives? Who will I be when the body dies?"

A note: As you attempt this *samyama*, you can expect your first set of responses to occur *consciously, subconsciously* and *superconsciously*.

If you have had previous metaphysical training and are open to mystical thought, your *subconscious* programming will probably allow at least a partially positive response to these questions, which will in turn spur a positive *conscious* response. If the reverse of this is true and you have not been exposed to mystical teachings, your first *subconscious* and *conscious* responses might be negative.

Yet even if both your *subconscious* and *conscious* responses to mystical questions in general are mostly positive, there will probably be at least *some* angst in your first reaction to these brazen queries. For this reason, it is advisable to preface your *samyama* with a yoga that brings you all the way into the *superconscious* bliss of *being*. Then, when you ask yourself from that inner platform of relative stability, "When death comes, who survives? Who will I be when the body dies?" you will be in a position to view your good, bad and mixed responses from the inside-out rather than the outside-in.

Certainly, your *superconsciousness* will perceive these questions as a motivation to dive more and more deeply into the bliss of *being,* for the deepest part of you knows *being* and its bliss will never die and will thus be there waiting for you as an ultimate refuge of peace when the time has come for your physical body to pass away.

Yet because this diving within can feel like a dying of sorts as you willingly and intentionally relinquish your grip on all you previously assumed was real, it can be an extreme sort of experience that requires some conscious and subconscious adjustment as it occurs.

Reflecting this adjustment, the concentration portion of your *samyama* might understandably consist of at least some wrangling with learned assumptions that previously brought you a sense of security. If you should decide during this wrangling that some or all of those beliefs need to be changed or dropped, you might go one step further to consider the radical possibility that no belief can offer a permanent safe haven of changeless security in manifest life—not because beliefs are not stabilizing, but because *there is no permanent safe haven of changeless security in manifest life.*

- After about a half hour or when you feel the time is right, relax out of your *samyama* back into the simple bliss of *being.* Then sit up in *sukhasana,* open your journal and under your title: "Who Survives?" record your answers to the questions: "When death comes, who survives? Who will I be when the body dies?"

105
Final Focus
The last use of thought

No one would deny the physical world of time, form and space looks plenty real while we are in it. Yet even the slightest effort to withdraw from it can reveal just how entirely the very existence of any *thing* is contingent upon our awareness of it.

When we are undistractedly aware of a flower, nothing else exists—literally. In that *now*—which is really the only time there is—there is only a flower. In another *now* or in the *now* of another awareness, the world of time, form and space will be perceived as something else, but that something else will always be comprised of nothing more or less than what any one awareness is aware of right *now.*

When we are completely immersed in the business of surviving life in a physical body, thoughts of past and future overshadow an awareness of *now* because we are extremely externalized. Consumed in a fear of a past and a desire for a future, all we care about is escaping the former as we chase the latter—life after life after life.

Yet somewhere in this process, as our knowledge from experience releases us from fear and desire enough for the cyclical nature of our physical existence to become apparent, we start to catch the idea that every detail of our life is playing itself out on some sort of preset, universal grid. Because this grid seems to maintain itself by itself without our detailed understanding of it and regardless of all the erratic things we do, we are left to assume we do not need to know how, when, where or why this grid was structured—nor do we even need to believe it exists—for it to be what it is and do what it does.

If knowing this does not fully appease our wanting to know more, we might be inclined to speculate reasons why life is the way it is. Eventually, however, the struggle and strain of our own life dramas drives us toward just letting life flow and flowing with life. Once we have become comfortable in this flow, which precludes a search for the "meaning of life," evolution moves quickly toward involution.

Those who have withdrawn into Nirvikalpa Samadhi know there is a realizable source of even existence and consciousness. They know this because they have been there. In this knowing there is no speculation. The Self Realization following a Nirvikalpa Samadhi is an experiential fact of looking back at coming back into time, form and space, from its timeless, formless and spaceless origin and realizing, at that point of return, a full absorption of awareness in Self has just occurred.

Before this full absorption has come to pass, we make our way within on faith—a faith born of what we have learned from our own experience. This faith based upon experience allows us to withdraw from complicated thought to simple thought to that *being* that is forever pulling our self into its Self.

The transition of the focus of our awareness from thought to the energy behind thought occurs as a result of our perception that no willed manipulation of thought can force a Nirvikalpa Samadhi to occur. With this simple perception we release awareness from unnecessary thought enough to realize the force of life has a mind of its own that can lead us within to its end of ends should we be willing followers.

106
Deepening
Seeking the source of being

In this practice, entitled "Deepening," we will intentionally invite a merger of *we* into *one* by directly seeking the source of *being*.

As we have already discovered, *being* can be experienced indirectly as the background of *doing*, or directly as the wellspring of *love, stillness, balance, peace, power, rapture, awareness, intuition* and more. Now, we will seek the *source* of *being* with full faith we will intuitively know how to accomplish this as we deepen our *being* experience.

As helpful as conjecture might have been way back when our need was to heed what we perceived to be a vague inner call, such speculation is now an obstacle and not a need at all. What's needed now, we know, is a simple focus on *being* with *an intent to pierce that being to its core*.

Deepening

- In the top right corner of the first page of your journal, write the date and time of this practice you are now beginning. In the top left corner, write the title, "My Depth of Being."

- Guide yourself through a preparation for deep introspection.

- When you are ready, sit in *sukhasana* facing east or south or lie in *shavasana* with your head positioned to the east or south as you focus upon going *inside* the bliss of *being*. To facilitate this internalization of awareness, slightly close and cross your eyes to focus upon the tip of your nose. As you begin to feel the centering of nonphysical force this physical action stimulates, try to purposely accentuate that centering by crossing your eyes further until you feel them closing with an inclination to roll in and up.

A Note: This syncing of a physical eye movement with an internalization of non-physical awareness is much harder to describe than it is to do, although "doing it" takes a little practice. So, start your implementation of this exercise slowly and easily by holding your eyes focused on the tip of your nose for only a few seconds at a time.

Breath control can assist in this effort. *Ujjayi* is especially effective when performed as follows:

On a breath measured nine-counts-in-hold-one/nine-counts-out-hold-one, cross your eyes to focus upon the tip of your nose during the in-breath, then release your eyes to a forward gaze during the out-breath. Once your cross-eyed gaze has become stabilized, maintain it during both the in-breath and the out-breath.

When you feel the inclination to take the next step in this process, roll your eyes in and up during the in-breath, then back to a cross-eyed focus upon the tip of your nose during the out-breath. Do this until you can hold your eyes in and up for both the in-breath and the out-breath.

- At some point during your practice of internalizing the focus of your eyes, you will experience an upward pulse of energy that seems to occur of its own accord and in its own timing. When you feel this pulse, follow it—even if it means dropping your structured breath control. As the duration of this pulse begins to lengthen, try to hold your awareness poised in that lengthening.

A Note: Again, this is easier done than said—and easily done, for all you are doing is following a powerful flow of energy with a sensitive submissiveness.

- When you ready, sit up and open your journal. Under your title, "My Depth of Being," describe your experience of "Deepening."

107
The End
The final yoking of yoga

Logic says knowing who we are should be fundamentally obvious. Yet it's not. The fact it's not indicates there is something powerfully illusory about what we've become involved with by getting born into a physical body—something beyond logic's reach.

When logic finally figures out it cannot figure out this ultimate identity of ours, it turns to intuition and asks, "What am I to do?" To this sincere query, intuition responds, "Take a break, you've done enough."

Once fear and desire have receded enough for excessive thought to diminish enough for us to discover that life has an innate capacity to turn its energies in upon itself by itself, and we have completely given ourselves over to this inwardly directed movement of primal life force, we can see that nothing known, not even wisdom, has much bearing upon the final yoga of involution.

We can also see our only part in this last yoking of yoga is to simply be still, and in that stillness, surrender ourselves—our awareness—into what feels like a centered intensity of power that grows in its strength because of our blending with it. Once this inner energy with which we are merging reaches a certain level of intensity, it starts to pulse like a physical heart. At times, in fact, this pulsing occurs in sync with the beating of our physical heart. At other times it flutters like a bird or holds itself poised at its peak.

The surge of this pulse is the lunging of our awareness in and up to an intensity of consciousness that is new for us. The pause following this pulse allows us to adjust to that new intensity as well as to ready ourselves for another lung in and up. With each adjustment we make in the peace of a pause, we prepare for lunge on a pulse. And with each lunge on a pulse, we land in a new pause of peace as we move progressively in and up, pulse-by-pulse and peace-by-peace.

While we are experiencing this intense pulsing and pausing of energy, memories will still rise on the periphery of our consciousness. Yet, as surely as these memories will rise, so will they fall. And when they have all finally fallen, all that will remain is that pulse and pause of pure life force, until—after one of those recuperating pauses of peace—there is a coming back from beyond.

And in that coming back, we know nothing of where we were, nor do we know any more than we did before about where we are now. All we know now is that what seemed unalterably fixed is not.

In a practical sense, the most significant change that occurs in the aftermath of a spiritual "coming back" like this is a shifting of life's priorities. In the fresh, new perspective that dawns after a genuine merging of self in Self, the inner comes first and the outer comes second. Everything we see, we see intuitively. And we can't avoid this. Every decision we make is dictated by the voice of our conscience that now can't be ignored. In the guidance of this inner voice, we are moved by an innate sense of righteousness to avoid a downward pull of consciousness even as we live in a flow of awareness that is free to see from all points of view in a love that feels at one with all and a wisdom that knows nothing at all but what it needs to know *now*.

108
Pulsing
Following the upward surge of life force

In this practice, entitled "Pulsing," we will be working to hold awareness at the center of the rhythmic surging-up of energy that naturally occurs during the latter portion of a prolonged yoga session focused primarily upon a deep piercing of *being*. So, get set. This session will last a long time—at least three hours. Yet it will be three hours packed full of involvements designed to keep you aware in the *now* with no laborious sense of slowly passing time.

Unlike the other practices described in this book, this "Pulsing" is not a sequential procedure. It is a set of yoga exercises (already learned and practiced) established as anchor-actions for you to work with as you strive to hold awareness hovered near the center of the power of your life long enough for that center to reveal its source.

If you feel a need to set a formal goal and procedure for this practice, let both that goal and procedure be *being*, for you are now working with a yoga of involution in which there is no goal but the goal of being what you already are and no procedure but the procedure of being what you already are.

Although the five exercise options presented below are listed in sequence, they are not meant to be practiced sequentially, exclusively. Each is available to be used according to a need felt *now*. The only stipulation is they should all be used.

As you embark upon this three-hour practice, allow your intuition to either jump freely or flow smoothly among your five exercise options. When distractions arise during your involvement with one of these practices, simply "jump" to another one. In this jumping, let intuition lead. If, on the other hand, one of these practices begins to morph into another of its own accord, simply follow that morphing with the flow of your awareness.

Pulsing

- In the top right corner of the next available page in your journal, write the date and time of this practice you are now beginning. In the top left corner, write "My In and Up."

- Once you have located a three-hour span of time and a ten-by-ten foot piece of empty and private floor space (with a rug or mat for *hatha yoga*), begin your practice of "Pulsing" by jumping or flowing within the "grid" of the five exercise options laid out below. Because these five exercises have already been fully explained, their descriptions will be truncated here.

1 • Preparing body: Lead yourself through *hatha yoga* postures you feel will prepare your physical body for meditation.

2 • Preparing mind: Perform the following six steps:

1. Sit in *sukhasana*, facing south or east, or lie in *shavasana* with your head positioned to the south or east. 2. Establish *ujjayi* breath con-

trol—nine counts in, hold one; nine counts out, hold one. 3. Feel the natural warmth of the physical body. 4. Feel the primal life force flowing through the nervous system of the physical body. 5. Feel the energy of the spine. 6. Pull your awareness from the feeling of spinal energy back into awareness aware of itself.

3 • Finding pulse: Sitting in *sukhasana* facing east or south or lying in *shavasana* with your head positioned to the east or south, gently cross your half-open eyes to focus upon the tip of your nose. As you feel a centering of nonphysical force, accentuate that centering by slightly intensifying the crossing of your eyes until you feel your eyes closing to roll in and up.

4 • Following pulse: Sitting in *sukhasana* facing east or south, or lying in *shavasana* with your head positioned to the east or south, follow the spontaneous upward pulse of energy flowing through the spine and up into the head. As the duration of this pulse begins to lengthen, stay with that lengthening. Try to hold it.

5 • Releasing in fire: When a negative memory involving another person arises, write—on a separate piece of paper—everything you can remember about that experience. After you have done this, compose a letter to the person with whom you had this experience (also on a separate sheet of paper). In that letter try to fully and freely express all of the negative emotion you feel. Don't hold back. Be explicit. When you are finished, burn both your description of the experience and your letter to the person involved.

Some Notes: This three hour yoga session will provide enough time for you to experience a repetitious cycling of physical, mental and emotional interruptions emerging both consciously and subconsciously. If these upheavals are negative, they will likely induce disagreeable thoughts and feelings. If they are positive, they can be expected to generate pleasurable thoughts and feelings. Physical, mental or emotional, negative or positive, conscious or subconscious, all of these intrusions upon your focus are distractions and must be dealt with as such.

With respect for the formidable potency of distraction, this nonsequential practice of "Pulsing" is intended to be flexibly efficient.

If, for instance, your awareness is nicely locked in and up as you are following the procedure described in "4 • Following pulse," yet you are also aware of an increasingly acute ache in your upper back, you can jump to the procedure described in "1 • Preparing Body" to become physically renewed for a continuing of your practice.

If, on the other hand, you are methodically working with "3 • Finding pulse," and you are suddenly accosted by a painful memory of an argument you had with a relative ten years ago, you can "jump" to "5 • Burning in fire" if there is a lot of emotion involved, or "2 • Preparing mind" if all you need is a reorienting of focus.

As you proceed, you will experience a simplification of this practice—especially as steps 1, 2 and 5 drop away for lack of need; and step 3 merges more and more with step 4.

• After at least three hours, open your journal. Under your title, "My In and Up," record your reflections upon internalizing awareness during an extended yoga session. As you write, please consider the following four mystical principles as they relate to your experiences during your practice of "Pulsing:"

1. All that prevents a conscious recognition of superconsciousness is the confusion of an unresolved subconscious working in conjunction with an undisciplined conscious state of mind.

2. When the conscious and the superconscious states of mind yoke together through a purified subconscious, they create a vacuum in which awareness gets pulled in and up.

3. When the in-and-up movement of awareness has been cultivated long enough for awareness to have become adjusted to its own highest intensity, a merging with Self is near.

4. Self Realization occurs during the retrospective experience of coming back from the one and only non-experience of Nirvikalpa Samadhi to *realize* experiencer, experience and experienced merged as one at the timeless, formless and spaceless source of manifestation.

- Finally, write in your journal, "Free Writing 6." Then close your eyes. Visualize a vacant space in front of your face. Allow that space to be filled with whatever comes. And whatever comes, open your eyes and write it down.

    Let what you write be the inspiration for Chapter 109 of this book, which is now your book, the book only you can write about the life only you can live as the Self of your self.

We wish you well.

Afterwords

That Self of one is Self of all.
That Self is Godly too.
What law of man could stand so tall,
That such might seem untrue?

In new lives made, the first good stretch
Of time is spent in doubt.
Yet if we're firm, we'll find we fetch
A secret, inside out.

Perseverance is the key
In piercing blinding veils.
To live in continuity
Is what this life entails.

That Self of one is Self of all.
That Self is Godly too.
What law of man could stand so tall,
That such might seem untrue?

At first, it's just a bliss that comes
And goes, but will not stay.
Yet if we're firm till mind succumbs
We'll find we've found a way.

There is no test of best or worst.
There is no one to win.
Those running last may come in first,
To yield a saint from sin.

That Self of one is Self of all.
That Self is Godly too.
What law of man could stand so tall,
That such might seem untrue?

Replenish pleasures of the head
Once debts stand paid in full.
Sit rocklike still, like living dead
Against the downward pull.

Higher still we fill and thrill.
We give our best and more.
We merge within — stone-locked and still —
We seek within the core.

That Self of one is Self of all.
That Self is Godly too.
What law of man could stand so tall,
That such might seem untrue?

A source of force is hard to feel
Unlike it's falling power.
This force of source, of course, is real,
Atop its mighty tower.

For it falls hard from highest heights
To land upon the dead
To bring to life brand new insights
Inside each newborn head.

That Self of one is Self of all.
That Self is Godly too.
What law of man could stand so tall,
That such might seem untrue?

New ways of thinking must evolve
New fish within the sea
Of consciousness that seeks to solve
Lost riddles of the free.

The war of worlds is won on one
Of two great battle grounds
Where night-bright moon and noon-day sun
Seek dusk-and-dawn-like sounds.

That Self of one is Self of all.
That Self is Godly too.
What law of man could stand so tall,
That such might seem untrue?

Thus night and day meet dusk and dawn
To stand on shores of peace.
Now twice as strong, they carry on
To gladly gain release.

Waters blending mighty force
To pool the best of all
Sets straight the steady, perfect course
Of souls thought bound to fall.

That Self of one is Self of all.
That Self is God in you.
What law of man could stand so tall,
That such might seem untrue?

GLOSSARY

Actinic The vibrational state of primal life force when it is functioning in the rarified superconscious substratum of manifestation.

Actinodic The vibrational state of primal life force when it is functioning as a mixture of *odic* and *actinic* force. When this *actinodic* force becomes strong, it acts as a conduit for the flow of superconsciousness out into externalized consciousness.

Adharma The opposite of *dharma*.

Advaita Vedanta A yogic philosophy, summarized as follows:
   God as Brahman is the only reality; the world of time, form and space is illusory; suffering is a consequence of ignorance; liberation is the eradication of ignorance in knowledge; and knowledge is understanding the true nature of God and the world.

Ahimsa "Non-violence."

Ajna chakra Sixth of seven chakras. Located in the soul body in a position corresponding to nerve ganglia between and about an inch above the two eyes of the physical body. It is through this sixth *ajna chakra* that psychic abilities are awakened.

Anahata chakra Fourth of seven chakras. Located in the soul body in a position corresponding to nerve ganglia near the physical heart. Through the refined energy of this *anahata chakra* we gain more than a periodic access to intuition, and through that access cognize a oneness binding the *all* of manifest existence. This sense of oneness blooms into a compassionate love that inspires selflessness over selfishness.

Ananda Bliss.

Anandamaya kosha The soul body.

Annamaya kosha The physical body.

Antarloka The astral plane of existence, which includes an upper region called *Devaloka* and a lower region called *Naraka*.

Anuloma viloma pranayama Known as "alternate nostril breathing" in English. Instructions for the performance of this breath control:

1. Sitting in *sukhasana,* rest your left hand on your left knee in any fashion that is comfortable for you. Then, close your eyes and curl the first (index) and second (middle) fingers of your right hand down the inside of your right thumb until the nails of those fingers rest against the base of that thumb.

2. Squeeze your left nostril shut with your ring finger as you breathe in slowly and deeply through your right nostril. At the peak of a full inhalation, release your ring-finger block of the left nostril and close your right nostril with your thumb as you breathe out slowly through your left nostril.

3. In a reverse of step 2 above, keep your right nostril closed with your thumb as you breathe in slowly and deeply through your left nostril. At the peak of this inhalation, release your thumb block of the right nostril and close your left nostril with your ring finger as you breathe out slowly through your right nostril.

Anuloma means "with flow" and *viloma* means "against flow." *Anuloma viloma pranayama* centers awareness in the power of the spine through a control of breath that equalizes the flow of air through the left and right nostrils.

The right nostril is governed by the sympathetic nervous system and corresponds to the left, masculine-aggressive, heating and "thinking" side of the brain. The left nostril is governed by the parasympathetic nervous system and corresponds to the right, feminine-passive, cooling and "feeling" side of the brain.

The sympathetic nervous system, part of the autonomic nervous system, mobilizes the body's resources under stress. It consists of nerves arising from ganglia near the center of the spinal cord. The parasympathetic nervous system, also part of the autonomic nervous system, aids the body in its ability to rest and recuperate. It consists of nerves arising from the brain and the lower end of the spinal cord.

When the sympathetic and parasympathetic nervous systems are allowed to work in close cooperation, the masculine and feminine nerve currents find balance. This establishes the internal equilibrium necessary for an easy ascension of awareness up through the soul body's seven chakras.

Aparigraha "Non-selfishness."

Asana Literally, "Seat" or "posture." In *hatha yoga*, *asana* refers to any of numerous poses prescribed to balance and tune the subtle energies of mind and body for meditation and to promote health and longevity. *Asana* is the third step of *ashtanga yoga's* eight-step method and is said to have given rise to the formation and practice of *hatha yoga*.

Ashtanga yoga A eight-step mystical system of introspection conceived in India by Patanjali (200 BCE) to catalyze an understanding of life as a consequence of seeking life's source. In his book, the *Yoga Sutras*, Patanjali establishes "eight limbs" or steps to spiritual illumination: 1. *yamas* (restraints), 2. *niyamas* (observances), 3. *asana* (posture), 4. *pranayama* (breath control), 5. *pratyahara* (withdrawal), 6. *dharana* (concentration), 7. *dhyana* (meditation) and 8. *Samadhi* (mystic oneness). *Ashtanga yoga*, said to be the first recorded yoga method. It is also called *raja yoga*, the "king of yogas."

Asteya "Non-stealing."

Asuras Demons. Entities who are impure due to ignorance in contrast to *devas* who are pure entities due to wisdom. *Asuras* can and will become *devas* through the gradual cultivation of purity gained from enduring the consequences of misdeeds.

Aum The first of the *bija* mantras, *Aum* is a sound catalyzing transmutation—the refinement of lower energy up into higher energy. During the chanting of *Aum*, this upward development of energy can be felt quite literally as its first sound, "aa" (as in law), vibrates within the chest; its second sound, "oo" (as in zoo) vibrates in the throat; and its third sound, "mm" (pronounced with mouth closed and teeth lightly touching), vibrates in the head.

Bhakti yoga A method of yoga focused upon worshiping God as the creator of life, a practice said to have been derived from the fifth *niyama* of Patanjali's *ashtanga yoga* entitled *Ishvara pranidhana*, which means "devotion to a personal Lord."

Bhramari pranayama A breath control performed by inhaling slowly and deeply through the nose, then exhaling slowly while producing a humming sound. *Bhramari pranayama* is a blissful practice that assists in the toning and balancing of the pituitary, an endocrine gland about the size of a pea that hangs suspended in a small blood-filled cavity off the bottom of the hypothalamus at the base of the brain in the center of the skull. The humming of *bhramari pranayama* vibrates the blood in which the pituitary is positioned. This soothes that gland into revealing the bliss for which this discipline is famous.

Bhuloka The physical plane of existence.

Bija Literally, "Seed Sound." Specifically, a sound syllable of power that can be used alone as a "bija mantra," or with other sounds to form longer mantras in the same way that letters are combined to form words and words are combined to form sentences.

Brahmacharya Literally, "walking with God." Specifically, "chastity."

Brahmaloka The spiritual plane of existence.

Chakra Literally, "wheel." A spinning vortex of energy in the body of the soul that stimulates and governs the flow of a certain instinctive, intellectual or spiritual energy. There are many chakras. Seven are primary. Because these seven non-physical force centers coexist with seven nerve ganglia along the spinal column of the physical body, the physical body is generally used as a frame of reference for indicating chakra locations.

Chandra bedha pranayama A breath control restricting breathing so that air is inhaled through the left nostril and exhaled through the right nostril with the assistance of the fingers and thumb of the right hand. *Chandra* means "moon." Thus, *Chandra bedha pranayama* stimulates the right, feminine-passive, cooling and "feeling" side of the brain, which influences the left side of the body.

Darshan "Sight of the divine."

Devaloka The upper region of the *antarloka,* or astral plane.

Devas Literally, the "shining ones"—angels. Entities who are pure due to wisdom, in contrast to *asuras* who are impure due to ignorance.

Dharma Both a principle of life and a method of living that perceives and respects an inherent order within the all of manifest existence—an inherent order that includes an inherent way of living. In a practical sense, following dharma means moving *with* the flow of life, not *against* it, being passive or aggressive when necessary, neither when possible.

Gloaming In a yogic context, "gloaming" means intentionally sustaining the transitional consciousness that exists on the threshold of sleep.

Guru "Teacher."

Hatha yoga "Hatha" literally means "sun/moon." *Ha,* "sun," refers to a subtle nerve current in the soul body called the *pingala nadi.* This nerve current is masculine in nature. *Tha,* "moon," refers to a similar nerve current in the soul body, but one that is feminine in nature and called the *ida nadi.* The practices of *hatha yoga* include manipulating the body and controlling the breath to calm and harmonize the *ida* and *pingala nadis* so the *sushumna nadi* can become activated and the *kundalini* can rise. The *sushumna nadi* is the central psychic nerve current of the soul body that coexists with the spine in the physical body. Most veteran yogis agree that *hatha yoga* was derived from Patanjali's eight-step *ashtanga yoga*—specifically, its third step entitled "asana."

Ida nadi A psychic nerve current that is pink in color and flows down the left side of the soul body. This current is feminine in nature and radiates emotional energy.

Ishvara "Personal Lord." God as the primal soul.

Ishvara Pranidhana "Devotion to a personal Lord."

Japa "Repetition." In yoga, *japa* is regarded as a form of focus in which a repeated action is used to keep awareness from wandering and to achieve an aim intimated in the unique energy of the action being repeated. In this yogic context, the "action" of *japa* is usually the repetition of a mantra.

Japa yoga A yoga method focusing upon *mantra* repetition as a means of attaining the specific benefit offered by the mantra being repeated. This practice, sometimes referred to as *mantra yoga*, can be performed silently or aloud.

Jnana "Wisdom."

Karma Literally, "action." Specifically, the principle of action/reaction or cause/effect that requires us to learn *from life* by enduring the consequences of our actions *in life*. "A karma" refers to a specific reaction not yet resolved in understanding.

Karma yoga A yoga method of seeking Self through selfless service. Most veteran yogis agree *karma yoga* was derived from Patanjali's eight-step *ashtanga yoga*—specifically, its fifth *yama* of *Aparigraha*, "non-selfishness."

Kosha Literally, "body" or "sheath." According to the *Vedas*, man has five bodies: *anandamaya kosha,* the "body of bliss;" *vijnanamaya kosha*, the "body of cognition;" *manomaya kosha*, the "body of thought, will and wish;" *pranamaya kosha*, the "body of vital force;" and *annamaya kosha*, the "body of food."

Kriya yoga A yoga method emphasizing breath control, a system of breathing exercises so elaborate and complete within itself it offers a path to God Realization through *pranayama* alone. Most veteran yogis agree *kriya yoga* was derived from Patanjali's eight-step *ashtanga yoga* —specifically, its fourth step entitled "pranayama."

Kundalini Pure life force flowing through the *sushumna nadi*.

Kundalini yoga A yoga method consisting of specific techniques performed to deliberately arouse *kundalini* power and guide it up through the seven *chakras* of the soul body into spiritual illumination. A common practice of *kundalini yoga* consists of meditating upon the feeling of the power that gets aroused as a result of performing certain *hatha yoga* postures in conjunction with specifically designated breathing exercises—especially a breath control called the "breath of fire." This "breath of fire" is a fast, light and shallow "sniffing breath" in which the inhalation and exhalation are of equal length and force.

Madhyama "Unstruck sound." In this context, "unstruck" simply means "not audible." Also referred to as "anahatha."

Manipura chakra The third of seven chakras, located in the soul body in a position corresponding to the solar plexus of the physical body. Empowered by the *manipura chakra*, we develop the faculty of will.

Manomaya kosha The emotional body—sometimes referred to as the "instinctive body"—in which urges and desires are fulfilled through the application of intentional will.

Mantra Literally, "instrument of reflection." Specifically, "an empowered sound"—a sound used as a word meant to express a specific power, which is that word's "meaning."

Mantra japa The repetition of empowered sounds.

Muladhara chakra First of seven chakras, located in the soul body in a position corresponding to nerve ganglia at the base of the spine in the physical body. Through the power of this *muladhara chakra*, we learn to live in the physical world with a sense of stability born of habit patterns we establish in memory. These habit patterns ground us in a lifestyle that feels secure.

Nada "Sound." According to the *Vedas*—life first manifested out of Self as sound.

Nada nadi "Life force as sound."

Nada-nadi shakti The sound of life force heard as the *Aum*.

Nada yoga A yoga method sometimes described as "the art of listening." Although inspired by the *Vedic* teaching that life first manifested as sound, *nada yoga* developed primarily out of an appreciation for the perceivable reality that every manifest thing consists of a vibration registering as sound. In *nada yoga,* the sounds listened for and heard are classified into four categories: 1. *Vaikhari,* also referred to as "ahatha," is audible sound. 2. *Madhyama,* also called "anahatha," is "unstruck" sound. In this context, "unstruck" simply means "not audible." 3. *Pashyanta* is subconscious sound comprised of noise emanating from unresolved karma. 4. *Paranada* is the original "sound of sounds," the transcendent "soundless sound."

Nadi Literally, "tube." In a mystical sense, a *nadi* is a nonphysical conduit through which life force flows from one point to another.

Naraka The lower region of the *antarloka*, or astral plane.

Nirvikalpa Samadhi The one-and-only non-experience of Self at the source of life manifest.

Niyamas Generally, the *observances* of yoga. Specifically, *shaucha:* "purity;" *santosha:* "contentment;" *tapas:* "fire," "austerity" or "self-discipline;" *svadhyaya:* "self-reflection;" *Ishvara Pranidhana:* "devotion to a personal Lord." The *niyamas* comprise the second step of *ashtanga yoga's* eight-step system.

Odic The vibrational state of primal life force when it is functioning in the physical realm. Odic force stimulates attraction and repulsion between people, between things and between people and things as it functions through a masculine (aggressive) and feminine (passive) movement of energy.

Paranada "Soundless sound." The first "sound of sounds."

Pashyanta "Subconscious sound" comprised of noise emanating from unresolved karma.

Patanjali (200 BCE) author of the *Yoga Sutras,* a work manual detailing the practice of *ashtanga yoga,* which came to be known as *raja yoga,* "the king of yogas." The "eight limbs" or progressive steps of *ashtanga yoga* are *yamas* (restraints), *niyamas* (observances), *asana* (posture), *pranayama* (breath control), *pratyahara* (withdrawal), *dharana* (concentration), *dhyana* (meditation) and *Samadhi* (mystic oneness).

Pingala nadi A psychic nerve current that is blue in color and flows primarily up the right side of the soul body. This current is masculine in nature and radiates intellectual energy.

Pranamaya kosha The "pranic body," also known as the "health body" or the "vital body." This body holds the life of the physical body.

Pranayama Literally, "life-force restraining." Specifically, the science of controlling vital energy (prana) by controlling the breath. *Pranayama* is the fourth step of *ashtanga yoga.*

Pratyahara The withdrawal of awareness from external consciousness. *Pratyahara* is the fifth step of *ashtanga yoga.*

Raja yoga Generally regarded as the "original yoga," *raja yoga*—literally, "The king of yogas"—is esteemed as the first and essential yoga, from which other yogas were developed.

Sahasrara chakra Seventh of seven chakras, located in the soul body in a position corresponding to nerve ganglia at the apex of the skull in the physical body. The power of this seventh chakra gives rise to spiritual illumination.

Samyama Literally, "holding together, tying up or binding." In Patanjali's use of this term (in his *Yoga Sutras*), that which is being bound into a one unbroken sequence named *samyama* is *dharana* (concentration), *dhyana* (meditation) and *Samadhi* (absorption).

Santosha "Contentment."

Satchitananda "Existence, consciousness, bliss." The first manifestation of life force out of its un-manifest source.

Sat Guru From an externalized point of view, the Sat Guru is perceived as a physical person. When recognized in this way, he is understood to be a purified spiritual preceptor who has realized God as Self and is therefore qualified to move others toward that same Realization.

From an internalized point of view, the Sat Guru is perceived as wisdom—wisdom revealed through a *live person*, a *life experience* or *direct intuition*. Intuitively, this wisdom is accessed directly from within ourselves. Physically, it is encountered indirectly through the presence of a physical teacher. Experientially, it is confronted, also indirectly, through the sometimes-difficult experiences of life.

Satya "Truth."

Savikalpa Samadhi Full emersion in the experience of *satchidananda*. *Savikalpa Samadhi* leads to *Nirvikalpa Samadhi*. *Savikalpa Samadhi* is enhanced after *Nirvikalpa Samadhi*.

Self The one ultimate source and identity of all life. The term *self* (in lower case) denotes the personal ego, an individual identity that contrasts its *self* with the *Self*.

Self Realization Although often used as an alternate name for the ultimate non-experience of Nirvikalpa Samadhi, *Self Realization* more specifically refers to the experience of realizing, after the fact, that a Nirvikalpa Samadhi has just occurred.

Shaucha "Purity."

Sivamaya kosha The body of God.

Surya bedha pranayama A breath control restricting breathing so that air is inhaled through the right nostril and exhaled through the left nostril with the assistance of the fingers and thumb of the right hand. *Surya* means "sun." Thus, *Surya bedha pranayama* stimulates the left, masculine-aggressive, heating and "thinking" side of the brain, which influences the right side of the body.

Sushumna nadi The principle psychic nerve current of the soul body that coexists with the spine in the physical body.

Svadhishthana chakra Second of seven chakras, located in the soul body in a position corresponding to nerve ganglia about six inches below the navel in the physical body. With the power of the *svadhishthana chakra*, memory and reason are manipulated to create plans for fulfilling desires and dealing with fears.

Svadhyaya "Self-reflection."

Tapas Literally, "fire." Specifically, "austerity" or "self-discipline."

Trataka The yogic discipline of fixing the gaze of open eyes on a physical object. In a sophistication of this practice, the eyes are closed and the physical object previously gazed upon is visualized.

Ujjayi A yogic breath control often called the "ocean breath" because its performance sounds like the sum-total monotone of a nearby sea. In practice, *ujjayi* is a deep breathing exercise that focuses upon slightly constricting the passage of air through the throat during both the inhalation and exhalation of air through the nose. This slight constriction of in-coming and out-going air not only produces the distinctive *ujjayi* wind sound, it also softens and slows the breath to yield a curious effect of soothing and calming the nervous system, even though it increases oxygenation and builds internal body heat.

Vaikhari "Audible sound." Also referred to as "ahatha."

Vedas Literally, "wisdom." Specifically, four companion scriptures—*Rig, Yajur, Sama, Atharva*—composed 1500-500 BCE and consisting of roughly 20,000 Sanskrit verses. The *Vedas* are Hinduism's foundational scripture.

Vijnanamaya kosha The mental body, sometimes called the "psychic body." In the *vijnanamaya kosha* intuition blends with high thought.

Vishuddha chakra Fifth of seven chakras, located in the soul body in a position corresponding to nerve ganglia in the throat of the physical body. The energy of this *Vishuddha chakra* inspires an unconditional love that seeks only to flood out as blessings to all. Although this *chakra* is often referred to as a force center of communication, its *real* communication is of a one-way emanational sort.

Yamas Generally, the *restraints* of yoga. Specifically, *ahimsa*: "non-violence;" *satya*: "truth;" *asteya*: "non-stealing;" *brahmacharya*: "walking with God" or "chastity" and *aparigraha*: "non-selfishness." The *yamas* comprise the first step of *ashtanga yoga's* eight-step system.

Yoga Literally, "to bind back." Specifically, "to bind back to the source of life." Ideally, a means of realizing life's fullest potential by merging with life's ultimate essence in the "I" of all.

www.ingramcontent.com/pod-product-compliance
Lightning Source LLC
LaVergne TN
LVHW051514070426
835507LV00023B/3109